VOLUME 522

JULY 1992

THE ANNALS

of The American Academy *of* Political
and Social Science

RICHARD D. LAMBERT, *Editor*
ALAN W. HESTON, *Associate Editor*

THE FUTURE: TRENDS INTO THE
TWENTY-FIRST CENTURY

Special Editors of this Volume

JOSEPH F. COATES
JENNIFER JARRATT

Coates & Jarratt, Inc.
Washington, D.C.

Ⓢ SAGE PUBLICATIONS   *NEWBURY PARK   LONDON   NEW DELHI*

THE ANNALS

© 1992 *by* The American Academy *of* Political *and* Social Science

Editorial Office: 3937 Chestnut Street, Philadelphia, PA 19104.

For information about membership (individuals only) and subscriptions (institutions), address:*

SAGE PUBLICATIONS, INC.
2455 Teller Road
Newbury Park, CA 91320

From India and South Asia,
write to:
SAGE PUBLICATIONS INDIA Pvt. Ltd.
P.O. Box 4215
New Delhi 110 048
INDIA

From the UK, Europe, the Middle
East and Africa, write to:
SAGE PUBLICATIONS LTD
6 Bonhill Street
London EC2A 4PU
UNITED KINGDOM

SAGE Production Staff: LINDA GRAY, LIANN LECH, and JANELLE LeMASTER
Please note that members of The Academy receive THE ANNALS with their membership.
Library of Congress Catalog Card Number 91-67478
International Standard Serial Number ISSN 0002-7162
International Standard Book Number ISBN 0-8039-4622-8 (Vol. 522, 1992 paper)
International Standard Book Number ISBN 0-8039-4621-X (Vol. 522, 1992 cloth)
Manufactured in the United States of America. First printing, July 1992.

The articles appearing in THE ANNALS are indexed in *Book Review Index, Public Affairs Information Service Bulletin, Social Sciences Index, Current Contents, General Periodicals Index, Academic Index, Pro-Views,* and *Combined Retrospective Index Sets.* They are also abstracted and indexed in *ABC Pol Sci, Historical Abstracts, Human Resources Abstracts, Social Sciences Citation Index, United States Political Science Documents, Social Work Research & Abstracts, Sage Urban Studies Abstracts, International Political Science Abstracts, America: History and Life, Sociological Abstracts, Managing Abstracts, Social Planning/Policy & Development Abstracts, Automatic Subject Citation Alert, Book Review Digest, Work Related Abstracts, Periodica Islamica,* and/or *Family Resources Database,* and are available on microfilm from University Microfilms, Ann Arbor, Michigan.

Information about membership rates, institutional subscriptions, and back issue prices may be found on the facing page.

Advertising. Current rates and specifications may be obtained by writing to THE ANNALS Advertising and Promotion Manager at the Newbury Park office (address above).

Claims. Claims for undelivered copies must be made no later than three months following month of publication. The publisher will supply missing copies when losses have been sustained in transit and when the reserve stock will permit.

Change of Address. Six weeks' advance notice must be given when notifying of change of address to ensure proper identification. Please specify name of journal. Send address changes to: THE ANNALS, c/o Sage Publications, Inc., 2455 Teller Road, Newbury Park, CA 91320.

The American Academy of Political and Social Science

3937 Chestnut Street   Philadelphia, Pennsylvania 19104

Origin and Purpose. The Academy was organized December 14, 1889, to promote the progress of political and social science, especially through publications and meetings. The Academy does not take sides in controverted questions, but seeks to gather and present reliable information to assist the public in forming an intelligent and accurate judgment.

Meetings. The Academy occasionally holds a meeting in the spring extending over two days.

Publications. THE ANNALS is the bimonthly publication of The Academy. Each issue contains articles on some prominent social or political problem, written at the invitation of the editors. Also, monographs are published from time to time, numbers of which are distributed to pertinent professional organizations. These volumes constitute important reference works on the topics with which they deal, and they are extensively cited by authorities throughout the United States and abroad. The papers presented at the meetings of The Academy are included in THE ANNALS.

Membership. Each member of The Academy receives THE ANNALS and may attend the meetings of The Academy. Membership is open only to individuals. Annual dues: $39.00 for the regular paperbound edition (clothbound, $54.00). California residents must add 7.25% sales tax on all orders ($41.82 paperbound; $57.91 clothbound). Add $9.00 per year for membership outside the U.S.A. Members may also purchase single issues of THE ANNALS for $12.00 each (clothbound, $17.00). California residents: $12.87 paperbound, $18.23 clothbound. Add $1.50 for shipping and handling on all prepaid orders.

Subscriptions. THE ANNALS (ISSN 0002-7162) is published six times annually—in January, March, May, July, September, and November. Institutions may subscribe to THE ANNALS at the annual rate: $120.00 (clothbound, $144.00). California institutions: $128.70 paperbound, $155.44 clothbound. Add $9.00 per year for subscriptions outside the U.S.A. Institutional rates for single issues: $23.00 each (clothbound, $28.00). California institutions: $24.66 paperbound, $30.03 clothbound.

Second class postage paid at Thousand Oaks, California, and additional offices.

Single issues of THE ANNALS may be obtained by individuals who are not members of The Academy for $15.95 each (clothbound, $25.00). California residents: $17.10 paperbound, $26.81 clothbound. Add $1.50 for shipping and handling on all prepaid orders. Single issues of THE ANNALS have proven to be excellent supplementary texts for classroom use. Direct inquiries regarding adoptions to THE ANNALS c/o Sage Publications (address below).

All correspondence concerning membership in The Academy, dues renewals, inquiries about membership status, and/or purchase of single issues of THE ANNALS should be sent to THE ANNALS c/o Sage Publications, Inc., 2455 Teller Road, Newbury Park, CA 91320. Telephone: (805) 499-0721; FAX/Order line: (805) 499-0871. *Please note that orders under $30 must be prepaid.* Sage affiliates in London and India will assist institutional subscribers abroad with regard to orders, claims, and inquiries for both subscriptions and single issues.

Printed on recycled, acid-free paper   92 1757

THE ANNALS

of The American Academy *of* Political *and* Social Science

RICHARD D. LAMBERT, *Editor*
ALAN W. HESTON, *Associate Editor*

––––––––––––– FORTHCOMING –––––––––––––

AFFIRMATIVE ACTION REVISITED
Special Editors: Harold Orlans and June O'Neill
Volume 523   September 1992

POLITICAL ISLAM
Special Editors: I. William Zartman
and Charles E. Butterworth
Volume 524   November 1992

WHITE-COLLAR CRIME
Special Editors: Gilbert Geis and Paul Jesilow
Volume 525   January 1993

See page 3 for information on Academy membership and
purchase of single volumes of **The Annals.**

CONTENTS

BOOK DEPARTMENT CONTENTS

PREFACE

The new millennium is only a decade away. We can already see the swell of interest and the almost magical effect of focusing attention on the future that the nearness of a change in century is producing. The millennium is a landmark, a point for stocktaking and reevaluation. For many, it seems to be a social inflection point marking the move into a world substantially different, for better or worse, from the one we now have.

Another force driving interest in the future is the rapid globalization of the U.S. and other national economies and the undeniably vigorous new competition accompanying this next level of socioeconomic integration.

Also emerging are global issues that are intrinsically long-term in their development and resolution. Consequently, they open up speculation about the future and evoke strong political positions. Examples are the threats of nuclear weaponry, the concern for nuclear power, and fear of global warming from the greenhouse effect.

As the interest in the new millennium grows, we can confidently expect that crackpot or insubstantial predictions, forecasts, forebodings, and anticipations will proliferate. Therefore, it seems timely to present a stocktaking of where we stand with regard to a solid understanding of the future. This issue of *The Annals* is a showcase for professional futurists, for people who earn all or a substantial part of their livelihood in the systematic exploration of the future.

Why the emphasis on professional? The reason is simply that one of the plagues on the exploration of the future is a tendency for prominent people to respond automatically and without serious, analytical thought to questions about the future of their activities or even about subjects with no connection to their activities. The result is intellectual noise that easily drowns out more coherent messages.

This issue of *The Annals* samples topics that have received substantial attention from futurists and demonstrates by example the richness of approaches useful in exploring the future.

For those who become hooked on the systematic exploration of the future, there is a bibliographic essay on how to dig deeper and how to keep up with futures literature.

The editors' hope for this issue of *The Annals* is that it will affect readers in several different ways. We hope to make them more aware that the future can be systematically explored and make them more sophisticated, skeptical readers of material about the future. Last but not least, we would lure them into launching or promoting a systematic study of the future of some subject of great interest and importance to them.

THE ARTICLES

An overview of the modern era and contemporary developments in the study of the future are provided in Joseph F. Coates and Jennifer Jarratt's introductory article. They identify some concepts that are shared by contemporary futurists irrespective of their topic of specialization or ideological proclivities. A general model of a futures study is presented. They also suggest some strategies that the reader or user of futures studies could adopt.

The article by Theodore Jay Gordon introduces tools for exploring the future that are widely used by practitioners. The article has special authority since Gordon is the developer or coinventor of a number of the most widely used techniques, such as the Delphi and cross-impact analysis. He is also a leader in the application of computers to futures research. A special twist that he gives to the use of computers is the direct involvement of the user or the decision maker in the exploration of the future. Specific assumptions and beliefs about the future held by the decision maker can be electronically integrated to show graphically some of the implications of his or her beliefs or plans.

The next group of articles was chosen because we thought they would be of interest to readers of The Annals. In addition, they illustrate approaches to their exploration.

Pat Choate, an economist highly regarded for his conceptualizing abilities and his forthrightness, takes up a particularly critical international issue in looking at the future of American-Japanese trade. To an extent greater than other articles in this volume, Choate engages his subject with advocacy and a specific policy agenda. Pat Choate has held positions in the U.S. Department of Commerce and the Office of Management and Budget and in the state governments of Tennessee and Oklahoma.

Taking a different tack on another macro issue, the information society, Vary T. Coates, senior associate at the congressional Office of Technology Assessment, probes the future developments and consequences of our massive commitment to information technology. Vary Coates is recognized for her seminal work on the exploration of the secondary side effects of technological developments, having spent a decade at the George Washington University's Program of Policy Studies in Science and Technology, where technology assessment has been methodologically and substantively explored.

Information technology is one of the great enabling technologies. Like electricity and the automobile, its impacts are important in themselves and more important for the waves of change they bring about. Because they open up so many new possibilities, they enable other technological systems to develop.

As a public policy area, the environment has matured in the last five to seven years. Prior to that, an environmental issue was likely to be site or topic specific, involving a relatively defined group of actors and particular sets of goals and points of resistance. In the last five to seven years, the environment has moved from a family of localized and site-specific issues to a national agenda item. The fundamental questions have shifted from "whether" to "when and at what cost" changes must be made. Every attentive citizen is alert to the macro- as well as the microenvironmental issues. Environmentalism has become the mirror image of an enabling technology. It has become a universally informing policy concern.

In his article, Richard Lamm, formerly governor of Colorado, strongly emphasizes and gives credibility to the policy aspects of the future of the environment. Governor Lamm, a lawyer by training, a politician by predisposition, is—if not unique—unusual among major American political figures in that he is a working futurist. The material he produces flows from his own deliberative thinking.

Jan Grell and Gary Gappert, of the Institute of Futures Studies and Research at the University of Akron, write on the future of governance in the United States. They argue that we must move from allowing ourselves to be governed, or perhaps misgoverned, in the old familiar bureaucratic style, to governing ourselves. This means we must take more individual responsibility for our own governance, forming partnerships and alliances that will help us tackle some of our emerging problems. The transition to governance from government will not be sudden, say the authors, but it will be powerful and sustained.

The future is in no way a North American monopoly, nor are the important issues of the world only North American. Professor Michel Godet holds the Chaire de Prospective Industrielle at the Conservatoire National des Arts et Métiers, Ministère de l'Éducation Nationale in Paris, France. This distinguished practitioner of the study of the future provides an article on European futures in the context of broader global trends and uncertainties. As an interesting cultural side note, "futurism," "futurology," and "futurist" all were in bad odor in France in the late 1970s and early 1980s. As a consequence, the French have chosen a new term—*la prospective*—for what we in North America generally consider to be the study of the future.

For the next article, we invited Professor Ian Miles of the Program of Policy Research in Engineering, Science, and Technology at the University of Manchester in the United Kingdom to provide us with an article on the consequences of women's participation in work life. His areas of special interest include information technology assessment and scenario construction.

The future of education is the topic undertaken by Professor Christopher Dede of George Mason University. Dede is known for his broad and deep knowledge of both the technology and the social aspects of education in the United States. Other special interests of his include the workplace and artificial intelligence. Dede discusses the emerging partnership between people and their intelligent tools, computers. He argues that education must prepare learners for these new human-machine cognitive relationships.

Although he believes we have a great opportunity to reconstruct education to meet this and other developing needs, he is somewhat pessimistic about the educational system's capacity to respond adequately.

Walter Hahn takes an interesting look at what must loom ahead as a wellspring of social change and unrest in the United States over the next decades, the rapid aging of the American population. Hahn, who for many years was a senior analyst at the Congressional Research Service, is broadly experienced in the exploration of scientific, technological, and social issues of concern to legislators. Walter Hahn is an active and dynamic member of the group about which he writes.

The long-term implications of an intensely politicized and important health issue, the acquired immune deficiency syndrome (AIDS) epidemic, are addressed by Jonathan Peck and Clement Bezold. Peck is trained as both a political scientist and a futurist. He has been extensively involved in foresight in pharmaceutical research and development. He has written extensively on pharmaceuticals, food, drugs, and related topics. Clem Bezold is the founding executive director of the Institute for Alternative Futures and president of Alternative Futures Associates. He has been extensively involved with state and local governments in strategic planning. He has worked over the years to encourage what he calls "anticipatory democracy." He directed several major projects on the future in the health and pharmaceutical area, as well as the forest products, food, and grocery store industries.

Having sampled the universe, interests, and work of contemporary futurists, it is appropriate to turn to the question of keeping up and digging deeper. Michael Marien's article is a bibliographic essay. Marien is a well-known futures researcher and author in his own right and a trenchant public speaker.

JOSEPH F. COATES
JENNIFER JARRATT

Exploring the Future:
A 200-Year Record of Expanding Competence

By JOSEPH F. COATES and JENNIFER JARRATT

ABSTRACT: The contemporary study of the future evolved from several directions: science, technology, military and business interests, sociology, history, and a literary tradition. Futurists may be working in a variety of organizations and situations, but they share beliefs in society's ability to explore, and take responsibility for influencing, the future. Lack of imagination and unexamined assumptions often cause forecast failure. Agreement and disagreement between several futurists is explored in this article, with the warning that pushing to achieve consensus on the future may mislead in times of rapid change. Finally, several key trends for the future of the world, and of the United States, are outlined.

Joseph F. Coates is the president of Coates & Jarratt, Inc. (formerly J. F. Coates, Inc.), a policy research organization specializing in the study of the future, and has worked as a futurist in business, industry, and government for over thirty years. He is adjunct professor at the George Washington University. His most recent book is Future Work *(1990).*

Jennifer Jarratt is vice president of Coates & Jarratt, Inc. She has an M.S. in studies of the future from the University of Houston—Clear Lake, where she taught in 1990-91 as a visiting instructor in the futures studies program. She is coauthor of Future Work *(1990) and* What Futurists Believe *(1989).*

12

THE contemporary study of the future evolved in the confluence of six separate streams of development. First, and most important, are scientific discoveries and technological inventions. Because of the long interval between a discovery and its practical applications on a large scale, science is increasingly recognized as offering early signs of what the future may hold.

Early in the industrial era through the nineteenth century, technology led science. Clever people came up with practical inventions that drew the attention of scientists and stimulated their interest. Today the reverse tends to be the case: science produces core new knowledge from which come new technologies and engineering. Science, technology, and engineering are increasingly important to society, and the anticipated long-term consequences concern those who advocate new uses of technology as well as those who are wary of its effects.

The second stream comes from military interests. On balance, the military has a long history of promoting technology in its own interest. In World War I, much of the nation's scientific talent was orchestrated to serve the military. At the end of the war, this concerted effort evaporated. At the end of World War II, to prevent this disappearance from happening again, the RAND Corporation was founded, with its task being to assess future needs for military preparedness. As a result, many of the tools and techniques of contemporary futures studies and many of its practitioners come from the military or from civilian organizations that, like RAND, work in support of the military.

The third stream flows from business. Since Henri Fayol introduced strategic planning to the corporation, the corporation's tools of anticipation have steadily grown more effective. Today, virtually no large organization considers operating without internal strategic planning. External to the corporation and to government are practitioners and institutions who work with them to establish a better understanding of the future as it relates to business interests.

The fourth stream has its intellectual source in sociology. Pitirim Sorokin is a landmark figure. In the contemporary world, Daniel Bell of Harvard and Amitai Etzioni of the George Washington University link trends to social theory and to anticipation of the future.

The fifth stream comes from the study of history. The contemporary historians Robert Heilbroner and Paul Kennedy discuss the implications of history's lessons for the future and draw out images of future worlds. Many academic historians have explored the roots of contemporary futures studies, particularly in nineteenth-century utopian and dystopian literature, developing courses on the history of the future.

Finally, reflecting and interacting with all of the aforementioned streams is the sixth: the literary tradition. Literature has always been ambivalent in its approach to the future. The tradition of writing about the future tends to reflect either strongly or weakly an interest in scientific and technological developments. These threads in literature—utopia, dystopia, fantasy, or science fiction—are a major source from which most people draw their first experience of systematic thinking about the future.

The nineteenth-century trend toward utopian and dystopian literature usually drew on a social ideology. That social focus is appearing again in social science fiction as interpersonal and intersocietal elements are introduced into what used to be purely science fiction.

WHO IS A FUTURIST

Futurists come from many backgrounds but can be sorted into a few categories. In one category are those who work within an organization and pursue a specialized interest. For example, in the food industry one might find someone concentrating on the future of nonalcoholic beverages. In the automotive-supply industry one might find an internal futurist looking at the future of rubber tires. Generally working from the outside in support of those specialized futurists are organizations and individuals that provide strategic planning and independent futures studies. The client can be a specific corporation, a trade association, or a government agency.

A second category of futurists concentrates on a professional and specialized audience, thereby creating a scholarly literature. The third and perhaps most prominent category comprises those futurists who have no specific client but who take society as a whole, the general public, as their audience. Alvin Toffler and John Naisbitt best represent this group today.

Fourth, there are those who are primarily concerned with the future as a source of entertainment. Their work often supports the television and film industries. The late Gene Roddenberry typifies this group.

Finally, there are the ideologues and the advocates who use many of the instruments, tools, and trappings of the systematic study of the future to promote their predetermined outcome. Julian Simon and Lester Brown, the latter of the Worldwatch Institute, might fit in this category.

SHARED BELIEFS

Whatever the category, futurists tend to share a half dozen implicit beliefs.

The first is that there is no single future. The forces at play are so complex that the most effective strategy for exploring the future is to recognize that the forces can come together in a variety of ways. The objective therefore becomes to identify and describe a useful range of alternatives and to plan in terms of a full range of plausible futures.

The second shared belief is that we can see those alternative futures. No serious futurist claims to be clairvoyant but only that we can see those alternatives to the extent that is useful in informing our judgment and shaping our actions.

The third belief is that we can influence the future. There would be little point in exploring the future if there were no practical consequences for actions that we can take now. A deep-seated belief that we can influence the future underlies the optimism characteristic of almost every futurist. While many are pessimistic in the short to midrange and see enormous obstacles to reaching a satisfactory or desired future, even the most pessimistic of futurists believe that if certain actions are taken, we can move to a new, higher state of human development.

The fourth shared belief is that we have a moral obligation to use our capability to anticipate and to influence the future.

A fifth belief, based on evidence, is that side effects of the human enterprise will increasingly dominate the future. There is little doubt that we can plan, design, and execute projects even on a global scale. We could begin social and economic programs to move us in any desired direction. Whatever we do, however, will be accompanied by unplanned side effects.

Futurists diverge on the appropriate actions that should be taken in response to an anticipated or desired future. At one pole are those who are structural in their orientation, believing that the future can best be influenced by grabbing control of the big levers of society and pushing them in a direction that will bring about change.

At the other pole are those who believe an approach to the future is most effectively promoted at the individual or personal level. They argue that one must bring about ethical, value, and behavioral changes first in individuals in order to reshape the trends driving the future. In this view, the drivers of change lie in some mass social movement. The structuralists argue that the mass of people need only accept the programs necessary for change and not necessarily new values. It is not crucial that they be committed with any strong ideological fervor.

HOW ONE EXPLORES THE FUTURE

Whether looking ahead five, ten, fifty, one hundred, or more years, there are characteristics common to comprehensive studies of the future (see Figure 1). No two futurists will agree on the details. Few futures studies give full, explicit attention to all of the components described in this section, but these components constitute the basis of a policy-oriented futures study, that is, a study explicitly designed to influence the behavior of an organization, the people within that organization, and the outsiders concerned with that organization's business or activities.

Anything worth studying the future of is usually complex enough to include many actors and interested parties and to involve institutions and social forces; it should therefore be looked at as a system. A system is a collection of elements or components linked in a dynamic structure that maintains itself.

One first tries to identify and define what the key elements or components of the system being studied may be. No system describes itself; hence it becomes a formal and a creative task to discover and identify all the elements of a system. A system is not simply an organization chart. It is not merely the physical plant or even an organization's employees and benefactors. It includes tradition, relations, habits, and many other elusive components as well.

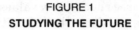
FIGURE 1
STUDYING THE FUTURE

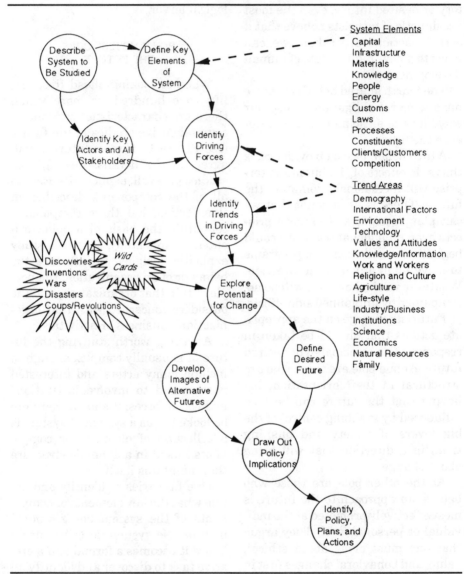

In the next stage, the futurist identifies the forces driving toward change or maintaining stability. Again, this task requires a combination of formal techniques and skill.

One would be on solid ground in arguing that every significant system in the United States today is being affected by population change, by information technology, by the globalization of the economy, by changing social values, and by new developments in science and technology. The futurist must tease out the specific trends that most influence the system under consideration. There are also more specialized factors working on or within any system.

Having identified the trends, the futurist must assess their force and their direction. Some trends are relatively stable, which can be extremely important for exploring the future. Some can undergo sharp changes in direction and strength. Some trends are cyclical or present other types of recurrent patterns or fall into some other interesting time patterns.

At this point, the futurist develops alternative futures, that is, ways in which the forces of change and the system components could come together to create new situations. The futurist knows that the study of the future is, to a large extent, a craft and an art. There are many tools and techniques to use, but it never becomes a formal, mechanical, or rigidly prescribed activity.

With alternative futures in mind, the futurist studies the implications and associated policy options. From there, the futurist identifies the actions that may be appropriate based on the picture of alternatives so far developed.

These actions are not actions to be taken five, ten, or fifty years from now. Rather, they are actions to be taken now to shape and influence the future, to promote desired outcomes, and to make undesired outcomes less likely. Sometimes it will be evident that no control can be exerted over particular changes. Therefore, another appropriate task is to begin to develop strategies to cope with the emerging alternatives.

By stopping now, the futurist would have a useful and comprehensive study of the future of the subject at hand, but it would still reflect severe limitations of a passive, almost a victim's approach to the future. Three other things must be done to round out the effort. The first is to go back to the alternative futures and develop preferable alternatives. These are not fantasy but sound alternatives reflecting the accumulated knowledge of the trends and the elements of the system. With desired futures in mind—"normative futures," in the jargon of futurists—the implications and the actions related to them can be reviewed in a new light.

The next step is to recognize that there are unexpected or low-probability events that may impact on that system. These so-called wild cards must be explored. They may involve discovery, invention, war, disasters, political upheaval—a seemingly endless list of events. They must be accounted for in the overall analysis; one option is to treat them as perturbations.

Finally, in the American system more than anywhere else in the world, few things will happen unless one has the support of the right people, and many things will not happen if the wrong people are in opposition. It is necessary to identify all the key actors or interested parties in the system and begin to explore their issues and concerns and motivations.

When the futurist has done all this work, what are the benefits? There are general and particular, institutional and private benefits from a study of the future. We all carry enormous baggage of implicit, unstated assumptions and beliefs about the future. A good futures study will force the revelation and testing of these assumptions. This leads to the next questions: "How do I know that my assumptions are right? What are the consequences of my assumptions' being right or being wrong?"

The second benefit from a good futures study will be to widen the range of considerations that enter into everyone's thinking about the future. If it does nothing else, a futures study should enrich a person's awareness of factors shaping what is of interest to him or her and the range of activities open to that person to influence. That widening of personal and organizational horizons should be accompanied by an increase in depth of vision. The future vision need not be limited to the next six months or year or two years. Significant things can be said and responded to concerning a time ten, twenty, or thirty years into the future.

A study of the future often reveals circumstances or trends that cannot be significantly influenced but that nevertheless must be coped with. The earlier a system begins to cope with them, the wider the range of choice ahead and the more positive that choice can be.

Finally, an understanding of the trends at work and their future possible outcomes can be a satisfying intellectual and conceptual frame-work for locating, reviewing, and interpreting everyday events and developments.

WHY FORECASTS FAIL

In forecasting, as in neurology and structural engineering, failure often reveals a great deal. Forecasts and forecasters frequently fail for several reasons. The most common source of failure is the mechanical extrapolation of trends. Today is the best indicator of tomorrow, but today decreases in value for points further in the future. All trends eventually slow down, stop, change direction radically, or reverse.

Another source of forecast failure is unexamined assumptions about the future. It is easy to overlook implicit and therefore unstated and unexamined beliefs.

A third underlying cause of failure is limited expertise, especially on the part of those who believe themselves experts on the subject in question. A classic in this field is the forecast made by Admiral William Leahy in a conversation with President Harry Truman in 1943. Referring to the atomic bomb, he said, " ' "This is the biggest fool thing we have ever done. . . . the bomb will never go off, and I speak as an expert in explosives." ' "[1]

Lack of imagination is another root of failure. *Harper's Weekly*, in August 1902, noted that " 'the actual building of roads devoted to motor

1. Admiral William Daniel Leahy, quoted in Harry S. Truman, *Memoirs*, vol. 1, *Years of Decisions* (Garden City, NY: Doubleday, 1955), p. 11, quoted in Christopher Cerf and Victor Navasky, *The Experts Speak* (New York: Pantheon, 1984), p. 252.

cars is not for the near future, in spite of the many rumors to that effect.' "[2]

The last two reasons for the failure of forecasts are opposite sides of a coin. One neglects the constraints on some future development, and the other suffers from excessive optimism. Both of these are characteristic of the inventor, developer, or promoter of a technology or cause. Secretary of the Navy John F. Lehman's plan in 1981-87 for a 600-ship navy failed to recognize the demographic trends—namely, the baby bust—that made a fleet of that size utterly impractical. With every new claim of a new scientific or technological development, the excessive optimist sees these developments rushing to market and entering society at a more rapid pace than is plausible.

THE USES OF
THE FUTURES STUDY

At a minimum, a futures study should serve as a framework for interpreting present events. It should give structure and organization to what otherwise seems deviant or exceptional behavior. Second, it should identify the likely developments that must be dealt with, whether or not the power exists to influence them. A study of the future should also act as a sorting rule between the choices that an individual or an organization may have. Usually it is best to go with the flow rather than to fight too many long-term trends. Of course, what is always hoped for in a study of the future will be the revelation of great

2. *Harper's Weekly*, 2 Aug. 1902, p. 1046, quoted in Cerf and Navasky, *Experts Speak*, p. 228.

new opportunity. This is unusual, but it does happen.

A serious futures study should nudge, if not force, those in positions of responsibility to examine and reexamine their own assumptions about the future. Finally, a systematic look to the future can help to set up guideposts to mark clear directions and to warn of possibly dangerous paths.

In using or interpreting a study of the future, there is a temptation to push too hard for consensus. If there is agreement among futurists, if there is agreement among the people involved in the production of a particular study, this all seems to add strength to the belief that a consensus exists. On the other hand, consensus can be misleading, particularly when an institution, an organization, or a society is in a period of rapid change and subject to new, powerful, and unfamiliar forces. Therefore, there is an important role for the outlier, the deviant thinker, the unusual, and the radical point of view in preventing a group from reaching a consensus too easily. The outlier is likely to bring to the discussion some unique or special perspective, some special knowledge, or some particularly interesting interpretation. The user of futures studies must endure an ambivalence between the search for and the desire for consensus and the uncomfortable awareness that the outlier may have something important, if uncongenial, to say.

This is particularly difficult advice for large institutions, for government agencies, or for many of the most influential bodies, such as legislatures, that one would hope to influence by a systematic study of the future.

Given, then, that consensus is not an ideal in the study of the future, are there things that most futurists agree about?

In our own recent book, *What Futurists Believe*,[3] in which the beliefs of 17 futurists were systematically reviewed and analyzed, there is consensus if not absolute agreement on some ideas, such as the following:

1. Complexity is an emerging characteristic of almost all human endeavors, institutions, and systems. The futurists differ on how to manage complexity, but they agree that new tools are needed.

2. Today's institutions and structures, such as government, are not the answer to the management of complexity. Most are out of date, bureaucratic, sluggish, with short time frames and attention spans and lacking in worldview. The need is for more flexible, faster institutions.

3. Science and technology are widely accepted as dominant if not the primary drivers of change. Among the most important of the new technologies are information technologies including telecommunications, computers, electronic applications, and information linkages of all kinds. Biotechnology is most important for its impact on agriculture and health, and material science for its revolutionary potential for manufactured products, construction, and eventually the development of human activity in space.

4. All see the end of oil as the dominant source of energy in the next

3. Joseph F. Coates and Jennifer Jarratt, *What Futurists Believe* (Bethesda, MD: World Future Society, 1990).

twenty to fifty years, and the key transition to various other energy sources. Most agree that that transition will be turbulent and will perhaps slow economic growth for a time until it is complete.

5. World economic growth has slowed down as a result of the increase of the cost of energy, world population growth, and the greater demand for resources and food. Some of the 17 feel the threat of global economic collapse.

6. Futurists generally expect great changes to occur within a framework of continuity that will keep the basic shape of society much as we know it. This means that we will make the transition to the information age and the switch to other forms of energy, bank electronically, and cope with great numbers of people and more diverse relationships in society, at the same time maintaining stability in our government and in our management of institutional structures.

7. The avoidance of nuclear war is one of the most important issues for the rest of the century and is a major threat to our ability to make our transitions smoothly.

8. Some of the 17 futurists believe that we will have one global system in the future, and we will increasingly need to integrate knowledge about this system in order to shape and manage it. As we become more interdependent, the implications of self-interested national strategies will become more serious.

9. Almost all of the futurists anticipate the economic and perhaps military decline of the United States, although for some the effect is more

apparent than real and for some the decline will be relative rather than absolute. The United States will take its place among the world's nations merely as one among equals.

10. Education, the futurists agree, requires much improvement, but they doubt the capability of the U.S. educational system to improve.

11. Demands in the information society for new standards of literacy and competence are at odds with the failure of the educational system in the United States.

12. The aging of the U.S. population represents a culture shock for a nation that has been young for most of its history. We can expect intergenerational conflict. U.S. society will stiffen and grow less flexible and more like the aging societies of Europe.

In contrast, the 17 futurists studied strongly disagree on a couple of points. One is the ability or capacity of individuals, groups, political systems, and nations to adapt to change or to create new and effective institutional structures.

Second, there is disagreement on how scientific and technological change is achieved in society. Some believe that science and technology are autonomous forces and cannot be controlled by social choice or political regulation. Alternatively, others believe that technological change cannot occur unless the social need for it develops. Most tend to agree, however, that its effects can be only partly anticipated.

A significant division exists between futurists whose images of the future are shaped by underlying optimism and those whose images of the future are based on pessimism. Futurists differ also on their assumptions about the effects of microelectronics on the global work force; the stability of the international flow of money and its relative importance to world economic health; the potential impacts of the USSR—now the former Soviet republics—and China on world trade; and the ability of less developed nations to catch up with the industrial revolution.

They are virtually all uncertain of or disquieted about four points:

— world population growth and what a world of 8 to 10 billion people could be like and its capacity to feed, house, and clothe that kind of population;

— the ability of the United States to support its military infrastructure at current levels for much longer;

— the future of Africa, which is generally believed to be dismal, although none of the futurists has analyzed the continent's prospects in any detail; what concerns them most is whether anyone else in the world will care or can act to head off inevitable disaster; and

— the influence of societal values on events, since that influence is achieved in ways that are not fully understood and that are unpredictable.

AS WE SEE IT

To conclude this introductory article, a brief summary of our own views seems in order. We concentrate on a few key issues facing the world and the nation.

The global trends

Twenty years ago, the Club of Rome attached the rubric "global problématique" to that knotty constellation of problems that characterized the contemporary world situation. No problem can be treated effectively in isolation and yet no mechanism exists for treating them in their totality. While agreeing that the problématique is a central idea, we see at least four trends that can only become more critical over the next two decades.

First is the status of women. It is unconscionable for the world to continue to keep the majority of its population in a state of complete or partial thralldom. Substantial progress in the United States and Europe, while still far short of social, economic, and political equality, has ignited a candle that is inextinguishable throughout the world. Led by the West and by the growing middle class in all the developing world, the traditional status of women will become increasingly economically insupportable and socially and personally unbearable. Throughout the world, the communications media, film, television, radio broadcasts, and the cinema bring to people everywhere an awareness of a different world from the one in which they are living. The dissonance between those two worlds cannot persist forever. Achieving equality of status for women is a first step. The long-term consequences of bringing women into parity in personal, social, and public life will have powerful effects on education, population growth, and world governance.

Second is international relations. The changing relationships between nations as a result primarily of the globalization of all economies will lead to fundamentally new bonds between nations. At the same time that a patent need for integration is growing, the world is experiencing an unprecedented unfolding of nationalism either as an innocuous marketing theme for international trade or in its more unstable and tribal aspects characteristic of Eastern Europe and black Africa. The most powerful institution extant for planning and managing a new world order has no political base, that is, the multinational corporation. Governments withdraw, resist, isolate themselves from the realities and generally ignore the need for integration, cooperation, common goals, and organized movement toward global management.

Third is population growth. Steep global population growth will be at the core of most of the emerging problems of the next three to four decades. The present world population is 5.4 billion, growing at roughly 93 million a year. Early in the next century, world population will reach 8 billion. The pressures associated with this increase—absolute demands on energy, food, clothing, and shelter; stresses on the environment; the need and the question of how to dispose of human waste—will be enormous. Furthermore, the world's population is rapidly becoming urban, thereby dissociating from agriculture and farming as these relate to human survival. The urban population of the world increasingly is dependent on fragile networks of supply, maintenance, and support.

In the past five decades of bilateral and multilateral assistance, the single greatest failure has been the promotion of population control. The likelihood of achieving any humane form of existence for all diminishes with each passing year without success in controlling population growth. Western nations tend to be paralyzed with guilt in approaching the population problem. The standards of privacy, fairness, and personal choice that make sense in advanced nations, as well as religiously based pro-birth imperatives that may have been appropriate a hundred years ago, are baggage that poor nations cannot afford. In desperate countries where the number of births far outruns the capacity to feed, house, or employ those who survive in anything like a tolerable standard of living, Western moralism on this subject must seem frivolous, if not incomprehensible.

The fourth issue is the impact of information technology on the world, a technology that, on the one hand, is informing potentially anyone of anything anywhere at anytime. On the other hand, information technology, particularly video, shows more of the poor what the rich have and tantalizes by offering no access to the goodies and privileges that it images.

The United States

Nationally, four of many issues come to the top as critical to the next two decades. The first is the growing crisis in governance and leadership. This is best characterized by an unbelievably short-term focus and by a degree of parochialism incredible for a continental economy that is at the core of the emerging global economy.

Legislators chop national issues of environment, health, energy, and scores of others into 50 little pieces, while at the same time deploring the fact that we cannot consistently and coherently move ahead as a nation. Congressional leadership and White House leadership have virtually become oxymorons. Ideology dominates the latter, and tangible fear of special-interest groups paralyzes the former.

The major corporation is barely more promising as a source of national leadership. Its totally unbalanced view of its duty to stockholders in the short run is creating a labor crisis. The consequences of the imbalance in power within business organizations, which was essentially glossed over by the prosperity of the 1950s, 1960s, and 1970s, became visible in the late 1980s with recession. The chiefs of the corporation know only one value, immediate return on investment. Their focus on the short-term prosperity of the organization is in sharp contrast to the outlook of the major Japanese firm, in which the firm exists more to provide a living for its employees than to serve the interests of the owners. Another alternative is European firms, in which some parity for the workers is built in at the institutional level. This shortsightedness of our public and private leadership is at the center of our inability to build a coherent approach to energy, the environment, demilitarization, health care, and scores of other issues.

The second issue is education. Education as the centerpiece of a democratic society and an essential ingredient of the technological era has been in catastrophic collapse for three decades. There is nothing new about the declining quality of education. What is new is that the pressures of competitiveness and the inability of the United States to perform well in the international marketplace, as well as the increasing inability of companies to find literate and numerate workers, have reached the point where the problem is more difficult to deny. In no year in the past decade do we find anything positive happening. The most powerful unorchestrated force likely to have an effect on education, namely, the corporate employer, continues to dabble in a thousand different ways with semi-philanthropic trivial and incidental intervention programs. The American polity and business act as if we did not know how to educate children, which we surely do. The core of the education issue is essentially political and calls for strong political action for its resolution.

The third issue relates to population but is not the issue of global population growth. It is rather the changing possibilities for population composition. Worldwide, oppressed people are migrating from wherever they are to the nearest neighboring countries. This is going on at a great pace in the Western Hemisphere, yet the United States lacks any clear policy about the integrity of its borders, and Americans do not know what their long-term wishes are as a nation with regard to these strikingly new forces for population diversity.

Finally, as the largest and soon to be merely second-largest economic entity in the global economy, the United States is confronted by the increasing awareness of the limited competitiveness of its products and its services. Yet there is no coherent mechanism for acknowledging this in government or in the corporate sector. We have no mechanism for defining our long-term collective objectives, and we therefore are devoid of policies for moving us toward them. The ideology of the present and recent administrations, the individualistic actions of corporations, and the myopia of the Congress will not lead the nation in a timely and speedy way to some new level of effective worldwide competitiveness.

These are all structural challenges to our society, and planet, that are within our capacity to meet. What we see as the key missing piece in many approaches to problems and challenges is constructive thinking about the future. As futurists, our long-term goal must be to enlarge the capacity for constructive thinking about the future as much as possible in our society. We, as most other futurists, refuse to accept the idea that progress is an outdated concept.

ANNALS, *AAPSS*, 522, July 1992

The Methods of Futures Research

By THEODORE JAY GORDON

ABSTRACT: In this article, the principal methods used in exploratory forecasting are described. These descriptions should serve two purposes. First, for someone who intends to make an exploratory forecast, they will provide information about the strengths and useful range of each technique. Second, they will also illustrate, directly and by implication, the frailties and limitations of the techniques so that forecasts, and plans based on them, can be better assessed.

Theodore Jay Gordon is the founder of the Futures Group and was its president and chairman from its formation in 1971 until his retirement in 1990. He is the innovator or co-innovator of several methods of futures research including cross-impact analysis and trend-impact analysis.

THE future will never be completely known or even knowable. The systems that, in intricate and virtually unlimited combination, determine what is and what will be are simply too complex, too delicately balanced, too dependent on chance or noise to allow complete knowledge of their workings. Yet, partial forecasting is possible; it usually involves limiting the forecast in time or scope, simplifying and modeling the system, and learning from history: all processes that make the vast complexity of the future less overwhelming.

Futures research is the systematic exploration of what might be. Its methods stem from economics, statistics, psychology, systems analysis, and operations research. The field encompasses both objective and subjective approaches. Its purposes are to provide early warning about problems that might lie ahead, to help identify and evaluate policies, and to illustrate the futures that are attainable.

In the most general sense, forecasts can be of two types: exploratory, that is, forecasts of futures that seem plausible; and normative, that is, forecasts of futures that seem desirable. Both exploratory forecasts and normative forecasts can be produced with quantitative and qualitative methods.

Planning—personal, corporate, or government—involves the search for policies that bring exploratory forecasts more in line with normative forecasts. The difference between the two, in engineering terminology, is an error signal. Planning is the process of identifying policies that, if followed, would make the forecast state of affairs approach the desired state of affairs.

Before beginning the description of some of the more prominent methods of futures research, it may be useful to mention a few warnings about forecasting and forecasts:

1. Forecasts can be very precise but quite inaccurate.

2. Extrapolation is bound to be wrong eventually. Simply extending historical trends into the future is easy, but this process suggests that nothing new will deflect the trends, that the only forces shaping the future are those that existed in the past.

3. Forecasts are incomplete. It is exceedingly difficult and rarely persuasive to include in any forecast future developments that are based on discoveries not yet made. As Herman Kahn once said, "The most surprising future is one in which there are no surprises."

4. Planning must be dynamic. Because of inaccuracies and incompleteness, all plans based on forecasts are subject to error. Therefore, as new information is gained, forecasts should be revised and the plans based on those forecasts, reviewed.

5. There are many futures. Most people in the field believe that policies can have an effect, that the future is shaped through action or inaction. Since we have choices, there are many possible futures that depend on what we and many others do.

6. Forecasting is not value free. For reasons not entirely clear, it appears easier to forecast bad developments than good. Furthermore, we tend to give higher probabilities to desired future events than undesired.

7. Forecasts can be self-fulfilling or self-defeating. By forecasting the

TABLE 1
AN OUTLINE OF FORECASTING METHODS

		Normative	Exploratory
Quantitative		Scenarios	Scenarios
		Technology sequence analysis	Time series
			Regression analysis
			Multiple-equation models
			Probabilistic models
			Trend impact
			Cross impact
			Interax
			Nonlinear models
Qualitative		Scenarios	Scenarios
		Delphi	Delphi
		In-depth interviews	In-depth interviews
		Expert group meetings	Expert group meetings
		Genius	Genius
		Science fiction	

possible existence of a new stack gas cleaning technology, for example, that technology may become more likely. The mechanism is clear enough: others reading about the possibility work to bring it about.

THE METHODS

Table 1 is a road map of the field in two-dimensional space. The upper left is the land of visionaries who can express their hopes in terms of numbers, such as a chief executive officer setting production goals for his or her company. The lower left is inhabited by visionaries who express their visions in nonnumerical terms: a Marx or Thoreau. The lower right houses forecasters who project the future as they think it will evolve but express their view in qualitative terms: Marshall McLuhan or Daniel Bell, for example. The upper right is the home of analysts, comfortable with mathematically based methods, who use equations to arrive at their conclusions about what the future might be. Methods in all quadrants can be systematic.

In this article, I will describe the principal methods used in exploratory forecasting, the right side of the two-dimensional space in Table 1. These descriptions should serve several purposes. First, for someone who intends to make an exploratory forecast, they will provide information about the strengths and useful range of each technique. Second, they will also illustrate, directly and by implication, the frailties and limitations of the techniques so that forecasts, and plans based on them, can be better assessed.

Genius forecasting

In this context, a genius is a person who can intuitively integrate diverse factors that impinge on the present to create images of the future and who can capture the imagination of others by describing that future and how it might arrive. Genius forecasting, whether expressed in science fiction or more formal futures research, often requires a measure of insight that cannot be evoked by more formal methods. But genius forecasting requires one ingredient that is difficult to obtain: a genius.

The Delphi technique

From a historical perspective, the contemporary rebirth of futures research began in the early 1960s with the Delphi technique at RAND in Santa Monica, California. To address questions about the military potential of future technology or potential political issues and their resolution, analysts used expert opinion. The reasoning went something like this: experts, particularly when they agree, are more likely than nonexperts to be correct about future developments in their field.

Bringing experts together in a conference room introduces factors that may have little to do with the issue at hand, however. For example, the loudest voice rather than the soundest argument may carry the day; a person may be reluctant to abandon a previously stated opinion in front of his or her peers.

Therefore Helmer, Rescher, Dalkey, and others at RAND developed the Delphi method, which was designed to remove conference-room impediments to a true expert debate.[1] In this approach, experts were

first identified and asked to participate in the inquiry. They were assured of anonymity in the sense that none of their statements would be attributed to them by name. The questions were pursued through a number of sequential questionnaires, each requiring persons with opinions that differed greatly from the group consensus to state their reasons for disagreement. These reasons for extreme opinions were fed back to the group in subsequent questionnaires, together with the consensus view. The participants were asked to reassess their opinions in view of the consensus and the reasons for disagreement. In a sense, this was a controlled debate, and more often than not, the group moved toward consensus. The two elements that mark a Delphi study are anonymity and feedback.

Because the number of respondents is usually small, Delphi studies do not—and are not intended to—produce statistically significant results; in other words, the results provided by any panel do not predict the response of a larger population or even a different Delphi panel. The value of a Delphi study rests in the ideas it generates, both those that evoke consensus and those that do not.[2]

The key to a successful Delphi study lies in the selection of the participants. In a statistically based

1. Olaf Helmer and Nicholas Rescher, "On the Epistemology of the Inexact Sciences," *Management Sciences*, 6(1) (1959).

2. For an example of the first published large-scale Delphi, see Theodore J. Gordon and Olaf Helmer, *Report on a Long Range Forecasting Study*, R-2982 (Santa Monica, CA: RAND, 1964). A check on the forecasts made in 1964 may be found in R. Ament, "Comparison of Delphi Forecasting Studies in 1964 and 1969," *Futures*, 2(1) (Mar. 1970).

study such as a public opinion poll, participants are assumed to be representative of a larger population; in Delphi, nonrepresentative, knowledgeable persons are needed. They are usually identified through literature searches—to find those who have published on the subject under study—and recommendations of other experts in a process known as "daisy chaining."

In general, techniques better than Delphi exist for short-term forecasting and for forecasting the future state of systems with well-known characteristics.[3] Delphi is most useful in forecasting long-range developments, future breakthroughs and their consequences, developments that can upset systems, and policy options and their outcomes.

Delphi through interviewing

Conventional Delphi studies are difficult to perform well. The questionnaires must be meticulously prepared and tested to avoid ambiguity; in addition, multi-round studies require a great deal of time. In-depth interviews have proven to be a more efficient way to gather expert opinion.

In using in-depth interviews, the same kinds of experts are first identified, invited to participate, assured of their anonymity, and, in most instances, promised a report based on the interview sequence. High-level staff members, familiar with the study's objectives, act as interviewers. Feedback can be introduced if

3. For one of the best detailed discussions of the Delphi method, see H. Lindstone and M. Turoff, eds., *The Delphi Method* (Reading, MA: Addison-Wesley, 1975).

two rounds of interviews are employed; however, single-round studies are used more frequently. In these, feed-forward is often employed, presenting to respondents information about emerging consensus derived from the prior interviews. True, this introduces differences between the various interviews, but the exercise is not designed to be statistically significant but rather to elicit ideas that can be important to subsequent analyses. Expert in-depth interviews are an excellent means of obtaining such ideas.

Electronically assisted Delphi

Delphi had its birth in the 1960s in the concern about spurious factors that limited the ability of experts to reach a consensus in group meetings. Today, for some applications, group meetings of experts have become more practical. Conference-room voting machines have proven useful; one such machine, the PC Voter, a device developed by the Futures Group, provides each participant a small terminal that is connected through a serial circuit to a personal computer. The computer's software integrates the answers of the experts and displays the group's opinion as a histogram on a monitor screen. A measure of anonymity is preserved because the inputs are private and unseen by others; the display provides feedback.

Since the 1970s, attempts have been made to perform Delphi studies using computer terminals on-line; the early experiments were generally cumbersome, and access to the appropriate technology limited the selection of participants.[4] New electronic networks and software called "groupware" may change the picture. These systems permit individuals at widely distant terminals to access and edit a common document simultaneously. For example, Xerox has groupware that interconnects simultaneous contributors to a document;[5] IBM has an "information warehouse" data access strategy that can serve the same role.[6] Clearly, on-line participation can be structured and controlled in a manner similar to the way a Delphi interaction can be.

In summary, the Delphi method and its derivatives can be used in almost any exploratory or normative forecasting. Since it is a method for eliciting and combining judgments, it is most useful when only judgments, rather than facts, are available. The market researcher might ask about the future of fashion; the manufacturer about the strategy of his or her competitors; the research and development lab chief about future scientific breakthroughs; the politician about the likely consequences of contemplated policies; the chief executive officer about a future vision for the firm. It is not the future that is produced in such exercises; rather, it is a composite view that draws strength from a controlled interaction of the opinion of experts.

4. Murray Turoff, "Conferencing via Computers," *Proceedings of NERM* (New York: Institute of Electrical and Electronic Engineers, 1972).

5. Joshua Greenbaum, "Xerox Groupware Bid," *Computer System News*, 10 Sept. 1990.

6. Martin Garvey and Robert Moran, "IBM Rolls out Distributed Data," *Information Week*, 16 Sept. 1991.

Trend extrapolation

Most people, most of the time, forecast by extrapolating trends. We see a system in change, moving in a particular direction, and ascribe to it, implicitly or explicitly, a momentum that will carry it forward until some limit is reached. This process can be completely subjective—we see the automobile in front of us slow down; our mind extrapolates the rate of closure and we hit the brakes to avoid a collision—or objective—the relative position of the two vehicles can be measured, an equation can be written describing their relative motion, and using this equation, the time of collision is forecast.

Whether the trend that is forecast comes from the mind or from equations, the underlying assumption is the same: the forces in motion will continue.

Time series analysis

Time series analysis refers to the mathematical methods used to fit trend data. These techniques can be simple or complex. The simpler approaches involve placing a curve through the historical data in a way that minimizes the error between the curve and the data. The curve can be a straight line or a curved line; statistical processes are used to place the curve through the data points. If the fit is good, the curve can be extended beyond the given data to make a forecast.[7]

7. Time series analysis is described in detail in Spyros Makridakis, Steven Wheelwright, and Victor McGee, *Forecasting: Methods and Applications* (New York: John Wiley, 1983); and in the excellent book by Robert

Modeling

The future value of some variables may depend on factors other than time; for example, the size of the market for gasoline depends on the average number of miles driven, the number of automobiles in service, and the average efficiency of the autos' engines. Models that relate a variable—for example, gasoline sales—to other factors—number of automobiles, miles driven, engine efficiency—can be constructed using a technique known as regression analysis.

Regression analysis is extremely useful, but great care has to be taken in specifying the variables that produce the forecast. For example, suppose we want to forecast gasoline sales. The price of apples in New York may, by coincidence, correlate precisely with gasoline sales, but one may have nothing to do with the other. The trick is to find factors that are somehow causally related to the variable under study.

In time series analysis and regression modeling, the equations are determined by statistical relationships. By contrast, in simulation modeling an attempt is made to construct equations that duplicate to a greater or lesser extent the actual functioning of the system under question. For example, a simulation model forecasting world population might involve the following logic: population tomorrow is simply the number of people today plus the number of people born, minus the number of people who die during the year. The coefficients of this model have physical significance and can be measured directly; they are not deduced statistically.

System dynamics models gain their strength from the inclusion of feedback loops. The method was popularized by Forrester and Meadows, who used the technique to simulate the growth of cities and global development.[8] Feedback simulates the regulatory systems found in most natural living and physical systems. Although system dynamics models have great appeal, some of the best-known applications have produced nonrealistic results for a number of reasons, including particularly the omission of future technology and corrective policies.[9]

Models of the sort previously described have several important strengths. First, they force the analyst to ask what makes the system he or she is studying work. The models often produce astonishingly accurate forecasts that can be validated by comparing the forecasts to actual data. Finally, the models permit exploration of alternative futures; by varying one factor or another, the analyst can get at least a preliminary feeling for the effects of pol-

---

Ayers, *Technical Forecasting and Long Range Planning* (New York: McGraw-Hill, 1979). A superb little book that contains basic computer programs that demonstrate most of these statistically based methods is Neil Seitz, *Business Forecasting* (Englewood Cliffs, NJ: Reston, 1984).

8. J. W. Forrester, *World Dynamics* (New York: Wright-Allen, 1971); Dennis Meadows et al., *The Limits to Growth: A Report for the Club of Rome's Project on the Predicament of Mankind* (New York: Universe Books, 1972). See also J. W. Forrester, *Industrial Dynamics* (Cambridge: MIT Press, 1961).

9. H. S. Cole et al., eds., *Models of Doom: A Critique of Limits to Growth* (New York: Universe Books, 1973).

icy or other developments on the forecast.

Probabilistic techniques

All of the techniques mentioned so far involve one basic assumption: past relationships hold all of the information required to forecast the future. This assumption may be correct only for a limited time and under limited conditions, however. In the real world, the future holds new developments that can and sometimes do change the relationships between variables. Furthermore, because models produce single-value forecasts, they suggest that there is only one future. This view of the future implies that actions that we or anyone might take have been totally anticipated in the equations, a fatalistic view that most planners would have to reject.

Probabilistic methods break the tyranny of the past and permit explicit introduction of factors that may make the future different. As a case in point, let us suppose that we wanted to forecast future demand for electrical power. Extrapolation might well be misleading. Any forecast of demand for power should take into account future developments such as the possible emergence of electric automobiles, cogeneration, changes in the price of fuel, and changing public concern about nuclear energy. Clearly, more than an extension of the past is required.

But there is no free lunch. Probabilistic methods add another layer of complexity to forecasting. The lists of potentially perturbing future developments can never be complete.

As an example of a probabilistic method, consider trend-impact analysis. The technique begins with an extrapolation of a time series. This is taken to be a baseline forecast, that is, the future of the time series if there were to be no trend-changing developments. Next a list of such developments is constructed; these developments might include unique technologies, societal changes, or political actions that could affect the future course of the variable. Each development on the list is expressed in terms of its expected probability of occurrence and its impact on the baseline, were it to occur.

Trend-impact analysis plays out all possible combinations of the events and their impacts, adjusting the baseline forecast in the process. The results are presented as a fan of outcomes, spread according to probability. In this way, the underlying uncertainty of the forecast can be assessed.

Another probabilistic technique, cross-impact analysis, focuses on the interaction between future developments. Events usually do not happen in isolation; when an event occurs, whole families of downstream happenings are triggered or made more or less likely. Cross-impact techniques focus on such interactions.

Imagine producing a matrix or table that displays the probability of an event, given the occurrence of other events. Begin anywhere and play through this matrix, deciding one event and then adjusting the probability of the remaining events. One scenario would be produced when all events were decided. Using a computer, thousands of scenarios could be produced in this way. By observing the frequency with which various scenarios occurred, probabilities can be assigned to scenarios, ranging from the most frequently occurring combinations of events to the rare combinations.[10]

In practice, the cross-impact method is cumbersome, and providing judgments about the conditional probabilities can be quite tedious if the number of events is greater than a dozen or so. Nevertheless, the method has been applied with some success to a number of problems, including assessment of the political stability of a troubled geographic region.

Interax is another probabilistic simulation technique; it is, in fact, a quantitative scenario generator, "a man/machine simulation that combines human analysts, stakeholders, and decision makers with a data base of possible future changes."[11] In essence, the model is a cross-impact simulation of a large set of events derived from a Delphi study. Some events have probabilities that depend on human inputs; these are addressed interactively by human players during an Interax run. The events that respond to human decisions typically are policies or resource allocations. The outcome of an Interax run is a particular long-term future including trend projections and probabilistic changes and their timing.

Scenarios

Scenarios can present the results of forecasts in a consistent and compelling way. The statistical probability of any scenario is low; its mark of excellence is its internal self-consistency.

Scenarios can be exploratory or normative, qualitative or quantitative. Scenarios can provide the backdrop for planning by sketching a range of possible situations in which policies may have to function. A city planner, for example, might produce three future scenarios of the city differing in the basic assumption made about immigration. With these in hand, certain tax policies can be assumed, and the results assessed.

Since scenarios can be written ad hoc, it is easy to produce a bad one. A bad scenario is one that is inconsistent, fails to describe how the future situation can be achieved—the path to the future—or is irrelevant to the policy study at hand.[12]

Technology sequence analysis is a quantitative scenario-like method developed by the Futures Group to forecast the time at which a future technology-dependent system could become available. The method is based on the perception of the future system as a network of intermediate technologies leading to the system. The time between each technology step is stated probabilistically; this permits the computation of the time of the availability of the target system, as opposed to its probability.

10. See T. J. Gordon and H. Hayward, "Initial Experiments with the Cross Impact Method of Forecasting," *Futures*, 1(2) (Dec. 1968).

11. See Selwyn Enzer, "Exploring Long-Term Business Climates and Strategies with Interax," *Futures*, 13(6):469 (Dec. 1981).

12. There are also many examples of excellent scenario studies; an illustrative study is D. L. Goldfarb and W. R. Huss, "Building Scenarios for an Electric Utility," *Long Range Planning* (United Kingdom) (Apr. 1988).

TABLE 2
APPLICATION CONSIDERATIONS

Technique	Relative Complexity	Forecast Horizon	Data and Training	State of Development	Current Domain*
Genius forecasting	Low	Infinite	Low	Unexplored	All
Delphi questionnaires	Medium	Medium/long	Low	High	All
Delphi interviews	Medium	Medium/long	Low	High	All
On-line expert groups	Medium	Medium/long	Low	Improving	All
Time series analysis	Low	Short	Medium	High	Not PO
Regression modeling	Medium	Short	Medium	High	Not PO
Simulation modeling	High	Short/medium	High	Improving	All
System dynamics	High	Short/medium	High	High	All
Trend-impact analysis	Low	Short/medium	Medium	High	Not PO
Cross-impact analysis	Medium	Medium	Low	High	All
Interax	Medium	Medium	High	High	All
Scenarios	Medium	Short/long	Medium	High	All
Technology sequence analysis	High	Medium/long	High	Improving	ST
Nonlinear models	High	Medium	High	Frontier	Not PO

*ST = science, technology; PO = political, policy.

The method is complex, but it is ideal when the problem involves forecasting the likely time of operation of a technology-based future system; furthermore, technology sequence analysis is very useful in identifying the specific pacing technologies that should be emphasized if the date of system operation is to be expedited.

Nonlinear techniques

"Nonlinear" means that output is not proportional to input. Imagine an economic model in which an increase in tax rate produces a commensurate reduction in consumer spending. In a linear model, doubling the tax rate might halve consumer spending. If the model were nonlinear, however, the situation would change: doubling the tax rate could result in an increase, decrease, or no change in consumer spending.

Chaos is a characteristic of nonlinear systems. It represents a frontier of futures research and is quite experimental.[13]

A model that includes nonlinear elements can be stable, oscillatory, or unstable. So can a model that has only linear elements. But a model that has nonlinear elements can exhibit a fourth state of behavior: chaos. A system in chaos exhibits apparently random fluctuations, and, in the course of such behavior, it may become static for a time, only to fall

13. See James Yorke and Tien-Yien Li, "Period Three Implies Chaos," *American Mathematical Monthly*, vol. 82 (1975).

back into noise later. Two analysts working with exactly the same nonlinear equations must have exactly the same starting conditions or the equations will produce different results. Thus a system in chaos is essentially unpredictable.[14]

If a chaotic system cannot be forecast, why should forecasters be interested in such a system? Because chaos studies may teach, eventually, what is and what is not forecastable and how real-world systems can be controlled. It may be impossible to forecast the exact future of a system but not impossible to anticipate its stability or instability.

SUMMARY

These, then, are some of the prominent methods of exploratory forecasting. They vary greatly in complexity, requirements for data, appropriate level of analyst training, and state of development. Table 2 summarizes some of these attributes.

Do the methods work? Certainly, under limited conditions and for limited intervals. Will they ever be perfect? Not as long as chance plays a role in determining the future and people can decide to take action. Will forecasts ever be complete? No. Is the activity, destined to be incomplete and inaccurate, worth the effort? Those of us in the field believe it is because, in the search for forecasting methods, we really search for how things, societal and political as well as mechanical, work. Understanding how things work provides a chance for avoiding the worst that the future may offer and steering toward the best.

---

14. T. J. Gordon and D. Greenspan, "Chaos and Fractals: New Tools for Technological Forecasting and Social Change," *Futures*, 34 (1):1-25 (Aug. 1988).

ANNALS, *AAPSS*, 522, July 1992

The Future of American-Japanese Trade

By PAT CHOATE

ABSTRACT: With the end of the Cold War and the dissolution of the Soviet Union, the conflicts between nations will increasingly be economic rather than military, but the existing international instruments for dealing with trade conflicts are antiquated and inadequate. The General Agreement on Tariffs and Trade (GATT), as a foundation for global trade, is fundamentally flawed. Japan has ignored its GATT obligations, taking advantage of open markets wherever it can while keeping its markets closed through a variety of formal and informal barriers. In contrast to Europe, the United States' response has been passive, resulting in a long history of failed process-oriented bilateral negotiations with Japan. In the final analysis, the difficulty lies not with Japan but with the United States. The solution is a result-oriented agreement with Japan. While this can be achieved through a variety of means, the guiding principle is results. That means an agreement that concentrates on outcomes, timetables and mutual responsibilities, levels of permissible trade imbalances, the composition of trade, allowable market shares, investment in both countries, and practices like dumping in third markets.

Pat Choate is an author and economist. His most recent book is Agents of Influence. *He lives and works in Washington, D.C.*

36

WITH the end of the Cold War and the dissolution of the Soviet Union, power and influence in the world will increasingly flow less from the instruments of war and more from those of science, technology, and economics. In the process, the conflicts between nations will increasingly be economic rather than military.

The existing international instruments for dealing with trade conflicts are antiquated and inadequate. Indeed, they are so ineffective and so susceptible to economic cheating that they actually encourage conflict.

Among the trade conflicts that are certain to dominate thinking and action in the 1990s and early twenty-first century, the most volatile will be that between Japan and the rest of the world, particularly the United States. Simply put, Japan's economic system of interlocking companies, state-sponsored cartels, exclusionary distribution systems, and a unique financial structure is incompatible with the economies of Europe, Canada, and the United States.

The world's failed experiences with the existing trade mechanisms and the failed U.S.-Japanese trade negotiations over the past two decades illustrate why new institutions and approaches are required.

THE GATT ILLUSION

The principal multilateral agreement on world trade is the General Agreement on Tariffs and Trade (GATT). Its purpose is to foster unrestricted multilateral trade by binding participating nations to negotiate trade rules and by mandating penalties for any deviation from these obligations. More than a hundred nations are contracting partners to the GATT, which is administered by a secretariat of 350 people headquartered in Geneva.

As the foundation for global trade, the GATT is fundamentally flawed. From the beginning, 1948, its coverage was limited to merchandise trade and tariffs, but the nature of trade has changed while the GATT has been unable to adapt. Another flaw is that, because the GATT was a contractual agreement, enforcement depended on the voluntary arbitration of disagreements between signatories.

To remedy these deficiencies, the United States has led other nations in seven major rounds of GATT negotiations—in 1949, 1951, 1956, 1960-62, 1962-67, 1973-79, and 1986 to the present. Notably, the time lags between negotiations and the time taken to conclude each round of talks have become longer and longer.

Regardless of the time demands, the GATT, now and in the past, has three principal limitations. First, it neither recognizes nor bridges the vast differences between the economic systems that exist in Japan, Europe, and the United States. Specifically, Japan and most of the dynamic Asian economies continue to rely on industrial targeting, and the line between government and business is blurred, if not nonexistent. These economies regularly rely on subsidies, protectionism, and dumping to both control their home markets and gain market share in foreign countries.

Europe has a mixed economy. Some industries, such as Airbus, are state dominated and subsidized. Others, such as the manufacture of auto parts, are market oriented.

By contrast, the American economy is primarily market oriented. Virtually no limitations are placed on market entry, and firms that fail are usually permitted to die. The GATT fails to accommodate these fundamental differences between the Asian, European, and American economies.

Second, GATT coverage is limited. The GATT covers roughly 80 percent of world trade in merchandise. Trade in services, agriculture, textiles, and investment and capital flows, however, are currently excluded. Consequently, the GATT covers not even 7 percent of global economic activity. The current GATT negotiations are supposed to expand this coverage, but so many exclusions have been agreed upon that any final agreement is guaranteed to be porous.

The third, and a principal, weakness of the GATT is that, when a nation does violate its treaty obligations, the dispute resolution process is ambiguous and slow. Most important, penalties are unenforceable.

Because the GATT is so ineffective, countries are pursuing alternatives. Europe, for instance, which has united in the European Community, has formed a trade bloc in which trade between members will be open. At the same time, trade with outsiders will be tightly controlled.

The United States is forging a de facto trade bloc through its negotiations on a North American free-trade agreement. Already, Canada and the United States have entered into a bilateral free-trade agreement, and negotiations are under way to create a similar arrangement with Mexico.

A major, but unspoken, motivation in both the European and North American actions is to deal with Japan's attempts to dominate world markets in key industries such as finance, automobiles, electronics, and high-technology goods. In the process, Japan has ignored its GATT obligations and has taken advantage of open markets wherever it can while keeping its markets closed through a variety of formal and informal barriers.

The Europeans have responded by negotiating tit-for-tat agreements with Japan. Thus Italy permits Japan to sell precisely the same number of cars in Italy that Fiat is permitted to sell in Japan, or roughly 3400 vehicles per year. In Europe as a whole, Japanese automakers are being limited to 16 percent of the market. Europe has also imposed limitations on Japanese sales of high-technology goods. European restrictions generally are inclusive of products imported from Japan or manufactured in Europe.

By contrast, the United States has taken a more passive path. When Japan was flooding the market with televisions in the 1970s, for instance, a temporary import quota was imposed. But it was set at such a high level, more than 1.5 million sets, and Japanese companies had stockpiled so many sets in warehouses, that it was meaningless. Likewise, when Japanese companies began to flood the auto market in the early 1980s, an import quota was established, but it was set at the level of existing imports and Japanese companies were permitted to build assembly facilities inside the United States, thereby skirting the restrictions.

Time and again when there have been trade difficulties with Japan, the United States has resorted to bilateral negotiations. And time and again, these negotiations have failed. Their failure is instructive as an illustration of the way not to go.

THE PATTERN OF FAILURE

The most striking feature of American trade negotiations with Japan is their sheer predictability. By now, we know in advance not only which issues will be discussed but also the approaches that will be taken by both sides and the results that will be achieved.

In August 1972, for instance, President Nixon met with Prime Minister Tanaka in Honolulu. The primary subject of this summit was the expanding American trade deficit with Japan, which that year had reached the unprecedented level of $3.8 billion.

In response to the deficit problem, President Nixon called on the Japanese to do a number of things.

1. First, he urged them to reduce their nontariff trade barriers.
2. Then he asked the Japanese to buy more American-made computers. Other U.S. negotiators pressed the Japanese to buy American-made aircraft and satellites.
3. President Nixon requested that the Japanese purchase more American agricultural products.
4. He said the Japanese should eliminate barriers to the establishment or purchase of retail outlets in Japan by U.S. companies.
5. Finally, he called on the Japanese to liberalize their business distribution system.

In response, the Japanese government promised to try to promote imports from the United States and to reduce the imbalance to a more manageable size within a reasonable period of time. They figured that three or four years would constitute a reasonable time frame.

The final Nixon-Tanaka communiqué emphasized the Japanese government's offer to improve its distribution system, to lower investment barriers for American retail firms, and to permit more sales of U.S. computer products in Japan. Specifically, the communiqué read:

The President also noted with appreciation the recent decisions by the Government of Japan to liberalize access to the distribution system by allowing improved investment opportunities in retailing, processing, and packaging as well as the decision to allow greater sales of computer products in Japan.

In the end, both President Nixon and Prime Minister Tanaka affirmed the commitments of both countries to initiate and actively support multilateral trade negotiations covering both industry and agriculture and the reduction of tariff and nontariff barriers as well as formulation of a multilateral nondiscriminatory safeguard mechanism.

Fast-forward in time to 19 October 1989, when U.S. Trade Representative Carla Hills addressed the Japan National Press Club in Tokyo. Ambassador Hills's main concern was the massive U.S.-Japan trade deficit—an unprecedented $50 billion. Her comments, while certainly timely, were also hauntingly familiar.

1. Like President Nixon nearly twenty years before her, Ambassador Hills encouraged the Japanese to reduce their nontariff barriers to American products.

2. She called on them to lower barriers to the sale of U.S. satellites and supercomputers.

3. She urged the Japanese to buy more American forest products.

4. She told them the story of how the Japanese government was keeping two of America's largest retailers —Toys-R-Us and McDonald's—from opening stores in Japan for two years while it deliberated on the firms' investment applications.

5. Finally, she asserted that Japan's closed distribution system not only hurt American producers by retarding U.S. exports to Japan but also affected Japanese consumers, who were forced to pay higher prices for those goods.

In the end, like President Nixon, Ambassador Hills reaffirmed America's commitment to the principles of free trade and the ongoing round of GATT negotiations. Between 1972 and 1989, little had changed except, of course, the size of the U.S. trade deficit with Japan. The Nixon-Hills example, moreover, is not unique. It reflects a long history of failed process-oriented bilateral negotiations with Japan.

Consider for a moment the following seven market-opening packages that flowed from bilateral U.S.-Japanese negotiations in the 1980s.

Package one

On 30 January 1982, a Japanese ad hoc committee led by former Ministry of International Trade and Industry Minister Esaki announced that the Japanese government would reduce 67 nontariff barriers—primarily in the customs and standards areas— as a package of market-opening measures. Japan established a new governmentwide channel for foreign grievances called the Office of Trade Ombudsman, and Japanese Customs authorities announced a five-point plan to improve foreign access to the Japanese market.

Following the announcement of this market-opening package, the Office of the United States Trade Representative commented that the Japanese initiatives were not exactly what they appeared to be. "Upon analysis," reported the trade representative's office, "it became clear that those 67 actions largely reflected a compilation of measures that had already been undertaken by various Japanese government agencies."

Package two

On 27 May 1982, the Japanese government announced a second major market-access package. Through this initiative, the Japanese said, they would reduce tariffs on 17 agricultural items, address problems with standards development, and allow foreigners to participate in Japanese technical groups of domestic industry organizations that were formed to draft specifications to submit to Japanese government ministries. Despite heavy U.S. pressure, though, the liberalization of agricultural production was not included in this package.

Package three

On 13 January 1983, Japan announced the reduction of tariff rates on 28 industrial and 47 agricultural products. This third market-opening package included a call for the simplification of import testing and certification procedures, including acceptance of certain test data generated overseas for veterinary drugs, feed additives, high-pressure containers, and electrical appliances. In addition, the Japanese government promised import-promoting administrative reforms, as well as the expansion of the number of retail outlets allowed to handle imported tobacco products.

Package four

On 21 October 1983, the Japanese reduced tariff rates on 40 items. The Japanese government also called upon its industries to import more foreign products.

Package five

On 27 April 1984, the Japanese government announced that it would take several new steps to open Japanese markets to foreign products. Among the measures that were promised were the elimination of tariffs on 7 items and the reduction of tariff rates on 60 others.

The package also included the liberalization of procurement rules on satellites purchased by Nippon Telephone and Telegraph as well as those purchased in the private sector. The Japanese government also accepted, through this package, the submission of test data from suitable foreign testing organizations to certify a range of products. Most important, this fifth market-opening package included the Japanese government's statement of intent to allow government agencies, government-related agencies, and private firms the option of purchasing space satellites from foreign suppliers in cases where purchase from a Japanese source was not necessary for the domestic development of technology.

But in the spring of 1984, when the Japanese announced these initiatives, the U.S.-Japan Trade Study Group—composed of businessmen from both the United States and Japan—reported that many of the allegedly new undertakings had been previously announced. The Reagan administration called the proposed tariff changes too little, too late, and asserted that many of the promises made by the Japanese government were simply too vague.

Package six

On 9 April 1985, Japan unveiled another package of market-access initiatives. This time, the Japanese said, they would eliminate many of the technical standards used to select telecommunications terminal equipment. The Japanese government also agreed to enforce procedural transparency in the telecommunications industry.

Package seven

On 30 July 1985, Japan announced an all-new "action program" for improving foreign access to its markets. At the center of this package was the Japanese government's pledge to reform its standards and approval processes. This package also outlined changes in tariffs, import quotas, government procurement, financial and capital markets, services, and import-promotion measures.

MOSS

In addition to offering these seven market-opening measures, the Japanese government was involved in a series of more specific market-opening negotiations with the United States. The biggest of these talks was the Market-Oriented Sector Selective (MOSS) on 2 January 1985, proposed by Japan. These talks focused on telecommunications, pharmaceuticals, medical equipment, electronics, and forestry products. A year later, the MOSS talks were expanded to include auto parts.

Maekawa report

In October 1985, Prime Minister Nakasone formed the Advisory Group on Economic Structural Adjustment for International Harmony, chaired by Haruo Maekawa, former president of the Bank of Japan. The Maekawa Group issued its final report on 7 April 1986. It called for a major restructuring of the Japanese economy—an increase in imports of manufactured goods, tariff reductions, streamlined standards and certification procedures, and a simplified distribution system.

Yet, today, after all of these market-opening processes and vast expenditures of time and energy on negotiations, the Japanese market remains only marginally more open in the 1990s than it was at the end of the 1970s.

RESULTS REALLY DO MATTER

The one clear lesson of U.S.-Japanese bilateral trade negotiations of the past two decades is that if process is what you want, process is what you will get. But what we really need is results.

In the final analysis, the difficulty lies not with Japan, but with the United States. Europe understands and negotiates for results. By contrast, U.S. trade policies remain locked in the past. They sit on three theoretical pillars, none of which are appropriate for the circumstances in which we now find ourselves. The pillars are the following:

— first, that open markets and free trade are the most efficient means to expand global trade and, therefore, should form the economic model that guides world commerce;
— second, that multilateral negotiations are the best way to open markets and promote free trade; and
— third, that the United States has a primary responsibility among nations to advance free trade.

The obvious flaw in U.S. thinking is that Japan's economy is like that of the United States. It is not, nor will it be, nor should it be. What's more, they keep telling Americans so, and Americans keep refusing to believe them.

Indeed, Japan operates in the world market using vastly different assumptions that serve vastly different ends from America's. The two nations differ in ways both manifest and subtle, reflecting basic differences in history, culture, national aspirations, and politics. Despite America's spirited urging of Japan to adopt the U.S. economic model—reliance on market forces, free trade, and deregulation—this system enjoys little appeal across the Pacific. While it suits the United States, it would never fit Japan—and the Japanese know it.

Put another way, Japan has the world's largest accumulation of savings, is the world's largest creditor, has the world's most advanced commercial technology, and possesses the world's most advanced manufacturing capacity. Japan also has one of the world's lowest unemployment rates and claims enormous social stability. Japan—with an economy half the size of the U.S. economy—is investing at a rate twice as fast as the United States is. Last year, in fact, Japan made more fixed capital investment than the United States and Canada combined, which means that its competitiveness and growth will surge in the 1990s. Japan has a $43 billion trade surplus with the United States, and its prospects for strong net national profits from trade surpluses continue for as long as one can calculate.

Why would Japan wish to abandon an economic system that serves its interests so well and adopt an approach that serves America's instead?

WHAT MUST BE DONE

If the United States is to reduce its trade deficits with other nations and particularly with Japan, a strategy far different from those it has used in the past two decades is required. The first step is to recognize and accept the differences that exist between the various economic systems throughout the world. These differences are neither good nor bad, just differences. The need is to accommodate them, and, in doing so, multilateral approaches involving many nations are generally a preferred route. At a minimum, this means completely rethinking our international institutions such as the GATT. They were ineffective in the past, and their ineffectiveness is positively dangerous for the future.

At the same time, the United States has an obligation to put its fiscal and economic house in order. This means balancing the budget and adopting trade-sensitive fiscal, monetary, and exchange-rate policies. In addition, the government must enforce domestic trade laws vigorously. The nation must also produce fully competitive goods and services. Nonetheless, it is important to note that the United States still produces hundreds of the most competitive and advanced goods in the world and still has the highest levels of productivity of any nation.

Until the GATT works or a new world trade organization emerges, the United States is left to its own devices in establishing a fair and reciprocal trade relationship with other nations.

In truth, the United States has few substantive trade and investment problems with either Europe or Canada. They accept our goods and investment and we accept theirs. In most years, moreover, U.S. goods are sufficiently competitive that the United States has either a surplus or a balanced trade account.

The same, however, is not true with Japan. For 26 years, Japan has run a merchandise trade surplus. In 1991 and 1990, Japan accounted for more than 60 percent of the U.S. trade deficit. Obviously, something is wrong. Equally obvious is that bilateral negotiations lead nowhere.

The solution is a result-oriented agreement with Japan. While this can be achieved through a variety of means, the guiding principle is results. That means an agreement that concentrates on outcomes, timetables and mutual responsibilities, levels of permissible trade imbalances, the composition of trade, allowable market shares, investment in both countries, and practices like dumping in third markets.

Access to America's markets for both Japanese imports and investments is the best—perhaps the only—negotiating chip the United States has. If the United States is unwilling to use it, it has no negotiating leverage. Indeed, if it is unwilling to use that leverage while keeping its markets open, why should anyone wish to do anything other than stall and delay negotiations?

To be sure, America must not succumb to the lure of old-fashioned protectionism. Rather, it must be sophisticated enough to discern the difference between closing U.S. markets to avoid foreign competition and closing them as a device to open Japan's markets.

And to be sure, America has permitted the fiscal and trade imbalance with Japan to go on so long that the process of adjustment guarantees that pain is inevitable on both sides of the Pacific. The only consolation is that the pain will be less horrible now than it will be if the United States waits even longer to take action.

In sum, geo-economics will replace geopolitics as the central obsession of nations in the 1990s and early twenty-first century. The danger is that our principal institutions—in particular, the GATT—are too limited to resolve today's economic conflicts, let alone tomorrow's.

For the longer term, a new set of institutions is required. Their basic function would be to permit the expansion of trade between economic systems that are fundamentally incompatible—institutionally, financially, politically, and culturally.

In the interim, the focus of U.S. negotiations must be tailored to the circumstances of individual nations. That is, with free-trade economies such as that of Canada, free-trade agreements are appropriate, much as now exists. With mixed economies such as those of Europe, mixed approaches are warranted—free trade in those industries where Europe relies on open markets and managed trade in those industries, such as Airbus, where commerce is subsidized and regulated. Finally, a managed trade arrangement is appropriate with those economies, such as Japan's, that are tightly controlled by a combination of government and a handful of large, export-driven corporations.

ANNALS, *AAPSS*, 522, July 1992

The Future of Information Technology

By VARY T. COATES

ABSTRACT: We are entering the age of information, in many ways analogous to the age of energy that began in the eighteenth century. This article calls attention to some of the paradoxes of the information age. It looks at social and economic macro trends that are shaping the era. A five-year outlook for information technology is presented. Finally, some implications for society and for its economy are suggested, and some issues are discussed that must be faced in the next five years as a result of the changes of the information age.

Vary Coates, Ph.D., is senior associate in the Telecommunications and Computing Technologies Program of the Office of Technology Assessment, U.S. Congress. Her areas of special interest include international telecommunications, technology assessment, technology forecasting, and science policy.

NOTE: The views expressed in this article are solely the responsibility of the author and not those of the Office of Technology Assessment or its governing board.

THE coordination, direction, and control of all social activity depend on information. As population and social networks increase in scale, institutions become more complex, and the physical environment is more thoroughly modified or synthetic, information becomes ever more valuable. Our social attention span or effective communities—the range of people and places that we perceive to be related to our own lives—have for many of us become global. The age of information that we are entering is in many ways analogous to the age of energy that stimulated the industrial revolution.

PARADOXES OF THE INFORMATION AGE

The concept of the information age carries with it some paradoxes. Information should be a great equalizer, but, while it encourages political democracy, it may also result in economic elitism. Information may be more widely dispersed yet become less widely shared. Our definition of "information" may narrow rather than widen. Systems that are designed to expand our capability for control may themselves grow beyond our capability to effectively control them.

The long-range social trends of expansion, intermeshing, and complexity led Zbigniew Brzezinski, Daniel Bell, and others to picture future society as the domain of bureaucratic experts or technocrats.[1] At a mini-

mum, greater coordination and control are increasingly necessary to conduct social and economic enterprises on a global scale or in a global network.

The information age was foreshadowed by telegraphy and telephony, but it truly blossomed when computers began to emulate the intrinsically human characteristics of memory, calculation, process control, anticipation, and decision making. Now the technology-dictated distinctions between processing information and transmitting it have begun to disappear. People and computers can communicate with each other over existing networks; messages are digitized and routed through any available technological channel by switches that are really computers; the telephone touch-tone pad often serves as a computer input device or the computer keyboard calls up a telephone connection. It is now fully appropriate to speak of information technology as a whole in terms of its social implications.

For the foreseeable future, information technology will continue to become more powerful, more pervasive, more accessible, more diversified, and more mobile, trends that have been apparent for four decades. Another long-standing trend is com-

1. Brzezinski spoke of a "technetronic age" of information technology and the rise of a "meritocratic elite" of technocrats, saying that "power will gravitate into the hands of those who control the information and can control it

most rapidly." Zbigniew Brzezinski, "America in the Technetronic Age," *Encounter*, Jan. 1968, p. 21. See also idem, *Between Two Ages: America's Role in the Technetronic Age* (New York: Viking Press, 1968). Bell spoke of the coming preeminence of a meritocratic elite founded on knowledge rather than property. Daniel Bell, *Toward the Year 2000* (Boston: Houghton Mifflin, 1968); idem, *The Coming of Post-Industrial Society: A Venture in Social Forecasting* (New York: Basic Books, 1973).

pression and miniaturization. Much information technology will be embedded in the form of minute brains on a chip in everyday surroundings and objects. Other information technology will take on the characteristics of social infrastructure—as do roads, traffic lights, utility lines, and public telephones—improving the quality of community life.

Information technology is in some ways inherently democratizing. The proliferating means by which information can be disseminated make it more difficult for authorities to monopolize the direction of social activities. The technology that facilitates centralized control also weakens control in some ways, as was demonstrated at Tiananmen Square. This is one of the paradoxes of the information age.

Another paradox of the information age is that much information may well become less commonly available, less universally shared, and thus less integrative of community and culture. Thanks to technology, an increasing amount of information is becoming standardized, priced, and subject to market forces. The age of information is really the age of data.

As energy resources moved into the market economy, growing differences in energy use between rich and poor resulted in greater disparity in the ability to participate effectively in all economic processes and social institutions. Similarly, information is becoming a monetarized commodity that drives societal processes as surely as energy drove industrialization. Disparities in terms of money, education, ability, and technology not only will be reflected in different degrees of access to information but also may grow as a result of that difference. While information technology can encourage political democracy, that effect may be negated as it reinforces economic elitism.

Information technology may subtly change the nature of what is accepted as information. Historical lore, school-transmitted common knowledge, and informally disseminated news—gossip—is devalued in comparison with formally distributed information and information-as-data, which are suitable for translation into binary impulses and billable by electronic data interchange. The all-important question is whether the systems that efficiently route and allocate such data in neat packets can also be used to convey to ordinary citizens information in the form of literature, art, political choices, and practical knowledge about the workings of the world we live in.

Another paradox of information technology is that, as computer systems take over more and more intricate monitoring and control, they tend also to extend beyond the direct intellectual grasp of their users. Very large systems are hard to document, monitor, diagnose, fix, and replicate. There are likely to be unrecognized sources of instability or possibilities of failure. Major networks, such as the switched public telephone system or the control system for a nuclear power plant, tend to malfunction in ways that are not fully anticipated or understood. Recent widespread telephone outages constitute a good example of this.

TRENDS SHAPING
THE INFORMATION AGE

The rapid development of information technology drives and is driven by the continuing shift toward a service-dominated economy. Most services involve the generation, processing, dissemination, and delivery of information. At least half of all such services are rendered not to individuals but to businesses. Making these services more efficient should raise the productivity of all sectors of the economy, providing a strong market impetus for the continuing development of information technology.

Another driving force is the evolution of a global trading arena, subjecting both American and foreign businesses to strong competitive pressure and encouraging the emergence of transnational enterprises. These far-flung corporations, gradually losing their national identities through mergers and acquisitions, can readily shift their sources of supply, their market focus, their production operations, their sources of financing and cash management, and their headquarters across national boundaries. Coordination of such corporate activity will require huge volumes of information and 24-hour capability to transport and share them. Many companies already operate their own elaborate communications networks, using a mix of microwave, satellite dishes, and circuits leased from public switched networks, often with hubs in several countries. They are like self-serving but benign spiders busily enclosing the world in a net of computer-controlled telecommunications channels.

THE FIVE-YEAR OUTLOOK FOR
INFORMATION TECHNOLOGY:
CONTINUING PROGRESS

The adoption of computers in large organizations has gone through four distinct phases: large central mainframes; personal computers and distributed data processing; the networking of microcomputers; and now the networking of networks. Each phase has added to, rather than superseded, the previous phase. In large organizations, there is likely to be a mainframe for central billing, inventory control, data processing, and system management, along with networked personal computers on clerical and executive desks throughout the organization.

Very large-scale integration has made it possible to put millions of components on a chip. Early microprocessors had about 2300 transistors; the new 486 personal computer has 1.2 million. The 586 computer, with about 4 million transistors, should be able to perform billions of instructions per second. The speed of processing, however, already exceeds the speed of input and accessing, so improvement in these two areas will be a major focus of research and development.

Another long-range trend is the increasing compatibility of hardware and more powerful, easier-to-use packaged software. Expert systems are increasingly available; these software packages make decision rules and knowledge gleaned from experts available to users through interactive dialogue with the computer.

Innovation literature speaks of the two factors of market pull and technology push. Market pull is response to demand or to perceived customer needs; technology push is the imperative to explore and develop new areas of technology long before potential applications can be discerned. Technology push drove the early stages of information technology development. Continuing developments are being driven by market pull.

NEW EMPHASES

For the rest of this decade, the most striking developments in information technology—already well under way—will be

— digitization of all data;
— new and more natural user interfaces;
— increasing mobility for information technology;
— specialization, miniaturization, and dispersion of information technology;
— multipurpose technology of broader capability and greater flexibility; and
— the networking of networks.

"Digitization of data" means the conversion of text, numerics, sound, and visual images to binary signals that can be manipulated, stored, transmitted, and reconverted to its original form for delivery. This makes possible integrated-services digital networks that can carry voice, data, text, and video signals simultaneously. Digitized data can be rearranged, combined, and otherwise manipulated with ease. These qualities make many information products or services interchangeable; customers can get the same data from many vendors

and reformat or analyze it as they choose. Competition drives prices toward real costs. Information service vendors, such as Dow Jones, who collect, generate, process, and distribute or transmit data for or to their customers, must increasingly compete by offering enhanced services or add-on features.

With the digitization of data, there is also a strong trend toward the capture of data at the source through automated teller machines, point-of-sale terminals, hand-held computers, and optical scanners and readers. For example, futures traders shouting and gesticulating in Chicago's turbulent commodity market pits will soon instantly record their trades on tiny computers strapped to their wrists that communicate with the market's central computer.

Great effort is going into the elimination of input devices, such as keyboards and mice, that tie the user to the technology in ways that impede other movements and activities. Speech-recognition capability is improving but may not be practically available on a wide scale within the next five years.

Scientists are working on technologies to combine computer capabilities and human sensibilities to create virtual reality, a simulation of physical and perceptual conditions through what some writers have called a "three dimensional interface."[2] People use goggles, helmets, gloves, and tools to project their bodily motions and to interact with computer-manipulated representations of reality on a screen. The user is in

2. "The Ultimate Interface," *Informationweek*, 25 June 1990, pp. 46-48.

the scene and sees and feels all the effects of the action in the scene.

Mobile communication is the fastest growing segment of telecommunications. Cellular telephones have found a ready market in the United States, primarily for use in motor vehicles. In Eastern Europe, where installed telephone systems are obsolete, cellular telephony is being used as an expedient until a new infrastructure can be built. If this opportunity causes cellular telephones to improve rapidly in cost and performance, they may become a viable alternative to wired communications in other situations. At present, cellular phones are not able to handle large-scale data transmission. But digital cellular telephony is just around the corner; digital compression technology, which can pack more phone calls into a given portion of the radio spectrum, will increase cellular system capacity up to twentyfold.[3] Personal communications networks are being promised by several companies. They involve miniaturized, hand-held radio telephones, possibly using a worldwide array of low-orbit satellites for transmission.

Hand-held notepad computers are just being offered that accept handwritten input. They can be used in tasks not easily done at a desk or limited to one location.

Information technology is moving in two contrasting directions: greater specialization and greater diversity.

3. U.S., Congress, Office of Technology Assessment, *The 1992 World Administrative Radio Conference: Issues for U.S. International Spectrum Policy—Background Paper*, OTA-BP-TCT-76 (Washington, DC: Government Printing Office, 1991), pp. 36-37.

Specialization in office technology and process control technology is attractive because of the growing diversity of white-collar work, workers, and workplaces, which have varying needs for technology. Computers are steadily becoming cheaper per unit of power, but general-purpose computers may become less cost-effective in many jobs because there is no need for so much power. This circumstance makes specialized equipment more attractive. At the same time, there is a complementary trend toward less specialized, multiple-purpose equipment. The capabilities of today's personal computers, telephones, fax machines, copiers, printers, and other equipment are being combined into multipurpose, integrated workstations capable of handling text, calculations, voice communications, graphic design, and video display.

Digitization of data makes inevitable still further convergence of computing and communications. Networks combine many kinds of transmission technologies and many kinds of terminals—telephones, computers, video screens, and so forth. There is a strong movement toward intelligent networks, with computer control distributed among switching centers throughout the network and even at the customer end.

Interconnectivity remains a serious problem, but it is being overcome by interface devices and services, such as client-server systems, that provide a link between, for example, a corporation and a bank. A payment instruction might move from the corporation's computer through the service vendor's computer to the bank's computer, even though the two end-point computer systems may not be directly compatible.

In the next five years we should see rapid progress in several areas. High-definition imaging systems are on the way. Parallel processor computers have recently demonstrated speeds one hundred times that of conventional supercomputers, and a teraflop computer capable of 1 trillion calculations per second is expected by about 1996. Scientists are working toward nanotechnology, including the development of molecule-scale computers, and photonic computers, which use photons—light rays—rather than electrons. Broadly useful applications are not widely expected from these technologies within the next five years, however.

INFORMATION AND EVERYDAY LIFE

The information age will have fully matured only when information technology permeates the everyday life of ordinary people. This will come about because of two related strong trends. The first is the embodiment of computers in familiar, everyday things, so that more and more objects—tools and toys, furnishings and fixtures, appliances and automobiles—are electronically responsive to their users or to their environment. The second trend is the adaptation of computers to familiar, everyday activities, in ways that are completely transparent, natural, and effortless for people with no interest in information technology as such. Eventually, the household environment and ordinary tools will react usefully and flexibly to simple signals or to subtle differences in the environment. This requires computers better endowed with sensors that pick up the same kinds of environmental clues that people use: sight, sound, movement, and so on. This will be a strong theme in industry research and development over the next decade.

The pervasiveness of information technology in things is passive; people need make little additional effort to operate or direct the technology. But a second trend is the more active use of computers in normal, familiar activity. Becoming accustomed to anticipation and control of change through information, people will increasingly expect to have this capability in all of their activities, even the most informal and personal, such as recreation, home life, family duties, and learning. To give people this computer-generated capability for control, computers must go where people go, unintrusively and unobtrusively, and the interface between people and computers must become transparent. In other words, computers must be mobile, very small, and freed from the keyboard.

Voice recognition is one way to get rid of the keyboard. Currently, computers can recognize only a few thousand words, or more from speakers for whom they have been especially programmed. Eventually, computers will be able to provide another bridge between people by translating human languages and by generating language for the mute and the deaf who lack it.

INDUSTRY IMPACTS

Nearly all economic sectors are shaped by the ways that information is used and by its availability and cost. Some sectors are particularly sensitive to the speed of transmission. Financial information, for example, has some peculiar characteristics. It may be immensely valuable for the first few minutes or seconds after its generation and almost worthless thereafter. It is often most valuable when available to the smallest number of people. Financiers and stock speculators were predictably among the first users of telegraphy in 1843.[4] Since then, telecommunications has radically changed the nature of banking and world financial markets.[5] It allows many kinds of institutions to provide most of the services once exclusively offered by banks. It encourages cross-national investment and enormously increases the speed and volume of monetary flow between national institutions and between nations. It ties together national currencies, decreasing the ability of national governments to enforce their own fiscal and monetary policies.

In education, information tends to be most valuable when widely disseminated and shared. Because information in this sector often has characteristics approaching those of a common good, there is relatively less incentive for the market to improve its distribution and to support

innovation in information technology. Fortunately, educational needs for information technology partly parallel those of business, government, and health care providers; thus education can have a share in an active marketplace for information hardware and services.[6] Technology is proving valuable in the classroom—although it falls short of the glowing promises made by its advocates in the past—and also in delivering instruction to remote or dispersed sites where personal instruction may not be cost-effective.

Many industries face possible restructuring as a direct or indirect result of technological change and convergence. Competing and complementary transmission technologies —microwave, cellular radio, fiber optic cable, satellite transmission— contribute to dramatic changes in telecommunications industries, which at the same time are undergoing privatization in some countries and regulatory liberalization in others. There is also strong secondary convergence between telecommunications systems (telegraphy, telephony, radio communications, broadcast). For example, radio networks could provide paging, electronic mail, and facsimile. Television broadcasters could offer teletext over the vertical blanking interval of the video signal, thus making fuller use of the broadcast spectrum. These impending developments mean that the media industries also face restructuring.

But while the long-range trend toward technological convergence is

4. Vary T. Coates and Bernard Finn, *A Retrospective Technology Assessment: Submarine Telegraphy* (San Francisco: San Francisco Press, 1979), pp. 70-76.

5. U.S., Congress, Office of Technology Assessment, *Trading around the Clock: Global Securities Markets and Information Technology*, July 1990; idem, *Electronic Bulls and Bears: U.S. Securities Markets and Information Technology*, Sept. 1990.

6. U.S., Congress, Office of Technology Assessment, *Linking for Learning: A New Course for Education*, OTA-SET-430 (Washington, DC: Government Printing Office, 1989).

clear, to users it can seem a long way off. It is delayed by segmented markets, by the failure to achieve interoperability, and by the persistence of obsolete regulatory categories (for example, distinctions between data processing and data communications, or that between carrying information and supplying it, which is difficult to apply to electronic bulletin boards).

PRODUCTIVITY
AND EMPLOYMENT

In industrialized nations, there are enormous enterprises whose need for information technology and services is still expanding. Many developing nations have hardly tasted the benefits of modern information technology. Improved information technology strongly contributes to productivity and innovation in other sectors of the economy, although it is hard to find empirical evidence as yet that information technology has made individual corporations more productive. Enthusiasts for information technology assert that there is a nearly insatiable demand for information technology, and a steady stream of technological innovation and improvement can be expected. If these assertions are correct, and there is much to be said for them, then those national economies that can produce information technology and services could expect to enter a sustained period of robust expansion.

But even if the market for information can expand indefinitely, a near-term consequence is likely to be strong constraint on growth in white-collar employment and, in the long term, a possible decline.[7] A decrease in primary keyboarding—entering data into a computer—will result from the increasing use of bar codes, scanners, optical character readers, point-of-sale terminals, and so on. An even stronger factor should be a decrease in the secondary keyboarding, which is the entry into one computer of data generated in another, incompatible computer, sometimes within the same organization. Some large companies are now using electronic data interchange services. These services allow the company, its primary suppliers, major customers, and service providers such as banks to exchange data directly from computer to computer via private communications networks. This exchange may eliminate clerical redundancy not just within a company but also within large groups of data interchangers.

With fewer clerical workers to supervise, with computers extending the scope of supervisory control, and with either clerical workers or top executives themselves using computers to generate reports, corporations are deciding to flatten their hierarchy by eliminating many middle managers. Data bases, new search and analytical tools, and expert systems may well reduce the need for professionals in some categories. Many of these tools can also in effect deprofessionalize and trivialize some professional work or allow it to be done by workers with far less training and experience and at lower wages.

7. U.S., Congress, Office of Technology Assessment, *Automation of America's Offices*, OTA-CIT-288 (Washington, DC: Government Printing Office, 1985).

Beyond the layoffs and cutbacks that can be attributed to the current economic recession, there is evidence of a long-range slowing of growth in clerical employment. Even as the U.S. economy recovers from its current recession, and even if it can resume a healthy rate of growth in today's highly competitive global economy, this trend will probably continue. This employment contraction is well under way, and, when the recession ends, current employment very likely will not rebound as it has in the past. The information age, paradoxically, may require fewer, rather than more, information workers. Looked at from the bright side, however, reducing the labor force should mean decreasing operating and transaction costs for business.

ISSUES FOR THE NEXT FIVE YEARS AND BEYOND

Increasingly, much personal data are stored in data bases. It is becoming cheaper to interconnect data bases, to search many data bases, and to merge and reformat material from each without the knowledge of the individual concerned and for purposes far from those for which the data were originally collected. Information thus aggregated, whether correct or full of errors, can be widely distributed, again unknown to the subject, who has no opportunity to correct it or stop its use.

Electronic sensors also threaten privacy. The U.S. Constitution, in the Fourth Amendment, forbids "unreasonable searches and seizures" by the government. When these words were written, search or seizure required a physical intrusion into or against people's "persons, houses, papers, or effects." But first by wiretaps, later by air or satellite surveillance and photography, and now by a variety of sensors, one may be searched, and evidence seized, without any physical intrusion or even approach.[8] Electronic surveillance technologies are powerful tools for the prevention, detection, and conviction of crime.[9] But in order to detect crime, one must watch noncriminals as well as criminals.

Some nations have enacted strong computer privacy laws. In the United States, laws governing the use of computerized data and the privacy of communications are limited, narrow, and inconsistent. Businesses argue that privacy laws may discourage the offering of enhanced information services. U.S. policy has been to act only when there is public indignation over demonstrated, widely recognized problems—for example, the recent controversy over caller ID.

The protection of intellectual property is another issue that is becoming more troublesome. Intellectual property is a unique representation or

8. U.S., Congress, Office of Technology Assessment, *Criminal Justice: New Technologies and the Constitution*, OTA-CIT-366 (Washington, DC: Government Printing Office, 1988).

9. Federal, state, and local criminal justice authorities now are able to use closed-circuit television, parabolic microphones, miniature radio transmitters (bugs), telephone taps, pen registers (which detect and record the dialing of telephone numbers), computer-usage monitors, electronic-mail monitors, cellular radio interceptors, satellite beam interceptors, pattern-recognition systems, and intruder-detection systems that pick up sound, vibrations, or infrared radiation.

embodiment of expression that is invested in an artistic, scientific, or intellectual work created by an identifiable person and separable from the medium in which it is embodied. In other words, a musical composition is intellectual property, separate from the record, tape, or sheet music that contains it.[10]

U.S. copyright law gives an author a limited monopoly right to his or her creation, so that creative work can be rewarded in the marketplace and writing and invention will therefore be stimulated. Now not only authors, musicians, and scientists but filmmakers, software designers, and other information workers also claim a right to the fruits of their intellectual labors. But information technology lets people easily copy music, video, electronic games, designs, and works of art for home use. Digital representations of such works also make it possible to generate successive copies without degradation of quality, and to cut from, add to, and otherwise manipulate these works. It is clear that most people believe it is acceptable to copy music and other works for one's own use or to give to friends so long as copies are not sold, but this cuts into sales and reduces royalty payments.[11]

Information technology can also genuinely confuse the perception or concept of what a product—such as a song, a joke, a computer game, or a graphic—is, whether or how it can be frozen in time and thus protected, detecting when it has become common property, and detecting when it has evolved into something else. Digitized information can so easily be edited or reformatted that it becomes progressively harder to separate original material from value-added analysis or interpretation.

Developing countries want to use intellectual products of the advanced nations to further their own social, economic, political, and educational development. Hence the issue of intellectual property rights is becoming an acutely troublesome one for national and international policy.

Troublesome issues are also likely to arise within the next five years over the use of information technology in decision making, in the form of expert systems, predictive models based on statistical data, and other tools. For example, in police investigations, historical data on crime are analyzed in an effort to predict future crimes, their locations, and their perpetrators. Models can also be used in attempts to predict criminal recidivism and help courts in making decisions about sentences or probation. By focusing not only on prior criminal history but also on factors such as age, race, marital status, place of residence, job history, and school records, such models may obscure differences between correlation and causality and encourage the misuse

10. Bruce W. Bugbee, *Genesis of American Patent and Copyright Law* (Washington, DC: Public Affairs Press, 1967). See also U.S., Congress, Office of Technology Assessment, *Intellectual Property Rights in an Age of Electronics and Information*, OTA-CIT-302 (Washington, DC: Government Printing Office, 1986).

11. U.S., Congress, Office of Technology Assessment, *Copyright and Home Copying: Technology Challenges the Law*, OTA-CIT-422 (Washington, DC: Government Printing Office, 1989).

of predictions to the detriment of individuals and of racial and ethnic groups.[12]

The most far-reaching issue for the age of information may be equity of access to information and to the services that deliver it to individuals. As already noted, some people and some nations will be less able than others to acquire information technology, to use it effectively, or to pay for information services. The currently prevailing free-market policy, which sees information primarily as a marketable commodity rather than as a prerequisite for a healthy community life, exacerbates this problem. For example, the principle and goal of universal service[13] that has governed the regulation of telephone service since 1934, when our basic communications law was passed, is rapidly eroding under current regulatory policy.

These are merely a sampling of the troublesome issues that are sure to arise in the next five years. Information is so critical to the nature of governance, and to all efforts to coordinate and direct social behavior, that it translates easily into power. It can increase either the power of government to enforce its authority or the power of people to thwart or resist authority. Inevitably, then, there will be perceived intrusions on the rights of citizens, conflicts of interest over access to information, competing claims to ownership or use of information technology, and attempts to regulate or to end regulation of information systems.

12. Office of Technology Assessment, *Criminal Justice*, p. 24.

13. The 1934 Communication Act stated that everyone should have reasonable access to basic telephone service. In practice, this required cross-subsidies, that is, charging large business users higher rates to help support residential service.

ANNALS, *AAPSS*, 522, July 1992

The Future of the Environment

By RICHARD D. LAMM

ABSTRACT: In terms of population growth and resource use, humankind is living on the upper slopes of some awesome geometric curves. Current growth rates have certain areas of the world doubling their population every 25 years. What is at risk is no less than the future of the whole globe. It will be hard for the world to avoid a demographic trauma. It is very difficult to motivate people when there is uncertainty and when the problem will manifest itself in the future. We really do not know what limits there are to population growth or resource use, and at what point ecological disaster takes over, but there are clearly limits on certain nonrenewables such as energy, land, and water. Additionally, humankind must decide how it will deal with a large number of environmental challenges: depletion of the protective ozone layer, global warming, deforestation, soil erosion, spreading deserts, and pollution of land, air, and water. To begin making the required changes, people must educate themselves and then educate each other.

Richard D. Lamm, formerly governor of Colorado, is now director of the Center for Public Policy and Contemporary Issues at the University of Denver.

IN terms of population growth and resource use, humankind is living on the upper slopes of some awesome geometric curves. Current growth rates have certain areas of the world doubling their population every 25 years. The world is growing 1.8 percent per year and adds approximately 93 million people a year to those of us already here; 92 percent of these additions are in the Third World. This geometric population growth requires geometric growth in amounts of food, minerals, forest products, and other resources and causes increasing stress on the environment. The question for the future is, How long can this continue, and what will be its impact?

One of the highest-stake debates in human history is currently taking place on the future of the environment. It is being fought out in academic journals, in Congress, and in the local pubs. The usual array of scenarios runs from the very Draconian to the nothing-to-worry-about perspective to the muddle-through scenario, with a range of alternatives in between. What is at risk is no less than the future of the whole globe. But, too often, the debate is a dialogue between the blind and the deaf. Futurists must objectively ask, How serious are the environmental issues facing us, and what are their solutions?

The debate, even in scientific circles, ultimately reduces itself to a battle of educated guesses in answer to important questions: What is the earth's carrying capacity, and what is the absorptive capacity of the ocean and the earth? Will population stabilize on its own, and, even if it does,

can Earth support even a stabilized but very large population at a decent standard of living? The questions are multiple and the stakes high.

Public policy has reacted to these questions in a number of ways. In the United States, the Carter administration prepared the comprehensive *Global 2000 Report*,[1] which was intended to start a major executive-branch effort to project the impact on the world of the then-current trends in population, resource use, and the environment. The report was published in 1980 and found a frightening potential for "global problems of alarming proportions by the year 2000."[2] It proposed some bold and far-reaching measures to correct the problems identified.

The Reagan administration dismissed the whole Global 2000 Project as foolish. It adopted the view that population was not a problem, and it was generally skeptical on all issues concerning the environment and resource consumption. To the extent that there were problems, it was thought that the market would solve them. At the World Population Conference in Mexico in 1984, the official U.S. position was exactly the opposite of what it had been ten years earlier.[3] Instead of viewing population growth with alarm, it was now "neutral" with regard to economic development. The environment ceased

1. Council on Environmental Quality and U.S. Department of State, *The Global 2000 Report to the President*, vol. 1 (Washington, DC: Government Printing Office, 1980).

2. Ibid., p. 454.

3. Werner Fornos, "Gaining People, Losing Ground: A Blueprint for Stabilizing World Population" (Pamphlet, Population Institute, 1987).

to be an issue with the Reagan administration.

But the rest of the world is moving ahead. In other parts of the globe, there is increasing interest in and concern with projecting the population and resource-consumption trends and trying to understand what they mean to the economy, the environment, education, trade, national security, and other related public policy issues. In programs often called, appropriately, "twenty-first century studies," nations like Canada, Japan, Mexico, the Netherlands, Norway, the People's Republic of China, Peru, the Philippines, Poland, South Korea, Taiwan, and the United Kingdom are examining alternative futures and trying to estimate the impact of these trends on their societies and on the world.[4] The United Nations has weighed in with the International Geosphere-Biosphere Program, a study of global change designed to examine the implications of these trends for long-term human habitability of Earth and to suggest alternate public policies.[5]

Thus, while the world will surely miss an official U.S. contribution, it will not be without projections of these trends and proposed solutions. While we could wish for far more, considering the stakes involved, the debate will be enlightened by these high-level studies from a variety of official sources. Most of the studies separate the issue into issues of population and issues of environment.

POPULATION

Degradation of the world's environment, income and equality, and potential for conflict exist today because of over-consumption and over-population. If the unprecedented population growth continues, future generations of children will not have adequate food, housing, medical care, education, earth resources, and employment opportunities.[6]

Humankind cannot continue to grow indefinitely. We are now adding more people to the world's population every decade than we used to add in a century. Between 1980 and 2000, the world's population is expected to grow by 1.6 billion. This is equivalent to adding 14 new countries the size of Bangladesh, with its population of 115 million, in 20 years. At current rates, the world's population of 5.4 billion people will double in 39 years. Three billion young people will enter their key productive years in this generation. The numbers add up very quickly. The United Nations Population Fund projects that without effective measures to slow growth, the world's population will likely triple to 14 billion in the next 100 years.[7]

4. Lester R. Brown, *A False Sense of Security* (New York: Norton, 1985), pp. 8-9. See also the statement of the seven major democracies issued in Paris, 15-16 July 1989; *North American News* (United Nations Environment Programme), 4(4):1 (Aug. 1989).

5. See World Resources Institute on International Institute for Environment and Development, *World Resources 1987* (New York: Basic Books, 1987), p. 1.

6. "Statement on Population Stabilization by World Leaders," signed by the heads of state of countries with over half the world's population, presented to the United Nations in 1985. For the complete text and list of signatures, contact Population Communications, 1489 East Colorado Boulevard, Suite 202, Pasadena, CA 91106.

7. Population Reference Bureau, "1989 World Population Data Sheet" (Population Reference Bureau, 1988).

The United States is not immune to this geometric growth. Consider, for instance, that the first U.S. census, in 1790, counted 4 million Americans. There have been 6 doublings of the U.S. population in the last 200 years. Six more doublings over the next 200 years would populate the country with more people than currently exist in the world. It is hard to imagine life in the United States with 8 billion neighbors. We shall have to stabilize the U.S. population and the world's sooner or later, and I suggest that sooner is better—much better!

The majority of scientists and other experts find the growth in human numbers ominous. Prince Philip, speaking for the World Wildlife Fund-International, has observed:

The population explosion, sustained by human science and technology, is causing almost insoluble problems for future generations. It is responsible for the degradation of the environment through the pollution of the air and water; it is consuming essential as well as non-essential resources at a rate that cannot be sustained. Above all, it is condemning thousands of our fellow living organisms to extinction.[8]

This view is not without dissent. A sharply different scenario is painted by Julian Simon, who has gained the ear of the Reagan and Bush administrations. Postulating that the "ultimate resource" is people, Simon criticizes the normal population concerns as a "closed world vision." He believes that more people in a country using more resources may create temporary shortages, but that the people then discover solutions to the shortages and, as a net result, the world is constantly moving toward less scarcity and a higher standard of living. "The trend is toward more and better rather than less and less nutrition even though the population of the world is growing. . . . There is no reason to believe that this trend cannot continue forever."[9] Simon makes some impressive arguments that, up to the present, the standard of living of the world's population has risen along with the size of the world's population. "Adding more people causes problems, but people are also the means to solve their problems."[10] While many would call this hubris, Simon's influence is growing.

Public policy is thus presented with a classic dilemma: no one can point out a specific physical or technical reason that the world will not be able to meet the basic needs of all of its people in the immediate future. The fact that people are starving and living in poverty is certainly due more to social and political structures than to physical scarcities. Humankind has been successful at overcoming many problems and obstacles. On the other hand, mathematics dictates that population and material growth cannot continue forever on a finite planet. We must ascertain first what the likely carrying capacity of Earth is—and do it soon enough to change the reproductive habits of billions of people. There is a

---

8. Rafael Salas Memorial Lecture, U.N. Population Fund, Mar. 1990.

9. Julian L. Simon, *Population Matters: People, Resources, Environment and Immigration* (New Brunswick, NJ: Transaction, 1990).

10. Ibid., p. 84.

twist in stopping population growth that Gunnar Myrdal called the "breaking distance": population continues to grow long after the birthrate has fallen to replacement levels.[11] Even if, beginning today, all the world's women limit the number of children they bear to two each, population growth will still continue for 70 years, and the population size will more than double. The lag time between recognizing the problem and solving it may turn out to be as difficult as the problem itself. There is yet an additional concern: how do we motivate people or nations to make sacrifices today that will avoid catastrophe tomorrow?

Most likely scenario

The most likely scenario, like beauty, lies in the eye of the beholder. I believe that it will be hard for the world to avoid a demographic trauma. It is difficult to write a happy scenario for Bangladesh, where 115 million people are crowded into an area 1.5 percent the size of the United States and whose population is projected to nearly double by 2025. Children born today in sub-Saharan Africa will, under current projections, see the area's population double by the time they are 22 and quadruple by the time they are 45.[12]

While biotechnology has made great strides in increasing the food supply, all of the experts warn us that these will only give us breathing room to stabilize population. We are losing the diversity of genetic mate-rial in our new food species; as a result, they are much more vulnerable to pests, blight, and drought. It would seem likely that at some point, the fragile food systems that now feed the world will be interrupted, and large-scale famine will result. Water shortages, aggravated by population, will likely cause new tensions in Africa and the Middle East. Environmental refugees will leave deteriorated areas and create pressures on their neighbors. Mostafa Tolba, executive director of the United Nations Environment Programme, has warned, "Throughout the world, there is copious evidence that the carrying capacity of many life support systems is being overloaded to the breaking point. Where such systems have collapsed, the option for the poor is stark: either to flee or to stay put and starve."[13]

Even before this, however, demographic pressures will likely cause large-scale migration and urbanization and tax the ability of many countries to provide political stability. Among the world's 120 governments studied for political instability, the 31 countries rated the most unstable all had high rates of population growth. Urbanization will aggravate all the problems caused by overpopulation.

The key factor of this scenario is the inability to change reproductive habits in time to avoid overtaxing an area's carrying capacity. The world has never faced a problem that required for its solution 3 billion individual changes in reproductive behavior. Is it possible? Yes. Is it likely? No.

11. Gunnar Myrdal, *The Asian Drama* (New York: Pantheon Books, 1971), p. 331.

12. "Keeping Food on the Table: Fighting Hunger in Our Growing World" (Pamphlet, Population Institute, 1988).

13. *International Dateline* (Population Communications International), Aug. 1991, p. 4.

THE NATURAL ENVIRONMENT

We are living in an historic transitional period in which awareness of conflicts between human activities and environmental constraints is literally exploding . . . never before in our history have we had so much knowledge, technology, and resources. Never before have we had such great capacities. The time and opportunity has come to break out of the negative trends of the past.[14]

The United Nations has given us a useful yardstick to gauge the interaction between population and the environment. It

has three components. First, lifestyle, income and social organization determine levels of consumption. Second, the technologies in use determine the extent to which human activities damage or sustain the environment, and the amount of waste associated with any level of consumption. These two factors determine the impact per person. The third meter, population, determines how many persons there are: it is the multiplier—it fixes the total impact.[15]

We are dealing with a multilateral equation, and the possible future scenarios that flow from this are infinite. Society has to steer between the twin poles of overreaction and underreaction. We know there is a significant lag time between taking an environmental problem seriously and effecting a solution. The challenge that faces us is to correctly identify the magnitude of the various environmental threats and adopt appropriate remedies in time.

There is a new note of urgency in current warnings about the environment. Twenty years ago, environmental problems were largely aesthetic or affected people's health or quality of life. Today, they threaten our very survival. Twenty years ago, environmental issues were immediately tangible and visible. Today, they are often intangible and less immediately perceptible. Acid rain, global warming, and loss of the ozone layer are less dramatic but have more of an impact. Twenty years ago, environmental problems were most often addressed by engineering solutions or the purchase of parks and wilderness and recreational areas. Today, solutions demand life-style changes—changes in how we transport ourselves, in how we recycle and reuse things, and in what we buy. Twenty years ago, solutions were generally imposed on corporations; today's solutions are increasingly sought to be imposed upon individuals. Under these conditions, it is hard to form a consensus. It is very difficult to motivate people when there is uncertainty and when the problem will manifest itself in the future.

A minority of experts believe that environmental threats are overstated or that the proposed solutions represent an overreaction. Professor Thomas C. Schelling of Harvard, for instance, has written thoughtfully that it would be cheaper to adapt to global warming than to take steps to prevent it. The economic and social price of dramatically cutting down on fossil fuel use is so large, in his estimation, that we would do better to

14. Gro Harlem Bruntland, prime minister of Norway and chair of the World Commission on Environment and Development, speech at the National Press Club, Washington, DC, 5 May 1989.

15. "The State of the World 1990" (Pamphlet, United Nations Population Fund, 1990).

wait and to use our resources to adapt to the warming if the warming occurs.[16]

But the principal debate revolves around the extent and magnitude of the actual harm. Some experts urge immediate and painful steps to save the planet, while others argue that the whole environmental movement is built on a false foundation. A cacophony of conflicting assessments makes solutions difficult.

It is impossible to cover all the possible scenarios. The scope of this article merely allows an overview. The possibilities are infinite, and, as Kenneth Boulding has observed, "The human dilemma is that all our experience is in the past while all our decisions deal with the future." We are left to speculate on so many variables.[17]

For instance, there is interesting evidence that some environmental degradations will create their own corrections. It is generally agreed that the amount of one greenhouse gas, carbon dioxide, has increased 25 percent since the beginning of the industrial revolution. The main question, however, has still to be answered: Is this increase causing a warming of the globe? Proponents point out that 7 of the warmest years of the last 100—1980, 1981, 1983, 1987, 1988, 1989, and 1990—have occurred in the last 11 years. Others say this pattern is within normal cycles.

In addition, scientists have long recognized that other factors, like cloud cover, can offset negative effects. There is a new urgency to identify possible feedbacks that could naturally help solve or ameliorate the trend of environmental deterioration. We must understand these feedbacks better if we are to fully assess the magnitude of the problem.[18]

Many environmental questions face us, and their number grows daily. China has announced a plan to put a refrigerator in every home in China by 2000. China has 1.1 billion people and adds 100 million every decade. Thus, in the 1990s, China alone could double the number of the world's refrigerators, which currently stands at 300 million. Ominously, China anticipates using ozone-damaging chlorofluorocarbons as the refrigerant, an economy move understandable in a Third World country—but the world impact could be immense. Likewise, China now uses the energy equivalent of 3 barrels of oil per person, mostly in the form of high-sulfur coal. What happens to the world—and downwind Japan—when China's usage increases to Russia's still relatively small use of 34 barrels per capita?[19]

Can the Third World industrialize along the pattern of the industrial world? Theoretically, the industrialized countries could help the Third World pay for cleaner technologies, but how can this be done when most of the industrial countries already

16. Thomas C. Schelling, *Global Environmental Forces* (Cambridge, MA: Harvard University, John F. Kennedy School of Government, Global Environmental Policy Project, 1990).

17. Kenneth Boulding, "1984: The Fallacy of Trends," *National Forum*, 64(3):19-20 (1984).

18. Most scientists are skeptical that the feedbacks will do much to reduce the total problem.

19. *The Global Ecology Handbook* (Boston: Beacon Press, 1990), chap. 4.

spend more than they take in via taxes? How can the Third World be prevented from using the quickest, cheapest, and dirtiest route?

Confronted by myriad scenarios, we must find institutions with the objectivity to make assessments and the jurisdiction to make a difference. The institutions set up to date to judge the magnitude of the problem increasingly are sounding an alarm. The U.N. General Assembly in 1983 created the World Commission on Environment and Development, which produced a unanimous report, *Our Common Future*, which set forth the challenge that the world is facing with regard to the environment. The report tries to balance both the good news and the bad but summarized it as follows:

When the century began, neither human numbers nor technology had the power to radically alter planetary systems. As the century closes not only do vastly increased human numbers and their activities have that power, but major unintended changes are occurring in the atmosphere, in soils, in waters, among plants and animals, and in the relationship among all of these. The rate of change is outstripping the ability of the scientific disciplines and our current capabilities to assess and advise. It is frustrating the attempts of political and economic institutions which evolved in the different, more fragmented worlds, to adapt and cope.[20]

The commission called for a new and dramatically different era of "sustainable economic growth" to improve the lot of the world's population.

We really do not know what limits there are to population growth or resource use and at what point ecological disaster takes over. But, clearly, there are limits on certain nonrenewables such as energy, land, and water. Additionally, humankind must decide how it will deal with a large number of environmental challenges: depletion of the protective ozone layer, global warming, deforestation, soil erosion, spreading deserts, and pollution of land, air, and water. These problems "evoke a classical Greek tragedy: Man, first by his ignorance and later by his indifference, has set in motion forces that he is unable to control—forces that are pregnant with consequences that could be grave, even disastrous."[21]

The challenge of environmental degradation to governance is immensely complicated, though less difficult than the challenge of population. The problems in this area are often called global, but in many cases they involve the cooperation of a handful of countries to start the solution—international problems rather than global. The developed world plus key countries in the developing world—such as Brazil—could make great strides in reducing the greenhouse gases. Similarly, acid rain, ozone depletion, and deforestation could be dramatically lessened by international cooperation between selected countries.

The most difficult challenge is likely to be the structuring of a form of international management of problems. Some halting steps have

20. World Commission on Environment and Development, *Our Common Future* (Washington, DC: World Commission on Environment and Development, 1987).

21. *Global Climate Change: A Challenge to International Governance* (Queenstown, MD: Aspen Institute, 1989), p. 12.

been taken, such as the creation of the Law of the Sea Treaty, the Outer Space Treaty, and the Antarctic Treaty. The models are there, but the hurdles are immense. Maurice Strong, head of the 1992 United Nations Conference on the Human Environment, put it succinctly: " 'Brotherhood, caring, sharing, working together are no longer simply pious ideals divorced from realities of life, but the indispensable ingredients for human survival.' "[22]

Most likely scenario

It is likely that, at a minimum, environmental protection will be incorporated into public policy and the price of goods. "We treat nature like we treated workers a hundred years ago," says one expert. "We included then no cost for the health and social security of workers in our calculations, and today we include no cost for the health and security of nature."[23] This situation will change, and the costs of the environment will be internalized, but the overarching question is whether a disaster scenario will occur.

It seems likely that some environmental trauma or disaster lies in our future. There are so many things that could go wrong that one or more probably will. The world has been constantly reducing its margin of error, constantly becoming more vulnerable. In a finite world, human population and consumption cannot increase

forever. The difficulty of changing the values, ethics, and beliefs built up over a thousand years will likely prove insurmountable. We will probably have to learn from disaster.

ACTION

No article on the environment should end without specifics on what can be done to avert disaster. First, people must educate themselves. Steps to take include finding out from local libraries and universities what books and other materials are available; joining one of the many environmental and population-related organizations; and ascertaining which government agencies relate to favorite concerns and lobbying the government. Simultaneously, individuals can think about their own life-styles. Gandhi's famous statement "My life is my message" relates in a way to all of us. People can reflect on their actions and how they relate to the environment. They can pledge to live in a way that has less impact on the environment and the world's resources. They can convert others to their viewpoints.

Once citizens have educated themselves, they must educate the public. Some channels include writing letters to the editor and speaking to local service clubs. During election campaigns, people can find out how their local candidates stand on environmental issues and can work for the ones who come closest to their viewpoints. They can tell their elected officials how they feel and what they want. They can organize others so that, together, they can speak with

22. Harlan Cleveland, *The Global Commons* (Queenstown, MD: Aspen Institute, 1990), p. 31.

23. "The Environmental Dilemma," *Economist*, 8 Sept. 1990, p. 4.

a stronger voice. There are infinite things that individuals can and should do.

We can press the World Bank to broaden its new ecologically sensitive philosophy on loans to include the need for reproductive control. We can, and should, press our own government to make population a priority and to stop caving into minority, anti-family-planning views. We can urge the U.S. government to make it a condition of extending aid to another country that the recipient country take effective action to control its population. We can better fund population-control measures. We can promote the use of RU 486 worldwide. We can, and should, pressure the U.S. government to take a stronger position on women's rights internationally, particularly in relation to health care, education, and political and economic freedom. Finally, we can push for the myriad public policies that will help promote conservation, such as a higher tax on petroleum.

Concerning conferences such as the U.N. conference on the human environment that convened in Rio de Janeiro, Brazil, in June 1992, individuals can lobby the local media to follow the proceedings and give adequate publicity to their results.

At any point in history, there are multiple Messiahs and multiple Jeremiahs who compete for our attention. Never, however, have the scientific community and thoughtful policymakers been more united in their warnings that humankind must change its ways. "No generation has a freehold on this earth. All we have is a life tenancy with a full repairing lease," Margaret Thatcher has said.[24] Wise words.

24. Ibid.

ANNALS, *AAPSS*, 522, July 1992

The Future of Governance in the United States: 1992-2002

By JAN M. GRELL and GARY GAPPERT

ABSTRACT: This article offers a ten-year perspective on the necessity for more governance and less government. The barriers to this conversion are not insurmountable, but they are political. Therefore, an individual, political, and institutional transformation is required. Currently, the United States is entering a new era of redefining the purpose of leaders and institutions, restructuring old ideologies, and redirecting the focus of responsibilities in order to meet the global challenges ahead; this era will continue well into the twenty-first century. This article describes the key elements necessary for successful governance. These elements include a new democracy; strategic cooperation; a new federalism; decentralization; a new moral infrastructure; individual responsibility and new leaders; collaborative partnerships and stability; and increased competition and technological growth.

Jan M. Grell is a research and planning associate at the University of Akron and the project director for the Ohio Policy Issues Network. She is the editor of Ohio Foresight *and is the author of articles on international politics, policy studies, and strategic planning. She received her M.A. in political science.*

Gary Gappert is the director of the Institute for Future Studies and Research and professor of public administration and urban studies at the University of Akron. He is the author of Post-Affluent America *and, most recently, coedited the urban affairs annual* Cities in a Global Society.

THE lack of majority consensus in the United States in the 1990s and beyond will necessitate a restructuring of ideas. New definitions that will reconstitute positive beliefs and value-laden opinions in American government will be needed. This major yet gradual shift toward more governance will begin at the local and state levels with grass-roots initiatives. The outcomes of this restructuring of ideas will include a new democracy, new leadership, and increased public participation.

This article presents a ten-year perspective that demonstrates the necessity for more governance and less government between now and 2002. Since 1989, the term "governance" has been used to describe the "roles and goals of the institution rather than the institution itself."[1] For the purposes of this article we take governance to mean an individual and collective act encompassing the ability to create and maintain the delicate balance necessary to act, process, and govern through, for, and with the needs and voices of a culturally diverse society.

Governance is different from government because governance is a broader concept, one that will eventually influence the government itself as well as its traditional institutions and actors. Carrying out governance in line with the foregoing definition will serve to create the linkage necessary to bring about a new democracy. More significantly, governance will include more balanced, collaborative actions by individuals, communities, and institutions.

1. Cynthia G. Wagner, "Challenges for Governance," *Futurist*, 25(5):35 (Sept.-Oct. 1991).

A MACRO PERSPECTIVE

The United States now has the great opportunity as well as the ethical obligation to redirect priorities. Currently, there is a growing sense that America must redefine the purpose of its leaders and institutions, ought to restructure its old ideologies, and should redirect its attention to individual human needs in order to meet the competitive global challenge of the twenty-first century.

There are major barriers involved in the shift from what has been seen as excessive government to increased governance. These barriers range from controversies over what makes good economic sense, to the power of agendas of vested interest. This is an ambitious undertaking, but it should not be an impossibility. It will involve institutional and political transformation. A gradual shift toward more governance will include alternatives that lessen reliance on traditional governmental institutions and foster dependence on collaborative partnerships that seek the delicate balance of political, economic, social, and cultural resources through the exercise of individual responsibility. For example, individuals from private businesses, the government, and nonprofit organizations are taking responsibility for the development of innovative programs and approaches to such problems as education, day care, hunger, and the homeless.

According to the Preamble of the U.S. Constitution, one of the purposes of government is to "promote the general Welfare." Government leaders have pursued a different purpose: winning the next election. Government policy highly influences the future of our national economy. Elected leaders work diligently to achieve credibility for concerns regarding national problems, but these leaders then avoid the risk of attempting to resolve those problems, especially if the proposed solution would agitate a majority of their voting population. Therefore, it becomes difficult to believe that our representatives can or will do what is necessary for the United States to survive as a world leader through the 1990s.

From 1965 through 1992, the United States has experienced some of its greatest challenges. Currently, we have either not dealt with these challenges at all or dealt with them ineffectively. The U.S. economy is threatened by high budget deficits, a banking crisis, children in poverty, the acquired immune deficiency syndrome, homelessness, and many other social and cultural problems. Researchers at the University of Texas tell us that "only 40% of American adults can write well enough to cope with job applications, government forms, and other daily problems."[2] Furthermore, Korea and Japan have surpassed the United States in producing practical technologies, although America is still ahead in research. These challenges must be faced or they will become insurmountable. At the end of the twentieth century, the United States has the opportunity to rethink and redirect society's priorities in order to begin to resolve problems long neglected. The United States can no longer hold to tattered policies

2. Marvin Cetron and Owen Davies, *American Renaissance* (New York: St. Martin's Press, 1989), p. 1.

in the face of new challenges. Therefore, one of the key tasks of emerging governance is to create mechanisms and linkages that foster equitable, effective policies that, in turn, will be adaptable to future conditions.

THE NATURE OF THE NEW FEDERALISM

The United States has a mature yet still dynamic system. Although concepts of the U.S. system have served as a model for federalist forms of government in other countries, the ideas and practices of U.S. federal government have changed, with profound effects.

During the last two decades, beginning with the advent of federal revenue sharing under President Nixon, there have been efforts to reverse a trend of centralization that began in 1932 with the election of Franklin D. Roosevelt in the midst of the Great Depression. At that time the states had many more problems than they each had resources to deal with them.

The return of powers and responsibilities to the states was accelerated under President Reagan. The irony is that in the last fifty years the nation has moved from a series of disaggregated and fragmented regional economies to a fully integrated continental economy. The new federalism works against the fact of economic integration.

Although the return of power to the states—and then to local governments in some cases—has worked effectively for many states, it may leave a vacuum where the increasingly important national and international issues are concerned, such as those dealing with the environment, technology, and international competition. David Osborne has detailed very well in his *Laboratories of Democracy* the apparent success of the new federalism.[3] The economics of the new federalism, however, have been devastating to many states because of the delegation of more responsibility with fewer resources.

It is less clear whether the devolution of governance responsibilities back to states and localities has effectively uncluttered the national government. Its international focus is apparent. Washington, D.C., has become an international city and decision-making center. President Bush was criticized in his first term not for his focus on important international issues but for the lack of a domestic agenda.

At the same time, many states and even some cities are establishing a global agenda, especially with regard to trade and investment. In the new federalism, state and local governments have been spurred by the old imperative, "trade or die."

The new breed of state governors expects to be full partners in national policymaking. For instance, at the February 1991 National Governors' Conference in Washington, a policy partnership proposal called for joint federal-state long-term action in the following areas: (1) restructuring of the health care system, (2) achieving national education goals, (3) developing a national energy policy, (4) enacting a new national transportation policy, (5) protecting and cleaning up

the environment, and (6) investing in human and physical infrastructure for renewed economic growth and a better quality of life.

In the new federalism, the different layers of government will need to be adept at the initiation and management of policy and program partnerships. Even if these layers reflect cultural and demographic diversity and different approaches to problem solving, the new federalism must reflect the American genius for creative complexity.

INSTITUTIONS AS FORCES OF CHANGE

There are many factors acting as forces of change. Science and technology are producing change the most rapidly. Raw data and knowledge will double between 1992 and 2002. Massive growth of technology will render some occupations obsolete. Perhaps for those individuals who prepare for the future work environment, jobs will be available; however, the changing nature of the work force will continue to have a significant impact on the economy. In addition to rapid technological changes, some factors driving governance in the United States will be social, cultural, and demographic trends. By 2002, minorities will become the majority population in many U.S. cities, and this shift may affect governance.

In this article two institutional forces of change will be addressed, education and legislation.

Education

Education is necessary for sound leadership. Therefore, education be-

3. David Osborne, *Laboratories of Democracy* (Cambridge, MA: Harvard Business School Press, 1988).

comes an important component of the new democracy. National success necessitates the elimination of piecemeal education policies and mandates a comprehensive, governable policy. The United States will not be able to maintain its world leadership and quality of life without a total restructuring of its educational system. By 2002, the U.S. educational system must serve all Americans throughout their lives. Educational reform will no longer be a fragmentary endeavor. The restructuring of the system will require the involvement of all Americans as well as shifts in our beliefs of how and to whom we provide schooling. Making tough, equitable decisions regarding existing funds and the most productive investment of new resources will challenge us. According to Governor Romer of Colorado, "In a world of rapid change and global markets, we must prepare our citizens to be lifelong learners, people who can think critically, communicate effectively, and perform at a skill level equal to their international competition."[4]

Legislation

The collapse of the concept of majority representation over the last twenty years poses the question, If representatives do not represent the majority of voters in their district, then whom have they come to represent? Additionally, an attempt to offset the power of the executive branch by the U.S. Congress has created its own bureaucracy. Congressional staffs have nearly doubled in size in the past ten years. Legislators have become more dependent on the judgment and advice of their staffs.

Effective governance over the next decade will necessitate a more participatory role for citizens in their own governance; increased representation of minorities; the creation of innovative, well-developed institutions at the multinational level; and more decision-making power at the state and local levels. Cumulatively, this suggests the growth of political participation and the emergence of governance through a delicate balance in which democratic decisions evolve out of necessity. Democratic participation is a necessary condition for freedom. According to the Kettering Foundation's recent report, *Citizens and Politics*, citizens are no longer apathetic about politics. To increase political participation, the report recommends (1) creating conditions necessary for reconnecting citizens with policies, (2) increasing citizen involvement in meeting public challenges in their own communities, and (3) encouraging the media to focus more on public dimensions of policy issues.[5]

KEY ACTORS ENCOURAGING CHANGE

In the 1990s and well into the twenty-first century, key actors, including some institutions, must create, implement, and maintain the process necessary for achieving an equitable balance of power through-

4. National Governors' Association, *The Governors' 1991 Report on Education* (Washington, DC: National Governors' Association, 1990), p. 37.

5. Richard C. Harwood, *Citizens and Politics* (Dayton, OH: Harwood Group, 1991), pp. 8-9.

out the nation. One set of actors comprises the justices of the U.S. Supreme Court. With a decisive conservative majority, the Court has many opportunities to reinterpret the Constitution. Such reinterpretations are likely to initiate an active legislative and judicial agenda. The influence of this Court will be felt through the 1990s and beyond. Responses to its reinterpretation of the Constitution will drive social change. Public reaction will include new movements and new coalitions. These will represent the concerns of the new American diversity. Increasing concern for issues that hit home will direct a more powerful, active involvement with public problems. Throughout the 1990s, ethics, values, and morals should become more significant in the social, political, economic, legislative, educational, legal, medical, and environmental decision-making process. If they do, leadership will be gained by those individuals whose aims cannot be reduced entirely to self-interest. The decentralization of infrastructures, as well as bureaucracies, over the next ten years will profoundly affect further distribution of power.

With greater competition, diversity, conservatism, and conservationism prevalent in American society, the new leaders will obtain and maintain their positions because of what they stand for instead of only whom they are affiliated with. Immigration, transnational corporations, and shifts in the labor force will create a more culturally diverse environment in which non-Anglo Americans—Japanese Americans, Chinese Americans, and so on—compete for leadership positions. Tomorrow's leaders must be able to anticipate the need for more balanced and effective governance. Furthermore, the new leaders should be able to do as well as to propose. Successful leadership will come from the strength of those individuals who seek a common goal. The challenges that face us will necessitate a pooling of resources, and it is unlikely that one individual will be able to produce all of the resources required for effective leadership of the whole. Although a central leader will still be present in many situations, ideas will be shared, power will be dispersed, and leadership will become more collective through networks and consensus.

In the 1990s and beyond, leadership and administrative action should be cemented in a normative structure in which the primary focus of governance is to augment the ability of citizens and leaders to act ethically. For individuals to become effective leaders, they must now begin contemplating a future of value-based competition, which will be necessary for sustaining development and maintaining the delicate balance of governance in a rapidly changing, interdependent, global environment.

Several factors will contribute to the remaking of the U.S. Congress in the 1990s. The reapportionment that will occur as a result of the 1990 census is one; a generational transfer of influence and participation is another; and recruitment of new candidates into congressional contests is a third.

Dramatic demographic changes between the 1980 and 1990 censuses resulted in the transfer of 19 congressional seats from Midwestern and

Northeastern states to Southern and Western states. This reapportionment means there will be a minimum of 19 new representatives in Congress. In addition, members of Congress from the states losing representatives are considering options for alternative careers. As a result of the 1992 reapportionment, Congress will be a substantially altered body, reflecting new voices, new issues, new districts, and new constituencies.

The 1992 reapportionment will also mean that the congressional class of 1992 will be substantially different from its predecessors. The baby-boom generation is likely to be more highly represented. The composition of the new Congress will include more women and non-native-born as well as some civil rights activists, more returned Peace Corps volunteers, and more Vietnam veterans. The Congress of the 1990s will reflect the coming-of-age experiences of the 1960s and 1970s.

The new members of Congress are also likely to reflect greater occupational and professional diversity. This will include the occupational experiences of the information society. Today's congressional leaders grew up in the midst of expansion. Their values reflect that experience.

Reapportionment, therefore, leads directly into new geographic, generational, and occupational representation. This shift will occur most dramatically at the congressional level, but it will also be mirrored in the composition of all 50 state legislatures.

FORCES OF STABILITY

The new leadership of the 1990s and the twenty-first century will require different individual competition. Ethics, values, and morals will become more significant in our interdependent, rapidly changing global environment. Since the philosophy of the 1990s is to do more with less, individuals will govern by being accountable for their commitments, assuming responsibility for others less fortunate than themselves, and holding others responsible for their actions. Throughout the decade, individuals can no longer only be part of the problems they expect government to solve. Individuals must act and collaborate as forces of stability within their families, schools, businesses, and communities. The stability created by these grass-roots efforts will facilitate a smaller yet smarter form of governance in which individuals become part of the solution.

Individuals are already taking a greater share of responsibility, while relying less on larger institutions for alternative options. Examples of this shift include more individual responsibility for employment, careers, personal health, and education. This can be seen in the growth in entrepreneurial activity, multiple careers, self-employment, home schooling, and preventive personal health care.

The reshaping of America has begun to redefine the roles of the public versus private sectors, as well as individual versus institutional responsibilities. Increasingly, individuals will no longer wait for institutions to provide solutions and opportunities. They will be more willing to act on their own and together within their multifaceted communities.

The United States, as well as the rest of the world, is in the midst of changes caused by advances in science and technology, lack of resources, and conflict created by immense desires for freedom, democracy, and equality. Increasing global change has produced a fragile, vulnerable, interdependent global system. Decisions concerning limited portions of the global population cannot ignore the impact on other individuals.

Since the new democratic order is a shift from government to governance, the ultimate purpose of human enterprise must be first to improve and then to maintain conditions of life within the capacity of available resources. Ethical and moral standards will be important if the United States wishes to remain a force for stability in the world.

Government's role has been that of dominant mediator; the new role should be of steward of public values. Ethics and authority will be of increasing importance in the public policy process. More specific laws could manage administrative discretion. More targeted and less complex conflict-of-interest laws could address wrongdoing stemming from corruption and envy. Furthermore, increased mediation, compromise, and conflict resolution could contribute to establishing moral standards, including virtues and values. Legislation in the 1990s should focus on outcomes that are advantageous to future generations of a reshaped America.

Legislators, attorneys, judges, and other public policymakers must adjust to their role as new leaders of the new democracy. They must assure themselves as well as their constituents that new technologies and policies meet the ethics test. Policymakers can no longer avoid the need to craft ethically based policies. New medical technologies that can improve and prolong our lives, for example, will underline the need for ethical policies, legislation, and paradigms to assist their integration into society.

To stabilize communities, the internal and external capabilities of the new family must be strengthened. Only 7 percent of the U.S. families fit the description of a nuclear family, defined as a working husband, a housewife, and two children. If this definition were extended to include two working spouses and any number of children, at best the category would include only 25 percent of Americans. Moreover, these numbers are still declining. A variety of family structures will predominate.

Today's American children will be tomorrow's new leaders. Therefore, new definitions and new models of the family are critical. It will be important to know how a sense of community and family is fostered as well as to build an educational model to fit multicultural diversity and the changing demographics of the family. Throughout this decade, the nuclear family will be only one of many familial styles. By 2000, approximately 53 percent of the work force in the United States will be female, necessitating learning centers, early childhood development, day care, and health care, among other supportive services.

Private corporations, as well as public and nonprofit organizations, must innovate in their methods and models for providing day care to their employees. As the new democracy and the next century unfold, decision makers should protect new and old forms of the family. A strategic family policy will be key to stable communities. That policy should encourage support of the family, an ongoing analysis of laws and regulations that support families of all types, necessary changes in the welfare system, greater involvement by corporations in support of better-functioning families—day care, schools, and flex time, for example—and more collaboration between corporations, universities, and other nonprofit agencies for the balanced development and welfare of America's children. The 1991 final report by the National Commission on Children, *Beyond Rhetoric: A New American Agenda for Children*, outlined this direction.[6] The National Commission on Children was established by Public Law 100-203 to "serve as a forum on behalf of the children of the nation."

Information technology will profoundly influence governance. Organizations today obtain power by monitoring information and government policy changes. By 2002, more sophisticated systems will be in place, which will add to the responsiveness of the governing process. Developments in communications technology will increase citizen participation in voting.

ECONOMIC IMPACT OF THE NEW DEMOCRACY

The United States has spent, or misspent, much of the last two decades mourning its loss of affluence and the advent of a postaffluent society. In a postaffluent society, values and life-styles face the constraints of resource scarcity and ecological security. Initial dissatisfaction with economic constraints should eventually lead us to an increased emphasis on community relationships and to a sensitivity to cultural diversity and environmental harmony.

The complex realities of the expanding global economy will also force a new competitive strategy that must reflect the humanistic concerns of the new democracy. Two aspects of this new competitive strategy should include (1) the response of cities to international forces and (2) the relationship between trade and education.

There are few, if any, U.S. cities that have not been affected by the growth of the international economy, new patterns of foreign trade and investment, and the influx of a new generation of immigrants reflecting a dramatic new cultural diversity.

As Jane Jacobs noted in *Cities and the Wealth of Nations*, society engages the dynamics of change in its cities.[7] The influx of an international focus into American cities reflects the global society.

Cities provide strategic linkages to the global economy. Such tasks as identifying opportunities, advancing and utilizing technology, financing and handling transactional flows, and structuring and servicing global markets will be carried out primarily in cities and will expand rapidly in the 1990s.

6. National Commission on Children, *Beyond Rhetoric: A New American Agenda for Children* (Washington, DC: Government Printing Office, 1991).

7. Jacobs, *Cities and the Wealth of Nations* (New York: Random House, 1984).

Cities can effectively compete in the global economy by developing a civic culture that respects the dynamics of a multicultural society and its learning needs. If a city is to sustain its development in a global economy and society, it will need to develop a cosmopolitan culture that is open to creativity and innovation. Moreover, according to a recent study, the most desirable urban sites for investment in the 1990s will be those in which there is a "commitment of individuals to collective relationships for community action."[8]

International trade is growing even faster than the global economy. The International Monetary Fund estimates that international trade transactions are growing at twice the rate of the overall world economy, or gross world product. As this expansion continues into the twenty-first century, global and holistic thinking will be essential to sustaining development in organizations and communities. The expansion of trade and the extension and linking of communications networks cross traditional geographic, conceptual, and cultural boundaries. This weaving together of global interests represents a profound educational challenge and opportunity.

The importance of an educational policy with a global perspective is increasingly evident. The feasibility of a global approach to education is enhanced by the dramatic improvements in communications made dur-

ing the 1980s and will continue to increase through information technology over the next two decades. Communities will be international in active trade, investment, tourism, sister-city affiliations, and cultural and educational exchanges. The new democracy will require vigorous participation in the global economy, and its educational imperatives will demand a considerable commitment of human resources.

JOINT PROBLEM SOLVING AND COLLABORATIVE COOPERATION

The conceptual framework for the future will include a new moral infrastructure, based upon a greater sense of spirituality, civic responsibility, mutual obligation, and social restraint. Governance begins with the individual. We will need to become better managers of ourselves, our children, our families, our jobs, and our local and national institutions and communities. Other elements of this conceptual framework are increased possibilities for social and cultural growth; the flourishing of human potential; alternatives to traditional work environments; intolerance of conspicuous consumption, waste, ecological abuse, and social injustice; expansion of education; increased citizen participation; a more stable, comfortable life due to advances in science and technology; and renewed responsibility to the entire human community.

The key to problem solving under the new governance will depend upon the strength of the foregoing conceptual framework, on which stability and collaboration can be implemented.

---

8. Dennis Rondinelli and Jack Behrman, "Where Will High-Tech Companies Invest during the 1990s? In Cities That Are Changing Their Culture," *Business in the Contemporary World*, 3(4):33 (Summer 1991).

State initiatives and responsibility have already increased due to the new federalism. Additionally, planning must address the broadening of the responsibilities of individuals, communities, corporations, and universities. Governance can be achieved by groups and regions' using power effectively by sharing it. The next decade will mandate strategic cooperation. If new administrations are to be successful, they must address these issues. Tomorrow's leaders must allow for the incubation of new programs and ways for achieving change. Increased individual and collective multisector involvement will provide the stability necessary for the foundation of governance.

CONCLUSION

The growing polarization of society into single-focus constituencies will increase the problems on the public agenda. The media will continue to identify problems and will create new ones. Suspicion of today's leadership minimizes the ability of government to solve problems. The shift from this highly politicized government to depoliticized governance will be a gradual, yet powerful, continual movement throughout the decade. The transition will include more individual responsibility and will foster dependence on collaboration. Moreover, the new strategic cooperation will provide a balanced process and an economically feasible foundation to address the needs of all in the new America and to allow everyone to flourish.

New perspectives on the future of governance in the United States are emerging because today's centralized hierarchical bureaucracies do not operate well in the rapidly changing, high-technology, information, multicultural society of the 1990s. We present three alternatives: a recentralization and regionalization alternative, a high-technocratic expertise alternative, and an alternative that involves rewriting the U.S. Constitution.

A recentralization and regionalization alternative could include regionalization of the federal government into the 12 districts of the Federal Reserve banking system. A number of federal agencies have already relocated to regional cities such as Denver and Kansas City. In addition, back-office functions such as data processing and specialized research are being moved out of metropolitan Washington. Regionalization is also occurring within several state governments.

A high-technocratic expertise alternative would be based upon the realization that many of the emerging issues involving the environment, public health, genetic engineering, multinational economic development, industrial policy, and so forth will require collaboration between experts and grass-roots coalitions. This alternative will recognize the importance of public input into the development of science and technology.

The alternative of rewriting the U.S. Constitution is an outcome of the growing concerns that the present Constitution does not adequately recognize and protect the interests of women and minorities and that it presents increasingly troublesome problems of interpretation. An equitable social policy that reflects diverse ethical concerns might require a constitutional convention.

Each of these alternatives recognizes the importance of the shift from government to governance and indicates structural changes that might be made toward that goal.

ANNALS, *AAPSS*, 522, July 1992

A Quasi Certainty:
Europtimism

By MICHEL GODET

ABSTRACT: This article is divided into three parts. First, a quasi certainty, Europtimism, is identified. Second, 11 probable trends in the national and international environments of the 1990s are noted. Finally, three major uncertainties are discussed.

Michel Godet is professor of industrial futures at the Conservatoire National des Arts et Métiers, Paris.

NOTE: This article is drawn from the author's next book, *From Anticipation to Action* (UNESCO).

T HE Old World has not uttered its last word, as one would believe.

FROM EUROPESSIMISM
TO EUROPTIMISM

What has happened to the Cassandras who, just yesterday, were predicting the inexorable decline of Europe? With the center of world gravity shifting almost inevitably from the Atlantic to the Pacific, the Old World was, according to them, doomed to become a peripheral zone, tagging behind the United States and Japan.

In fact, it was only a few years ago, at the moment of the flash in the pan of the American recovery and when the dollar was at its highest, that it was almost automatic to point to the technology gap in Europe, Europe's weak economic growth, endemic unemployment, and social and political rigidities. The analysts of Eurosclerosis had forgotten that a crisis can be a harbinger of hope provided that it jolts a nation into overcoming the forces of inertia and habit that slow change and adaptation.

The majority of the European countries have learned over the past few years to win the battle against inflation by reducing wage escalators, to apply the value-added tax in a manner more favorable to business, to acquire flexibility—although still insufficient—in matters of employment and salary, and to establish limits on protectionism.

We have seven good reasons to hope.

1. Like a sea serpent, the theme of the decline of Europe resurfaces periodically. Already in the 1960s, a false alarm was sounded with *The American Challenge* by J.-J. Servan-Schreiber, and, nonetheless, Europe experienced a rate of growth even stronger than that of the United States during the period between 1967 and 1973. Since then, economic growth in the two regions has been comparable.

2. Europe has maintained its position as a turntable of international trade: more than one-third of international commerce is conveyed through Europe, and Europe is the principal supplier and the principal channel for trade for most of the other regions of the world except Japan.

3. European countries, even if, in this instance, the United Kingdom is excluded, had the good sense to significantly reduce their energy dependence, down to 53 percent for France and Germany. Europe has thus done better than Japan, which continues to be dependent by over 80 percent.

4. Europe also had the good sense, with the European Monetary System, to endow itself with relative monetary stability in a turbulent international environment.

5. Europe possesses the strongest scientific potential in the world and showed with Airbus and Ariane that cooperative research and development can be profitable.

6. Industrial renovation in the Old World is being accompanied by a higher level of investment and higher productivity gains than are being realized in the United States (this is the counterpart of less job creation). Europe has had the sense to gain strategic positions in key industrial sectors—aeronautics, space launch capabilities, nuclear energy, communication—and it also reinforced its

place in traditional sectors, such as agriculture, chemicals, and textiles.

7. Last but not least, the sociocultural diversity of the European countries, often seen as a barrier to Europe's cohesiveness and as an element of weakness, represents a potential advantage for adapting in the face of future uncertainty.

EUROPE 1993: THE DREAM AND THE REALITY

Europe, the greatest solvent market in the world, is offered as the new El Dorado for European enterprises in the 1990s. The Europessimism so prevalent until the mid-1980s is no longer in fashion. Europe had previously seemed to be stagnating in a phase of decline and rigidity, incapable of emerging from crisis and unemployment. The world's focal point was supposedly shifting from the Atlantic to the Pacific. The strong dollar and the Japanese economic triumph were irrefutable evidence of this apparent shift. But today, Europe, the world's leading trading power, has once again become the economic focus for the end of the twentieth century. What has happened?

Announcement of the great internal market of 1993 did not have an immediate effect. Indeed, the signing of the Single European Act by the European Council of heads of state in December 1986 in Luxembourg passed almost unnoticed, with the council's deliberations marked by dissension and apparent failure. This historical context has been strikingly analyzed by Jacques Nemrod.[1]

1. Jacques Nemrod, *Le mal Européen: Le surprenant trompe-d'oeil de l'Acte Unique*

In Nemrod's book we learn that, in addition to the Single European Act, there is also a Final Act, which is never publicly mentioned. It is composed of 20 declarations, some made jointly and some made unilaterally, which express many reservations.

Among the joint texts adopted we find that "fixing the date of 31 December 1992 does not have any automatic juridical effects."[2] Reservations are also expressed, notably by West Germany and the United Kingdom; these reservations are concerned with maintaining national sovereignty over areas such as health, consumer protection, the environment, and so on. Nemrod states that "most of the infringements of the principle of free circulation of goods rest on these pretexts . . . if we do not change anything, why do we wish to persuade people that everything is going to change?"[3]

In fact, the Treaty of Rome in 1957 envisaged the full realization of a Common Market by 1 January 1970. It is therefore highly unlikely that on 1 January 1993 the great European internal market will be fully realized. Nevertheless, the goal of "Europe 1992" plays a beneficial mobilizing role, since it encourages people to think about coming changes and about habits that will have to be called into question.

The road to the realization of these ambitions is now harder than ever. The easiest part has been done, and, in order to achieve further progress, states will have to agree to give up

(Paris: Rivages—Les Echos, 1987). See also Michel Godet, "Europe 1992: The Dream and the Reality," *Futures*, 21(2):183-87 (Apr. 1989).

2. Nemrod, *Le mal Européen*.
3. Ibid.

part of their national sovereignty, which does not seem likely.

LIMITING THE COSTS

It is probable that the internal market will not be achieved in the short term. While awaiting the putative benefits, we should take care to limit the costs of a single Europe. The establishment of a single market with universally accepted norms could first benefit Japanese and U.S. businesses, which, moreover, will enjoy dominant positions in their own countries with complete impunity. The benefits of the European market must not be bestowed on the rest of the world without compensatory measures. New competition within Europe must be balanced with greater protection from external competition.

ELEVEN PROBABLE TRENDS[4]

At the heart of the numerous uncertainties bearing down on the future of Western societies, several very probable trends can be discerned:

— new demographic imbalances, and the prospect of South-North migration flows;
— threats to the physical environment and the negative legacy of past growth;
— a lawless and turbulent international scene;
— slow growth that is irregular, unequal, and interdependent;
— new energy price rises;

4. A large part of the following draws on a document prepared with Remi Barre as part of a prospective study of the period to 1995 undertaken in 1987 for the Elf group.

— an explosion of new technologies, yielding a new competitive order;
— deregulation linked to new international and regional regulations;
— economic competition on a global scale, with states playing a key role;
— a decrease in the number of industrial jobs, and a rising tide of service industries;
— crisis of the welfare state; and
— a rise in social tensions.

Demographic imbalances and North-South migratory flows

A population explosion in the poorest countries accompanied by absolute population decline in the richest countries is the marked trend that, if it continues for two or three more decades, will alter the map of the world and cause upheaval in our societies. By 2020, for example, the population of Europe will be comparable to that of Nigeria or Brazil. In 1990, the population on the southern shores of the Mediterranean exceeded that of the northern shores. In 2030, if current trends continue, it will be twice as great.

The United States, Japan, and Europe are no longer securing the replacement of generations and are aging in the face of Third World countries that are increasingly young and densely populated.

Beyond the inevitable questions concerning pension provisions and health expenditure, will we be able to continue excluding people from economic activity through retirement when their life expectancy is still 20 or 30 more years?

These projections are not forecasts and are unlikely to correspond to future reality, if only because of migratory pressures. By 2030, some of today's minorities could represent one-fifth of the total population in some countries, such as Germany, France, or the United Kingdom. Is this a passing phenomenon or a lasting concern?

The physical environment

At the start of the 1980s, it was believed that the environmental policies of the preceding decade had borne fruit. The improvement in air and water quality, facilitated by the restructuring of certain primary activities that were among the most polluting—production of chemicals; steel making—gave the impression that most environmental problems were soluble. Today this calm assurance is no longer apparent since several major future environmental problems have already burst onto the scene and are fueling a number of controversies.

First, it is thought that the regular increase—by over 10 percent in the last 25 years—in the levels of carbon dioxide in the atmosphere will gradually cause the atmosphere to become warmer—the greenhouse effect. This could increase rainfall in certain regions, such as the Mediterranean, and could cause some deserts to recede. Will yesterday's worries come to be considered as a hope for tomorrow? Although most experts are in agreement over the trend, they are much more divided over the degree of the significance of the phe-

nomenon and the scale of its eventual consequences; the same applies to the erosion of the ozone layer. Thought needs to be given to regional agricultural specializations that could find themselves overturned.

Second, the degradation of the environment in the Third World is a very worrying phenomenon because it will affect the daily lives of hundreds of millions of people. The unconsidered development of human activities, unplanned demographic and urban explosions, excessive deforestation, overexploitation of land, the perverse effects of irrigation such as soil salinization—all these trends hold the beginnings of a number of crises: over water, firewood, and cultivable land. This environmental degradation will aggravate certain natural phenomena such as drought and floods.

Third, the risk of a reduction in biological diversity is great, owing to the rapid disappearance of animal and plant species, particularly in the tropical forests, whose still considerable surface area is expected to shrink by as much as one-third between now and the end of the century. Here again, it is information that is lacking. All those spectacular figures, such as that 1 million of the 5-10 million species of living organisms will disappear,[5] are almost meaningless. How can we appreciate a reduction in stock that seems to be five times smaller than the margin of error on the size of the stock itself?

5. Council on Environmental Quality and U.S. Department of State, *The Global 2000 Report to the President* (Washington, DC: Government Printing Office, 1980), 2:331.

Fourth, acid rain, with its catastrophic effects on the lakes and forests of Europe and North America, is a typical example of a problem identified long ago but whose identification gave rise to no preventive action or even to enough research to allow the real causes to be identified. Some scientists believe it would be unreasonable to set up expensive control systems that would have no effect on this phenomenon of transborder pollution whose sources are diffused and multiple, such as exhaust fumes. Conversely, some ecologists fear that proof of links between causes and effects will not become evident until it is too late; after all, 25 percent of German forests were struck before there was any reaction.

Finally, some environmental problems emerging today are a result of the vulnerability and negative fallout of environmental protection policies carried out up to now.

Beyond the need for information and scientific knowledge, the major problem for the environment is anticipation, prevention, and responsibility toward future generations.

A *lawless and turbulent international environment*

The lack of regulators appears all the more critical as we have to expect internal social explosions within the Third World and an upsurge in the number of regional or local conflicts.

The seeds of tomorrow's social eruptions are buried in today's trends: rapid population increase; glaring inequalities, where luxury sits side by side with poverty; and massive urbanization in gigantic megalopolises that are nearer to slums than to cities.

Beyond the multiple uncertainties of the lawless and turbulent international environment, two permanent factors can be discerned: first, international monetary instability—currency reflects geopolitics—and particularly the persistence of a strongly fluctuating dollar in relation to other currencies; and, second, the self-centered development of themselves by developed countries.

Slow, irregular, unequal, and interdependent economic growth

Interdependence is a reality that can be measured by means of many indicators, such as the ever-increasing proportion of national production devoted to export. This increasing openness to the outside means that no country can claim to be in sole command of its own growth: the accelerator is international, and only the brakes remain national.

Because of the impossibility of establishing international and national structures and rules adapted to the new context of interdependence and technical and economic change, a new phase of general, concerted economic growth seems unlikely. I would add that population aging is hardly likely to stimulate growth.

It is irregularity, rather than slowness of growth, that will have serious consequences for investment decisions, as it will lead to forecasting errors and to erratic behavior shifting from optimism to pessimism and vice versa. Periods of recession will be followed by periods of recovery as if the powers of recall were acting to maintain growth rates around a low average of about 2 percent—which, considering levels of development, is considerable. These rates are four to five times higher in absolute terms than the rate in an average year in the last century.

There is no longer one Third World but many. Their unequal development is expected to be another source of tension between neighboring countries, some of which are developing rapidly, with medium population levels, while others are prey to the difficulties of underdevelopment and overpopulation.

New energy price rises

Expensive energy is abundant, and rising prices encourage economy measures and energy substitution. Unfortunately, the fall in the real value of oil prices in the 1980s makes further sudden price rises—shocks—more likely after the mid-1990s.

The flood of new technologies

New techniques of production and organization bring the hope of productivity gains, new products, and new services but also threats to jobs and freedom. Precisely what emerges will depend on the political and social choices that are made concerning these new technologies and on their rate of diffusion, which constitutes a major uncertainty.

Competitive differentials between companies will increasingly stem from quality of organization and mastery of the information systems that surround new technologies.

After the hardware and software, the "orgware" will be a determining productivity factor in a company's competitive position. Five major trends that will have serious consequences are the following:

— mass production of variety by small-scale production systems;
— the comparative advantage of low salaries becoming less and less important;
— the flexibility of production equipment, indispensable for adapting to the fluctuations of changing markets;
— the need for alliances and cooperation with other companies at the level of precompetitive research, or development and industrialization; and
— a stronger coupling of scientific research and marketing, within the framework of an efficient strategy for managing a company's technological resources.

Deregulation associated with new international and regional regulation

The process known as "deregulation," which started in the United States almost 15 years ago, is being reproduced throughout the world. In reality, it is an evolution rather than a disappearance of regulations. This evolution is taking place along two fundamental axes, each with its own specific consequences.

First, certain types of activity—transport, telecommunications, or, more generally, services—are opening up to competition in certain types of market—certain public markets, for example—or in geographic regions—Japan—that until now have been excluded.

Second is the increased effectiveness of regulations on hygiene and health—for consumers and workers—safety, and the environment. The current trend is to make regulations more coherent and precise in order to improve their effectiveness. On the whole, this does not lead to a relaxation of constraints—quite the contrary—but it does guarantee that the same rules are applied universally, and this makes their development easier to forecast correctly, which makes international harmonization easier. At the European level, regulation and the introduction of standards will be a factor reducing uncertainty over the rules of the game but also generating new areas of competition and hence of turbulence, even in protected services such as banks and insurance.

Finally, the methods of instituting these new regulations are themselves evolving. The strategic decision-making bodies are increasingly the European Community, international organizations such as the General Agreement on Tariffs and Trade, or even the United States Congress.

Economic competition
on a global scale, with
states playing a key role

The transnational arena is the place for competition between the large multinational corporations that are tending to form global oligopolies through broad sectors of activities. To this competition will be added increasing cooperation and strategic alliances in, for example, the technological field, which will tend to reinforce still further the barriers to entry for companies not co-opted into the oligopoly. Those multinationals that function as global information systems have two characteristics that distinguish them from other companies: first, the ability to take the results of fundamental research and transform them in their own laboratories into adaptable technologies; and, second, the ability to access the world capital market, a huge source of finance, which moreover allows the continuous fluctuations in interest rates and exchange rates to be used as an opportunity.

These multinationals interact with many small and medium-sized enterprises, which are rooted in regional, social, and economic realities. These regional companies are specialized subcontractors and product innovators and often maintain a symbiotic relationship with the multinationals, each needing the other to ensure its competitiveness and longevity. Increasingly, the interface between the transnational, national, and regional space forms the basis of a company's competitiveness.

Between the transnational and the regional, the national level determines often very different comparative advantages, through three distinct mechanisms. In the first place, a nation's public policies on training, standards, and public markets define the technical environment of the companies. Second, national social dynamics determine collective attitudes toward distribution of value added, toward the rules of the game between social groups, and toward the individual's relationship to work and the company.

Decline in industrial jobs, and rise of service industries

The decline in industrial jobs started in the early 1970s in Europe; between 1970 and 1990, industrial output rose by 40 percent in Europe, and at the same time employment fell by 30 percent. This decline is expected to spread to all developed nations; the numbers of industrial jobs have been declining noticeably in the United States since 1980, and in Japan they have remained constant since 1973. It appears that what happened in the agricultural sector is being reproduced in the industrial sector; because of technical progress, an increasingly small proportion of the population is sufficient to produce growing quantities of industrial goods.

This uncoupling of production and classical industrial jobs could reach the point where, as in agriculture, the labor of 10 percent of the active labor force will be adequate for production needs. It is the knowledge workers who will take over. They will become more numerous, even within industry, than traditional blue- and white-collar workers.

Services—namely, commercial and financial activities, transport, leisure, utilities, public administration, education, and health care—today employ 55-65 percent of the active labor force in the industrialized nations. This growth of employment in services is as huge as it is recent. The proportion of household consumption spent on services is growing continually—it is currently 45 percent of the total—and it appears that expenditures on health and education can only continue to grow.

As for companies, functions other than production are developing rapidly. At each stage, from raw material to finished product, activities involving organization, stock control, maintenance, repair, coordination, and information have increased to the extent that they now make up the most significant proportion of product cost.

This tertiarization of the secondary sector also affects the product itself, which is often made up of an integrated whole of products and services. In addition, investment is becoming increasingly nonmaterial, targeted at training, software, research and development, and marketing, and is growing at four times the rate of material investment. This development of services, both within and outside the firm, is central to performance improvement.

The rise in services, however, is running into three different kinds of limitations that are mortgaging their growth in the medium term. First, collective services see their development limited by public finance problems. Moreover, financial restraints are bringing to a head the problem of the growing differentiation of some consumer services—health care, social security, education—as they are privatized. Second, the growth of services for the home is reaching its limits as consumers produce these services themselves by purchasing the product that performs the service. Finally, and more fundamentally, technological advances have still not produced a new wave of activities that go beyond mere gadgets and that satisfy real needs.

Services are creating three times fewer jobs in France today than 15 years ago, and they do not compensate for the reduction in jobs in agriculture and industry. Thus the "white tide" has not managed to defeat unemployment. Will opportunities arise out of strengthening service exports? (France is well placed on this score, ranking second in the world, just behind the United States.) Tourism makes up a large part of this item. When a country does not have enough products to export, it sells its landscapes and its way of life—another reason to preserve them.

Crisis of the welfare state

In most developed countries— countries in Europe; the United States; even Japan—the size of compulsory deductions—taxes and social security payments—in relation to gross domestic product has increased sharply since 1973 and now, in Europe, represents 45 percent of national product. This percentage, which has climbed by 10-15 points in the space of 10 years, cannot grow indefinitely without damaging general economic activity. In many cases, limits are imperative, particularly in Europe, where social security is facing exponential growth in health expenditures.

Reducing the scale of compulsory contributions and at the same time diminishing the role of the state in the economy would seem indispensable in order to help restore the ability of companies to finance themselves and to avoid penalizing those who wish to work more and thereby earn more. If this reduction in the tax burden is to happen without worsening the budgetary deficit, it can only be at the cost of either a reduction in the wage bill of public employees or imposing limitations on social transfers. The choice has to be made. Public expenditure must also be considered. In France in 1990, public expenditure represented 52 percent of gross domestic product, and public debt rose from 20 percent to 40 percent of gross domestic product in a few years. This debt will have to be repaid, and the return of inflation could prove politically convenient.

Beyond the financial crisis there is also a crisis in the legitimacy of the welfare state. The state must, however, support the infantry of the economic machine and tend those wounded and left out for the count by the savagery of the market. To preserve social peace, it must brandish the imperatives of solidarity and give a quasi wage to the unemployed, being ready to recoup the corresponding costs—unemployment benefits, national insurance payments—through taxation.

Finally, there is a crisis of effectiveness: the administrative machine is no longer accountable. The state is the worst of bosses. Financial crisis is forcing it to accept the relative impoverishment of public employees. In many administrations, absenteeism has increased threefold since 1980. Perhaps what is needed is fewer, better-paid civil servants.

When taxation kills work, when the state holds its civil servants in contempt and sets a bad example to its citizens, when the state plays a disruptive rather than a regulatory role, then it becomes intolerable. I would add that crises in effectiveness and legitimacy are merging. In reality, power is in the hands of a state aristocracy.

Rise in social tensions

In a world where everything is changing, advantages must also change. Unfortunately, there is good reason to believe that in this clash between forces of change and forces of inertia, some people will fall by the wayside in a rearguard battle—young people, older workers.

The unemployed are often excluded from the job market by those who control the education system. Unemployment is very destructive in a world where work has become the essential channel for social recognition and value and where the overworked man or woman is the symbol of success. Exclusion from the job market is a form of social death.

THREE MAJOR UNCERTAINTIES

If the foregoing trends seem probable, what exactly would result from a conjunction or confrontation between them is a question full of uncertainties. Here I call attention to three uncertainties that are important.

Will the rate of diffusion of new technologies be as rapid as forecast?

It can only be postulated that, generally, progress in the diffusion of new technologies will remain slow, due to the inertia inherent in production and social systems. Resistance is perhaps stronger in the tertiary sector, to the extent that this sector has, so far, been less affected by the stimulus of international competition. Many factors combine to explain the slow rate of this penetration. In the first place, there is the question of reallocating time freed by new techniques of production, organization, and so on. What is the point of investing in order to obtain productivity gains that cannot be translated into expanded production due to saturated markets, slow growth rates, or staff reduction? The staff are there, and must be kept busy, and a reduction in working hours can only be gradual if it is to be equitably shared between sectors.

In the second place, the spread of office technology means that the world of work becomes relatively transparent, which works against established hierarchies. Information technologies are not neutral vis-à-vis power structures. It is therefore not surprising that certain actors at the heart of companies, often managers, feel threatened and resist innovation.

What is technologically possible is not necessarily economically profitable—we should beware of creating a Concorde in the field of telematics—or socially desirable. It is unlikely that working at home will develop to the point that a significant amount of office work disappears. The physiognomy of urban housing developments in France—their pokiness, their lack of comfort, and the mediocrity of the environment—makes it unlikely that they will be lived in for whole days at a time. Moreover, work is a social activity and meets a need for communication that is satisfied less and less elsewhere.

Metamorphosis of work and employment

Unemployment today affects 10 percent of the active labor force in France. Tomorrow it may well affect 15 percent, then 20 percent or more if there is no change in structures, organizations, rules of the game, and behavior. This means we are heading for a dual society, with a growing proportion of the population—the young and the old, who are becoming younger and younger—excluded from the labor market. Such a scenario can only be explosive.

Ultimately, there is only one way out—a sharing of work and income, matched with greater mobility of existing jobs. If there are only four jobs for five workers, this is not a problem if the jobs are rotated; moreover, an opportunity exists to increase creative breaks from work. A reduction in working hours seems probable and desirable to me, but it does not have to mean a decrease in hours of real activity. People want not to work less but to work differently.

In order to avoid the dual society, we must promote the pluralistic society where each individual could have several jobs and where each job could be occupied by several people.

Evolution of life-styles and social organization in developed countries

The most persistent question concerns the evolution of values and ways of life. At this level, conjecture fails, as futurists do not see clearly and sociologists have difficulty in understanding the present or even the recent past. As for analyses of life-styles, these have no predictive value. In technical terms, the percentage of variables explained by life-styles is almost systematically negligible. In all cases, it is 10 times less important than any sociodemographic indicator, such as the level of education of the housewife or her profession.

After World War II, new values emerged to replace the traditional values of fulfilling one's duties, making one's efforts pay, saving, and hierarchies. New values were to become dominant during the 1960s that gave priority to consuming, the attraction of novelty, and the importance of keeping up appearances. After the end of the 1960s, however, this model found itself challenged by new values, characterized by the rejection of the criteria of social excellence, the motives of status, and large organizations and bureaucracy, in order to give importance to conviviality, personal and cultural life, relationships, the quality of one's personal and collective environment, decentralization of small groups, autonomy, and self-realization.

As they spread, the new values combined in a heterogeneous way with the values of the consumer society that assimilated them. Conviviality was translated into Club Med, autonomy into the suburban detached house, and self-realization into stereos.

Double social fragmentation

Beyond the current phase of adjustment of demands and behavior to new opportunities and new constraints, it seems that we are heading toward a double fragmentation of the social scene. The first involves a deepened and renewed fragmentation at the level of the classical major social partnerships—employers, unions, the state, socioprofessional actors—that are negotiating over the way revenue is distributed and over the status and development of the welfare state.

The second is the fragmentation of the representatives of new values into many groups and minorities, expressing different values or even different interfaces between common values and varied opportunities and constraints. This juxtaposition of the believers in moral excellence (the so-called militants), the small, more or less closed groups (even sects), the new consumers, those who live for the moment, the minority who have a satisfying job, the new agriculturalists, those without work or without declared work, and so on will translate into growing disparities in lifestyles, demands, and behavior.

In this variety we shall find all the possible degrees of compromise between partially contradictory trends developing in parallel, such as the search for both autonomy and security, for both freedom and a sense of roots.

ANNALS, *AAPSS*, 522, July 1992

Consequences of the Changing Sexual Division of Labor

By IAN MILES

ABSTRACT: The trend of women's entering parts of the labor market that were traditionally male dominated is common across most Western industrialized economies. It looks set to continue, with more role models available for girls and more financial and educational resources released that women can use to improve their circumstances. Though some prejudices will be dispelled by the performance of competent women workers, some men will seek to contain women's activities, on account of threats to their power and prestige in both home and work life. Women will still have to battle to realize the opportunities that are presented—as well as coping with, or transforming, the double burden of housework and formal employment. The ensuing conflicts are liable to intensify the critique of traditional concepts of masculinity and femininity. Suppressed grievances and insecurities are liable to come to light. This ferment has the potential to increase social justice—in family life, formal work, and more broadly—but this outcome cannot be taken for granted.

Ian Miles is professorial research fellow and associate director of the Programme of Policy Research on Engineering, Science and Technology at the University of Manchester, United Kingdom. He has published several books on issues connected with new information technology and in the area of social indicators research.

THE male experience has often been taken to be the norm in studies of working life, with women's lives treated as deviant exceptions to this norm—as in the case of many other areas of life.[1] Though for men such terms as "work" and "work life" refer mainly to formal employment, for women there is also the experience of substantial volumes of housework, unpaid domestic labor. The home is also a workplace, even if it is not so defined in terms of the male norm. This article concentrates on the role of women's formal employment in social change, but it will be important to remain alert to the double meaning of "work life" for women.

This theoretical and empirical literature concerning women's changing role in the formal economy has, with a few exceptions—for example, the work of sociobiologists—overwhelmingly rejected the notion that gender differences in working lives are simple reflections of our biological differences. While there are many nuances in the alternatives to biological determinism, most analysts relate the different experiences of men and women in employment to the typical responsibilities placed upon women to service men and children in the family.

TRENDS IN
WOMEN'S EMPLOYMENT

In the postwar period, women's participation grew in the labor markets of Western industrialized nations, and the share of employment taken by women is now between 40 and 50 percent in countries such as the United Kingdom and the United States. Many women's jobs are part-time, and there are high levels of occupational segregation, with female employment remaining concentrated in particular industries and occupations. Comparative analyses of U.K., U.S., and French surveys for the early 1980s[2] identify areas where women's presence is greater or less than would be expected from their overall participation in the labor force. Women were overrepresented in the "other services" and the banking and finance sectors; they were underrepresented in the agriculture, energy and water, extractive, metal manufacturing, and building and civil engineering sectors. They were overrepresented in clerical and service occupations, and underrepresented in administrative and managerial, agricultural, and "production and related" occupations. Women tend to occupy lower rungs of the occupational ladder[3] and to receive lower wages than do men.

Despite these features of women's employment, women in large numbers have entered many work activities that were formerly exclusively or almost exclusively male. Occupational segregation appears to be decreasing in countries such as the United Kingdom and the United States. In addition to—and perhaps stimulated by—the expansion of ser-

1. See, for example, Dale Spender, ed., *Men's Studies Modified* (Oxford: Pergamon Press, 1981).

2. Angela Dale and Judith Glover, *An Analysis of Women's Employment Patterns in the UK, France and the USA*, Research Paper no. 75 (London: Department of Employment, 1990).

3. Shirley Dex, "Gender and the Labour Market," in *Employment in Britain*, ed. D. Gallie (Oxford: Basil Blackwell, 1988).

vice and white-collar jobs, more women have been pursuing higher education and training and thus gaining formal qualifications to compete for more senior positions. The evolution of wages and of aspirations for higher living standards has made dual wage-earning a necessity for many families, while increased availability of contraception has made it easier to plan families in the light of employment prospects. The experience of two world wars, where women proved they could take over many male jobs, is often said to have had an impact on attitudes. And women have been active, both directly and through influencing policymakers, against sex discrimination at work.

In considering future developments, it would seem reasonable to expect that both the structural trends in employment opportunities and the widening ambitions of women will continue. Countertrends may emerge, however, such as reactions to changes in the structure of economic costs and to challenges that women's employment places upon men. The future implications of women's activity in formal employment can be understood only with reference to housework and family arrangements. Given the absence of strong empirical evidence as to the emergence of substantially new living patterns, I will assume that relationships of heterosexual and nuclear-family form remain the dominant form of living arrangements, with the continuation of the increasing number of people living alone—especially as a consequence of the growing proportion of single elderly people—and of high levels of marital breakup and of subsequent remarriage.

CHANGING WORK ORGANIZATION

There is widespread agreement among forecasters as to some of the broad patterns of change in employment opportunities over the coming decades. In particular, we can expect the structure of employment to continue to shift toward white-collar and service jobs, which have typically been areas of so-called women's work, with some growth in occupations connected with demographic change, such as nursing. Many of these developments will favor women's employment, as will the shortage of skilled staff associated with the exhaustion of the abundant supply of labor associated with the baby boom.

Two factors may offset these developments, however. First is the growing technology intensity of service—and other—work, which means that many employees will be required to possess or acquire technical skills, especially skills associated with the information technologies. These have typically been skills that men have been most willing and/or able to acquire, and, unless efforts are made to ensure more female competence in them, the likelihood will be a reinforcement of male dominance in many senior posts in service organizations. The second factor is the redesign of organizational structures that is being undertaken by some organizations and that is promoted for many more by a variety of articulate advocates. It is proposed that leaner

4. Ibid.

firms can reduce management hierarchies through the use of telematics and other innovations, doing away with layers of middle management. If this strategy is a viable one for more than a vanguard of advanced companies, the likely consequence would be fewer opportunities in office and white-collar work for women and, probably, more obstacles in the way of a progression in occupational status through the steps of an internal labor market.

Organizations are also being urged to attempt to become leaner by restructuring work and applying new technologies so as to relocate production in space and time—and there are some notable steps in this direction, albeit on a small scale to date. Some of these developments, such as the relocation of routine office work in remote, low-wage areas, may create more employment opportunities for women in such locations, though perhaps at a cost to those in the traditional heartlands of corporate headquarters.[5] Probably the most widely touted of these innovations, telework, is often portrayed as a mode of employment that will be particularly valuable to women. "Telework" refers to paid employment carried out at a distance from the employing organization, usually at the employees' homes or in local telecottages—where employees of different organizations may work together—and linked to the employer by new telecommunications facilities such as electronic mail and facsimile.

As well as the common benefits of reduced travel time to work and the like, telework is seen as providing more flexible working conditions and as allowing women to spend more time in the home—both of which should make it easier to combine household responsibilities, especially child care, with employment. In practice, however, telework seems for many women to be reinforcing their isolation within the home.[6] As with remote working, bringing the job to the woman in this way may provide new employment opportunities, but it may also serve to restrict her contact with the informal network of communication within the organization that is so important for career advancement.

The future evolution of employment, along with its implications for women, is thus a complex affair. On balance, there is good reason to expect that structural changes in the economy, and strategic choices by firms, will provide more scope for women to enter areas of work that have been heavily male dominated. The possibility cannot be ruled out, however, that there may be higher barriers to progress up occupational hierarchies within companies. These barriers may be overcome by efforts to ensure more equality of opportunity—efforts by women in employment themselves and those allies they may find among men—and by policymakers whose motivations may be as various as anxiety to secure women's votes, keenness to ensure that their potential as economic resources is not wasted, and, last but not least, concern with social justice.

5. Annie Posthuma, *The Internationalisation of Clerical Work*, Occasional Papers no. 17 (Falmer, Brighton: Science Policy Research Unit, 1987).

6. Cf. Ursula Huws, "Telework: Projections," *Futures*, 23(1):19-31 (Jan.-Feb. 1991).

So far, I have concentrated mainly on the more formal dimensions of employment—on the job contract, the hours worked, and the skills required. There has been considerable attention to how women may be disadvantaged in respect of these dimensions. In addition, it is important to note that employment has important informal dimensions. Workers form social groups, often out of the workplace as well as in it. The informal norms and working practices set up by these groups have sometimes been studied from the economic standpoint, for example, the effect that they have had on productivity levels. But social groups formed at the workplace are an important source of interpersonal relationships, too. Informal practices are often difficult for managers and policymakers to intervene in. They can be powerful influences on the experience that both male and female employees have with work; they may constitute barriers to women in employment; and they may be affected by the increasing entrance of women into many areas of employment.

FEMININE IDENTITY

To what extent do men and women bring the same attitudes concerning employment into the workplace? Despite the heterogeneity of both male and female populations, and changes in values over time, recent U.K. survey research[7] suggests that meaningful generalizations can be drawn.

This study finds aggregate differences between employed men and

employed women in "work involvement," with men more likely than women to say that they would continue in paid work even if they could afford not to. But it should be noted that majorities of both sexes—three-quarters of men, two-thirds of women—did represent themselves as involved in work in this sense. In terms of "instrumental reasons for having a job," men were more likely than women to portray their reasons for working as being a matter of securing money for necessities; in contrast, more women described themselves as earning money to buy extras.

In contrast, there was little difference between the sexes in terms of "labor market individualism," defined here in terms of such statements as "Unemployed people can get another job if they want one," and "The welfare state reduces the will to work." Likewise, there was little difference in "expressive reasons for having a job," defined as saying that one is working in order to use one's abilities to the full or to "do something worthwhile."

Michael Rose has demonstrated that the great bulk—96 percent—of the difference in work values between women and men vanishes when nongender factors such as skill, labor market, and occupation are held constant.[8] He thus suggests that many more women will develop a

---

7. Michael Rose, "The Work Ethic: Women, Skill and the Ancient Curse" (Presidential Paper for Section N [Sociology], annual conference of the British Association for the Advancement of Science, Portsmouth Polytechnic, UK, 25-30 Aug. 1991 [available as a mimeo from the Centre for European Industrial Studies, University of Bath]). See also idem, "Attachment to Work and Social Values," in *Employment in Britain*, ed. Gallie.

8. Rose, "Work Ethic."

strong—"masculine"—work ethic once the conditions that force many women into low-skill part-time jobs, such as skill deficits and lack of child-care provision, are alleviated.

Other survey evidence supports this argument, showing, for example, that women who consider themselves unemployed share the negative experiences of unemployed men, though professed housewives are in a less problematic situation. These problems include not only loss of income but also reduction in social contacts, meaningful activity, time structure, and status.[9] Employment has become much more important as a source of important social experiences and relationships in the course of the evolution of industrial society, for men and women alike. With increasing female labor participation and the entrance of women into more fulfilling jobs, together with the breakdown of many traditional community structures that might otherwise provide such relationships, this trend is liable to persist. Women's identities will be more tightly bound up with their occupations, their self-images will draw upon both the associated technical skills and proficiencies and the social relationships. Greater female participation in a wide range of occupations means that more role models will be available for girls and young women to use as reference points in thinking about their own futures. In turn, this might promote the widening of girls' educational aspirations and performance, which are frequently restricted.

This emphatically does not mean that feminine identities will come to resemble the normal masculine identity, since gender differences are not just a matter of formal work or housework. They are in part products of the differential treatment of children from babyhood onward, by parents, teachers, and other significant adults.[10] Change in such practices is frequently slow and partial. Biological differences—menstruation, genitalia, pregnancy, and so on—though open to interpretation in many ways, are also bound to affect the individual experiences of boys and girls.

If the trends in women's work force participation continue as described, women may be expected to gain more material and cognitive resources that they can use in constructing their own identities—on the basis of the character formations established in childhood. They will appropriate some behaviors that are traditionally regarded as masculine ones, though these may well carry subtly different meanings. They will also seize the opportunity to promote some traditionally feminine values and practices that have been undervalued by the dominant male culture. The results are likely to be multiform. We can expect to see a variety of ethnic, occupational, and other styles of behavior incorporated into our already pluralistic cultures.

MASCULINE IDENTITY

Traditional notions of masculinity, no less than those of femininity, are

9. Felicity Henwood and Ian Miles, "The Experience of Unemployment and the Sexual Division of Labour," in *Unemployed People*, ed. D. Fryer and P. Ullah (Milton Keynes: Open University Press, 1987).

10. H. Moss, "Sex, Age and State as Determinants of Mother-Infant Interaction," in

under threat. Some men welcome this challenge, resenting the way, for example, that men's career success frequently means working patterns that make it very difficult to spend adequate amounts of time with their children. Many men are more cautious but are prepared to shoulder some of the burden of housework and to accept the legitimacy of women's grievances—at least to an extent. Others are defensive, seeking to maintain the power and prestige traditionally accorded to their gender. The workplace becomes an important site for the ensuing conflicts.

Having a job corresponds with the notion of man as the breadwinner: unemployed men frequently face severe problems associated with the loss of this role.[11] This may be felt as a loss of authority within the family. Efforts may be made to compensate for the loss of authority by recourse to noneconomic means of coercion, namely, verbal or physical violence. Other reported reactions include loss of sexual potency, and, less frequently than might be expected, efforts to construct more egalitarian family relations.[12]

Many particular jobs are bound up with traditional forms of masculine identity. With manual laboring jobs in numerical decline, dilemmas are posed for male working-class cultures that place high value on physical strength, control of powerful machines, and so on.

The decline of traditional manual work may be compensated for, in principle, by the emergence of other sources of male pride. For example, pride in intellectual acumen, competitive entrepreneurialism, or adept control of information systems can be fostered in white-collar occupations. While managerial and technical positions have expanded, however, the more typical white-collar jobs that the sons and grandsons of manual laborers find available offer little scope for autonomy or display of individual competence. The alienation and rowdyism displayed by young men faced with such career prospects may be responses to the lack of opportunities to develop work-based alternatives to the forms of male self-esteem valued by their fathers.

The sources of masculine identity in employment extend beyond the formal features of the workplace, such as the nature of the task and occupational hierarchy. Less formal features are also important. It is notable that the atmosphere of many largely male workplaces is one of a boy's club, with banter, prestige, and informal decision making following men's norms. Horseplay of various forms may be manifested in the free spaces of highly alienating jobs.[13] Often the rhetoric of such occasions is antiwomen, although there is little corresponding emotional support offered by men to each other.

Readings in Child Socialisation, ed. K. Danziger (Oxford: Pergamon Press, 1970).

11. Cf. Leonard Fagin and Michael Little, *The Forsaken Families* (Harmondsworth: Penguin Books, 1984); Peter Kelvin and Joanna E. Jarrett, *Unemployment* (London: Cambridge University Press, 1985).

12. Lydia Morris, "Employment, the Household and Social Networks," in *Employment in Britain*, ed. Gallie.

13. Jeff Hearn, "Men's Sexuality at Work," in *The Sexuality of Men*, ed. Andy Metcalf and Martin Humphries (London: Pluto Press, 1985).

When women are present in the workplace, masculine identity may be measured against the relations between the sexes. The traditionally subordinate position of women in employment may have served to bolster men's feelings of power and superiority. In such cases, the rise of women to senior positions should undermine this complacency. They may be perceived both as competitors for job and promotion opportunities and as threats to men's power at work and, by extension, at home. The means whereby men act to resist equality of the sexes in working life have been well documented by Cynthia Cockburn in a recent study.[14]

One notable form of control of women through informal practices in the workplace is sexual harassment. The phenomenon shares similarities with certain other pathological gender relationships, such as child abuse, incest, and rape. The scale of these phenomena is only just being recognized, since victims are often silenced by (1) the public opprobrium, including doubt of one's testimony, that is often cast upon the victim in court and elsewhere; (2) the need to retain close relations, in the employment situation or family, with the perpetrator; and (3) a sense of guilt and self-blame, sometimes generated by the (usually male) oppressor. The growing presence of women in employment is likely to lead to growing awareness of sexual harassment in work situations, even if the incidence of such behavior might be hoped to decrease, given more women's escape from subordinate positions and increased efforts to stamp out harassment by employers who are becoming aware of the potential legal consequences of permitting it.

Sexual harassment is an extreme, if common, case of men's exercise of power over women in employment. With the growing presence of women in equal or superior positions in the workplace, men will have to confront the ways in which they collude with such power displays there. It remains to be seen to what extent men's behavior out of the workplace will also be affected. While some men may well accommodate by reappraising their assumptions about gender power relations in the family and elsewhere, it is plausible that others will seek to reinforce their threatened identities by retaliating against women in the outside world. The growth of extreme neoconservative political movements and religious fundamentalism, both typically seeking a return to traditional sex roles, may draw on men's desires to maintain their superiority in the home and workplace alike. Such backlash movements can be highly influential, as the whittling away of abortion rights and other social reforms over the 1980s demonstrates vividly. This suggests that as well as documenting the positive gains that women can achieve from new gender relationships, proponents of sexual equality must demonstrate viable and attractive new models for masculine identity, which can help to assuage the fears that underlie these movements.

14. Cynthia Cockburn, *In the Way of Women: Men's Resistance to Sex Equality in Organisations* (London: Macmillan Education, 1991). See also her excellent earlier case study, *Brothers: Male Dominance and Technological Change* (London: Pluto Press, 1983).

EMPLOYING ORGANIZATIONS

It was suggested earlier that the development of some new forms of work organization—such as telework—is driven more by the internal needs of employing organizations than by those of female workers. The same case could be made about more familiar nontraditional forms of women's work, such as part-time work and flexible hours. Nevertheless, these developments are in part responsive to the availability of female employees, and the need to recruit women into a wider range of positions in companies is liable to lead to more experimentation with arrangements of work that do not impose a male norm on all workers. This push is likely to be reinforced by pressures from women themselves and by policies on equal opportunities—and, perhaps, by efforts to provide better child-care facilities, which might offset some of the educational underachievement that is a source of concern in many Western countries.

Among the developments that are likely to become far more common than at present, then, are

— provision of maternity and paternity leave;
— provision of child-care facilities and procedures that accommodate to the need for absence from the workplace to cope with childhood health problems;
— more flexible working hours;
— revision of existing training programs, whose content and structure often reflect male priorities, to accommodate women better, and establishment of new programs to train women for more senior positions. These programs will be offered both by in-house groups in large companies and by specialist public and private agencies;
— development of corporate schemes for mentoring women, putting them onto promotion fast tracks, and providing them with role models;
— efforts to place strict limits on the display of sexism and the emergence of sexual harassment at work, perhaps including educational activities aimed at men, as well as support for women protesting such practices; and
— perhaps most unpredictably, efforts to design alternatives to the old boys' networks and to the use of typically masculine sites like the bar and the golf club as locations for important business activities. In addition to creating parallel women's networks, there may well be informal interaction organized around activities that are less sexually stereotyped—with the proviso that these may also need to be ones where there are few pressures to engage in flirtation, courtship behavior, and the like.

The picture is unlikely to be all rosy, however. Many firms will be laggards in these initiatives. Small firms are often slow to undertake such developments (there are, of course, shining exceptions, pioneers among small firms). If Western societies are moving into a post-Fordist organization of production, with a great increase in the role of small firms and a reduction in scale of some large firms, there may well be less change than would be expected by extrapolating from the strategies now being pursued by supposedly vanguard firms. Even if the case for such a trend is overstated, my earlier suggestions about the implications of organizational restructuring for management hierarchies and promotion patterns also point to factors that would tend to offset these trends. The challenges that such developments pose need to be carefully investigated by trade unions, women's movements, training bodies, and others.

Women can play an active role in organizations, beyond encouraging the reshaping of working arrangements to better meet their needs. Pressures to act as honorary men, behaving like one of the boys, should decrease as more women acquire power in managerial, scientific, and related professions. The values and practices that women bring with them to the workplace are liable to begin to affect organizational culture, with the prospect of creating more nurturing and humane work environments.[15] The extent to which this happens will be conditioned by the demands of a competitive economic environment, of course, and it is quite possible that the imperatives of making hard business decisions will push many women toward tougher attitudes than they would

have anticipated at the outset of their careers. Putting women at the top of major institutions will not bring about a utopian society, but it is safe to predict that it will lead to change in a whole range of corporate cultures and practices.

DOMESTIC WORK AND FAMILY LIFE

Housework is still overwhelmingly women's work, though there is evidence that substantial inequalities between the sexes in household labor time tend to open up with the birth of the first child. Time-use studies show, too, long-term trends in the allocation of domestic work, with a slow shift toward greater male-female equality.[16] This trend in large part reflects reductions in female domestic labor time through the use of labor-saving domestic technology—even if standards of cleanliness and the like have been raised—and through the reduction in family size. Less important is a small growth in men's contribution to housework. This may reflect women's case for more equality, their greater contribution to household incomes, or factors such as the conversion of some aspects of domestic work into opportunities for pleasure—leisure—or display of prowess, as in hobbies. Examples include shopping, cooking, child care, and gardening.

15. For example, Rianne Eisler, "Women, Men and Management: Redesigning Our Future," *Futures*, 23(1):3-18 (1991). See also Judy B. Roesener, "Ways Women Lead," *Harvard Business Review*, Nov.-Dec. 1990, pp. 119-25; and the subsequent debate in *Harvard Business Review*, Jan.-Feb. 1991, pp. 150-60.

16. Jonathan Gershuny et al., "Time Budgets: Preliminary Analyses of a National Survey," *Quarterly Journal of Social Affairs*, 2(1):13-39 (1986); Ian Miles, "Time Use and Information Technology: Present and Future Developments of Private Households," in *Industrial Societies after the Stagnation of the 1970s*, ed. Burkhardt Strumpel (Berlin: Walter de Guyter, 1989).

New domestic technologies are unlikely to make any substantial savings in housework over the next few years.[17] While further decline in family size may be limited, as more women's jobs acquire professional values and promotion prospects, there is liable to be more postponement of first births until later points in the woman's life.[18] This will be offset to the extent that provisions for child care and work advancement are introduced. We could expect more demand for domestic service of various sorts—au pairs, temporary home-based child care, and, perhaps, help with routine housework. The reemergence of domestic service in Britain over the last decade has caused much soul-searching among feminist professionals; efforts to support service workers by legislation, training initiatives, and informal norms are a possible consequence.

Earlier it was suggested that women are liable to accord the experience of employment a more central role in their identities. What does this mean for home and family life?

There is potential for conflict between the demands of family members and the beliefs and values that stem from participation in formal employment. The material and psychological resources that derive from employment may empower women to refuse more of these demands; in other words, family conflicts may become more overt as they are less routinely settled by the exercise of male dominance. Some strain may be experienced by family members caught in conflicts whose resolution is difficult. But the family is, equally, less likely to face the strain of being the sole source of everyday gratifications and consolations for women. This is a burden that, some commentators argue, is putting nuclear families under increasing strain—and that is certainly implicated in the prevalence of depression among women.[19]

Those who seek to stabilize existing family practices by restricting women's opportunities would do well to consider the oppressive aspects of current arrangements. But proponents of sexual equality would do well to recognize that some of these fears of family conflict raise issues beyond the maintenance of male power, such as the collateral damage that may be sustained by children and other family members. Social innovations such as family and workplace counseling support may be required to ease the transitions that are probable, if not inevitable, and that represent steps toward a more just society.

END NOTE

As a man, I am aware of drawing upon the research and practical experience of numerous women in preparing this article. By drawing attention to the complex implications of women's increasing role in formal work, and in particular to the potential for backlash and dysfunctional male responses, I am in no way arguing that

17. Miles, "Time Use and Information Technology."

18. Joseph F. Coates, Jennifer Jarratt, and John B. Mahaffie, *Future Work* (San Francisco: Jossey-Bass, 1990).

19. George W. Brown and T. Harris, *The Social Origins of Depression* (London: Tavistock, 1978).

their efforts to achieve greater equality are misplaced. Far from it: they need to be reinforced.

To acknowledge the fears that many men have about the changes that are under way as a real social force does not mean substituting compassion for men's angst for concern with women's oppression. Rather, it indicates that we need to find ways of making much clearer the benefits that both men and women stand to gain from a transformation of gender relations at work. Men will need to learn to support each other in the process of forging new masculine identities, as well as supporting women in the transformation of male institutions. The future, as always, will be the product of the choices that we—both men and women—make.

Education in the Twenty-First Century

By CHRISTOPHER J. DEDE

ABSTRACT: America's multiple educational systems are its major long-term mechanism for shaping the future, but this infrastructure for human resource development has remained static rather than shifting its mission as the societal environment has changed. The emergence of a global economy with a shift toward cognitive partnerships with intelligent tools, and the growing challenge of diversity when excellence and quality depend on a pluralistic understanding of a worldwide market are underscoring the decline in the effectiveness of America's instructional environments. Building on societal discontent with traditional educational models, the evolution of advanced technologies for teaching, learning, and management and the initiation of a restructuring movement for educational reform both provide contexts for innovation that may foster the implementation of new paradigms for education. Nonetheless, a future of little or no change in American education is all too probable; similar opportunities for innovation always slipped away in the past.

Christopher Dede is a professor at George Mason University, with programmatic responsibilities in education, information technology, and public policy. A former Danforth Fellow, he received his doctorate from the University of Massachusetts. His research and consulting center on artificial intelligence, education, and strategic planning. He has been a policy fellow at the National Institute of Education and a visiting scientist at the Massachusetts Institute of Technology.

OF all of society's institutions, education has been the most stable. An inhabitant of eighteenth-century America transported forward two centuries would find most modern organizations confusing but would instantly recognize the teaching methods and much of the instructional equipment that characterize education in today's schools, communities, and workplaces. Multiple organizational and contextual factors have rendered traditional approaches to teaching and learning almost impervious to change.[1]

Nonetheless, many believe that this conventional paradigm for education may alter dramatically over the next decade. Early in the 1990s, an unprecedented confluence of external trends and discontinuities is driving forces for educational reform; simultaneously, technological advances and societal discontent are empowering the institutionalization of alternative models for learning. By the turn of the millennium, radically different educational approaches may be permeating school districts, businesses, and communities. In this article, the structural shifts undermining the dominance of the traditional educational paradigm will be delineated first; the factors leveraging competing models of teaching and learning will be discussed later. Given the space constraints for the article, the focus of the discussion is on educational institutions concerned with kindergarten through grade 12.

1. Christopher J. Dede, "Futures Research and Strategic Planning in Teacher Education," in *Handbook of Research on Teacher Education*, ed. R. Houston (New York: Macmillan, 1990), pp. 83-97.

TRENDS INFLUENCING THE U.S. EDUCATIONAL INFRASTRUCTURE

Two major structural shifts are eroding the effectiveness of U.S. schools. These trends are creating a situation in which—for the first time in a century—society is willing to reconceptualize its fundamental model for education.

The emergence of a global marketplace

One significant external trend affecting everyone with a stake in an educated American population is the emergence of a worldwide economy. Society mandates school attendance in part to prepare pupils for productive participation in the workplace; in the past, preparing learners to compete effectively with other Americans in our domestic economy was sufficient to ensure their prosperity. The evolution of worldwide markets, however, means that U.S. employees must be more adept than their global competitors at meeting the needs of a very diverse range of customers.

In this new economic ecology, each nation is seeking a specialized niche based on its financial, human, and natural resources. Developed countries, which no longer have easily available natural resources and cheap labor, cannot compete with rising-star developing nations in manufacturing standardized industrial commodities. But a nation with America's strengths—technological expertise, an advanced industrial base, an educated citizenry—could develop an economy that uses sophisticated people and information tools to produce customized, value-added products.

Such a strategy to build U.S. prosperity in a global marketplace necessitates a shift in work roles away from smart machines manufacturing standardized commodities toward cognitive partnerships with intelligent tools. As this transformation to a postindustrial economy occurs, an evolution of job requirements toward higher-order thinking skills is taking place in all types of occupations, blue-collar as well as white-collar.[2] With advances in artificial intelligence during this decade, workstations will evolve to be more intelligent through embedded expert aids for decision making, and the thinking skills required of the human role in person-tool partnerships will become even more sophisticated. People's creativity and flexibility will be vital because the standardized aspects of problem solving will be absorbed by the machine.

Transforming the U.S. economic system from mass-produced commodities to customized products will not be easy or painless. On the contrary, advanced technology eliminates occupations as well as creates them, and, in an automated workplace, people with low-level skills may have access only to dead-end, minimum wage jobs—or to no work at all.[3] The United States must find ways to work smarter—as the America 2000 initiative championed by President Bush discusses[4]—or its prosperity will continue to wane due to competition from nations with lower wages and cheaper natural resources. Growing public awareness of this situation has created massive pressure for improving educational effectiveness in schools, workplaces, and communities. People who care little about learning as an intrinsic value are increasingly concerned about the pragmatic consequences of an ignorant work force and are demanding educational reform in order to enhance their prosperity.

*The growing challenge
and opportunity
of diversity*

Intellectually sophisticated, highly motivated human resources have always been important to economic success, but developed nations now need a work force that also understands the diverse range of needs in the world market.[5] Creating customized products requires a deep understanding of quality as seen through the eyes of each individual consumer. In a global market, this understanding necessitates a rich comprehension of and empathy with many diverse cultures. Being able to design products that are flexible enough to be tailored to a wide variety of needs

2. This issue is discussed in detail in Shoshanna Zuboff, *In the Age of the Smart Machine: The Future of Work and Power* (New York: Basic Books, 1988).

3. A good resource in this area is G. Burke and R. W. Rumberger, eds., *The Future Impact of Technology on Work and Education* (New York: Falmer Press, 1987).

4. U.S., Department of Education, *America 2000: An Education Strategy* (Washington, DC: Department of Education, 1991).

5. National Center on Education and the Economy, *America's Choice: High Skills or Low Wages* (Rochester, NY: National Center on Education and the Economy, 1990).

demands the ability to see a situation from multiple perspectives.[6]

Thinking about workplace skills in this manner requires a shift in attitude for many Americans, who until recently saw the rest of the world more as an interesting theme park in which to vacation than as a marketplace they must understand in order to prosper. The Japanese have been very successful in the global economy by studying other cultures and creating customized products to meet their needs. The United States could gain an advantage over its international competitors by excelling at cross-cultural design; working in its favor are this nation's great diversity and long tradition of pluralism.

Our society must, however, overcome deeply rooted problems of racism and prejudice to achieve that goal. To market to the world, the United States must move from a melting-pot to a salad-bowl mentality. Cultural diversity is a strength rather than a weakness, but it can only be harnessed when every group benefits equally from cooperation toward shared goals. To date, other than at times of war or other manifest crises, this nation has been unable to leverage its diversity into a unified, pluralistic action. Education provides a potential lever for accomplishing such a synergy.

At present, however, the widening range of diversity in schooling between kindergarten and twelfth grade poses more of a challenge than an opportunity. Due to changes in family structure, in socioeconomic and ethnic distribution, and in political policies, about one-third of preschool children are destined for educational failure because of poverty, neglect, sickness, handicapping conditions, and lack of adult protection and nurturance.[7] Teachers are asked to be parents, moral counselors, bulwarks against drugs and sex, linguists, and custodians of holding tanks—in addition to communicating an expanding range of skills and knowledge.

Excellence and equity are usually presented as contrasting, rather than complementary, educational goals. Both prosperity in the global marketplace and truly democratic domestic governance require a new type of excellence made possible by pluralistic equity: quality based on multiple perspectives and intercultural partnerships. Current governance crises have their roots in school, workplace, and community-based instruction that fails to leverage the power of diversity—and in a societal context that dooms many children to educational failure because of intolerance and neglect. Increasingly, business and community groups are lobbying for educational reform out of the recognition, in Ben Franklin's words, that "we must all hang together, or assuredly we shall all hang separately."

The erosion of school effectiveness

In part because of the trends discussed previously, Americans are dissatisfied with the performance of all

6. U.S., Congress, Office of Technology Assessment, *Worker Training: Competing in the New International Economy* (Washington, DC: Government Printing Office, 1990).

7. Harold Hodgkinson, "Reform versus Reality," *Phi Delta Kappan* 72(1):9-16 (1991).

types of classroom settings and dismayed with the difficulty of sustaining even modest improvements in educational effectiveness. Over the past three decades, successive waves of reform have come and gone; little fundamental change has occurred.[8] Because school instruction and worker retraining have drifted further from meeting the needs of a rapidly evolving society, the public has shifted its definition of "education reform." Parents and communities, industry leaders and politicians have reached a consensus: fine-tuning traditional models of education is fruitless; fundamental changes in the mission, content, and methods of all types of teaching and learning are essential.

Over the past few decades, the effectiveness of traditional teaching and learning settings has eroded in part because society's other educational agents—families, communities, the media—have abdicated their responsibilities. The trends discussed earlier necessitate partnerships for education between all of society's institutions to make learning a continuous, lifelong activity. Given America's current economic malaise, however, making the expenditures that quality educational experiences require will be difficult. In particular, the recent shift of social welfare funding from youths to the aged has placed this nation in the position of eating its seed corn.

The long-range costs of not educating are even greater than the resources required for lifelong learning. Welfare, prisons, the inability to compete in the global market, incompetent juries, and ignorant voters are just the tip of the iceberg; skilled human resources are the nervous system of a society. The challenge lies partly in providing increased funding—although surveys show that Americans are willing to pay substantially more for quality educational experiences—and partly in guaranteeing that the resources expended will be well spent by using more sophisticated assessment mechanisms than standardized tests.[9]

In summary, the emergence of a global economy with a shift in work roles toward cognitive partnerships with intelligent tools and the growing challenge of diversity when excellence and quality depend on a pluralistic understanding of a worldwide market are underscoring the decline in the effectiveness of America's instructional environments. But need alone does not create innovation; a discontinuity in education's tradition of stability must be driven by alternative models for teaching and learning. The next section details two types of levers that could empower massive educational reform over the next decade.

EMERGING OPPORTUNITIES TO RESHAPE AMERICAN EDUCATION

The trends described previously amount to an impressive set of external forces for change in all of society's teaching and learning environments. Nonetheless, the forces for stability

8. Larry Cuban, "Reforming, Again, Again, and Again," *Educational Researcher*, 19(1):3-13 (1990).

9. Raymond Nickerson, "New Directions in Educational Assessment," *Educational Researcher*, 18(12):3-7 (1989).

in education are strong, and a baseline scenario in which instructional settings a generation from now look much like those today is all too plausible. Fortunately, two opportunities that could empower change from within education have emerged in the early 1990s. The evolution of advanced technologies for teaching, learning, and management and the initiation of a restructuring movement for educational reform both provide contexts for innovation that may foster the implementation of new paradigms for education.

New models of teaching and learning

During the 1990s, the information technologies could leverage the creation of alternative models for teaching and learning by altering education in a manner parallel to their current impact on the workplace. Emerging information tools are enabling business to achieve new levels of effectiveness, rather than simply improving efficiency. In the industrial workplace, now rapidly disappearing, two types of jobs dominated. Many people manipulated mindless tools: using a wrench on the assembly line, drafting with a pen, looking up precedents in law books. Others followed the orders of a smart machine: pushing the "hamburger" key on the cash register at a fast-food restaurant, keypunching information into an automated data base, feeding lab samples into a medical analyzer.

Educating today's students for those jobs is a guarantee of intellectual obsolescence. In every American industry, devices based on artificial intelligence are taking over all forms of standardized problem solving. As one illustration, accountants are graduating from our universities in droves, expecting a stable, well-paying career—but the majority of those jobs will disappear within a decade as expert systems automate financial operations. Similarly, middle-management roles—collecting and summarizing operational data—are rapidly vanishing, since top decision makers can get sophisticated analyses of organizational functioning directly from information tools.

Over the next generation, intelligent information technologies will eliminate every industrial-era occupation that centers on complex but routine processing of data. What remains will be a mixture of low-level jobs, such as janitor or waiter; high-level professions, such as director, politician, or therapist; and the new roles that the postindustrial, global economy generates. Occupations as we know them are about to become history; America is entering an era of smart machines working independently of people, and people working in partnership with intelligent tools.

Imagining civilization a generation from now may be as difficult for people today as visualizing a commodities broker electronically monitoring soybean options would have been for eighteenth-century farmers contemplating a steam tractor. America does not have much time to understand and shape what is happening; the Industrial Revolution took more than a century to reach fruition, but global economic competition and the pace of technological advance will drive the next transformation much more quickly, over just a few decades. Unintelligent workers and nations with obsolete economic approaches will face difficult times.

What do these changes mean for people with a stake in an educated society? During the 1990s, advanced information technologies will increasingly amplify people's intelligence through cognitive partnerships between users and intelligent tools. Computers are capable of a type of cognition complementary to human thought; they excel at sophisticated manipulation of formulas, while people are flexible, creative, and adept at recognizing complex patterns. The use of technological devices as cognition enhancers will drive a new definition of human intelligence centered on higher-order mental attributes.[10]

Education at all levels must alter its focus to prepare learners for cognitive partnerships with intelligent tools. Changing workplace needs will reshape the goals, clients, and content of instruction. Shifts in pedagogical methods, the organizational structure of teaching and learning settings, and the locus of education will inevitably follow. Sophisticated information technologies can provide the leverage to make evolution to a new educational model possible; the same advances that are transforming the economy can empower new models of teaching and learning and of organizational management.

Only new models for both instruction and institutional management can accomplish such a shift. The core of developing a new paradigm for teaching and learning must be based on insights drawn from the leading edge of practice in cognitive science, developmental psychology, and pedagogy. Similarly, institutional restructuring requires understanding recent advances in organizational management, economic development, and strategic thinking. To implement innovations based on these two sets of insights, information technology must be a drive shaft on the vehicle of educational reform, rather than, as in its current role, a hood ornament on the traditional classroom model.

Advanced information technologies are a necessary but not sufficient factor in transforming to new models of teaching, learning, and management.[11] Individualized learning and decentralized institutional structures require improvisational scheduling, flexible roles, the distributed coordination of interacting organizational processes, and accountability and incentives based on performance. All types of organizations are finding that sophisticated computational and communications capabilities are necessary for orchestrating such complex operational practices. In addition, using instructional technologies in classroom settings helps to prepare learners for mastering the intelligent tools

10. Christopher J. Dede, "Imaging Technology's Role in Restructuring for Learning," in Restructuring for Learning with Technology, ed. K. Sheingold and M. S. Tucker (New York: Center for Technology in Education, Bank Street College of Education and National Center on Education and the Economy, 1990).

11. Alan C. Kay, "Computers, Networks, and Education," Scientific American, 265(3):138-49 (1991).

and interactive media that will pervade workplaces and communities.[12]

Even though use of sophisticated technology in teaching and learning settings seems vital to educational reform and to economic development, the availability of a technology does not guarantee its acceptance or its effective implementation. A second driver for change that seems likely to couple with advanced technology to leverage educational reform is the emerging restructuring movement.

The restructuring movement as a paradigm shift

Educational reformers who describe themselves as restructuring schools believe that past efforts to change the traditional model of teaching and learning have failed primarily because they focused on altering only one aspect of the dominant educational paradigm. Institutions are complex systems that, through mutually reinforcing cultural structures, incentives, regulations, and norms, resist change. Any single instructional reform—such as an interdisciplinary approach to teaching global economics—will atrophy because the scheduling, staffing, reward structure, curriculum, and governance of the overall educational system work against that innovation.

The restructuring movement differs from prior reforms by taking an integrated, systemic approach in which every aspect of the organizational structure is reorganized to support alternative models of education. The fundamental attributes underlying emerging restructured models of teaching and learning can be categorized as goals, pedagogical strategies, organizational strategies, and assessment and evaluation.

The goals include

— basing accountability on outcomes important to the society, rather than on those metrics of educational accomplishment most easily measured;[13]
— setting challenging goals for student learning and staff accomplishment;
— helping every student to grow in meaningful ways, recognizing that all learners must succeed if our society is to prosper;
— focusing on mastery of higher-order knowledge, rather than emphasizing performance fluency in basic skills;
— making affective and motivational outcomes—such as self-worth, curiosity, ethical understandings—as important as cognitive accomplishments; and
— attracting and retaining outstanding staff through a combination of salaries, working conditions, collegiality, respect from society, and the innate worth of the enterprise.

The pedagogical strategies are the following:

— viewing students as active constructors of meaning rather

12. Christopher J. Dede, "Emerging Technologies: Impacts on Distance Learning," *The Annals* of the American Academy of Political and Social Science, 514:146-58 (Mar. 1991).

13. Lauren B. Resnick, "Learning in School and Out," *Educational Researcher*, 16(9):13-20 (1987).

than passive assimilators of data;[14]

— seeing instructors as facilitators of learning, who are themselves still growing in their knowledge, rather than as imparters of truth;[15]

— creating environments for learning that promote diversity, mixing different ages, developmental levels, and cultural backgrounds;

— utilizing a repertoire of pedagogical techniques, including cooperative and self-directed learning approaches;[16]

— integrating curricular content around real-world issues rather than isolating subjects based on discipline-centered content;

— tailoring instruction to each student's learning style and individual needs; and

— situating learning in an environment similar to that in which the knowledge will be used.[17]

The organizational strategies are these:

— tailoring the organization of the educational setting to the needs of students and teachers, rather than subjugating teaching and learning to those practices easiest to manage, such as standard time slots for all class periods;

— attempting innovative high-risk, high-gain strategies to enhance educational effectiveness rather than using a traditional teaching and learning approach with extra finances or effort;

— intensively supporting human resource development to meet continuously changing role expectations; and

— utilizing a systemic approach that simultaneously reconceptualizes the curriculum, pedagogical methods, theories of learning, definitions of "quality" and "equity," organizational approaches, and the involvement of all society's interested parties.[18]

Finally, assessment and evaluation include the following:

— aligning authority and responsibility, while decentralizing decision making to the operational level; classroom-based, site-based, and community-based management;[19]

— evaluating teams that share responsibilities and rewards rather than individuals held accountable for doing a particular job;

14. John D. Bransford et al., "New Approaches to Instruction: Because Wisdom Can't Be Told," in *Similarity and Analogical Reasoning*, ed. S. Vosniadou and A. Ortony (New York: Cambridge University Press, 1989).

15. David C. Dwyer, Cathy Ringstaff, and Judy H. Sandholtz, "Changes in Teachers' Beliefs and Practices in Technology-Rich Classrooms," *Educational Leadership*, 48(9):45-52 (1991).

16. David K. Cohen, "Teaching Practice: Plus Ça Change . . .," in *Contributing to Educational Change: Perspectives on Research and Practice*, ed. P. Jackson (Berkeley, CA: McCutchan, 1987).

17. John S. Brown, Allan Collins, and Paul Duguid, "Situated Cognition and the Culture of Learning," *Educational Researcher*, 18(1):32-42 (1989).

18. Albert Shanker, "A Proposal for Using Incentives to Restructure Our Public Schools," *Phi Delta Kappan*, 71(5):345-57 (1990).

19. Jane David et al., *State Actions to Restructure Schools: First Steps* (Washington, DC: National Governors' Association, 1990).

— assessing effectiveness based on outcomes rather than on following prescribed procedures;[20]

— rewarding practices that succeed with additional resources, while allowing failing approaches to die;

— respecting every role, giving rank no special privileges, and allocating incentives by merit; and

— conceptualizing quality and excellence as moving targets.

While not by any means exhaustive, this list is suggestive of indicators that exemplify emerging restructured models of education. Parents, business leaders, and community organizations have been very supportive of this approach to educational reform because restructuring situates the goals, assessment methods, curriculum, and instructional practices of schools in the larger context of societal needs. Space does not permit presenting scenarios of future learning situations based on these design principles, but vignettes illustrating this type of education are presented in other articles by the author.[21]

At present, these two reform movements—restructuring advocates, and innovators using sophisticated educational technologies—are not strongly linked. Combined, however, they could muster considerable resources to challenge the dominance of traditional teaching and learning models. Given society's overall dissatisfaction with the current functioning of educational institutions at all levels, the next decade is likely to be fertile ground for these seeds of potential sweeping change.

Actions for initiating educational redesign

What follow are two incomplete lists of present actions that practitioners and policy setters could take to initiate a reform process for all levels of education in response to the external trends described earlier. The focus of these potential actions combines both movements for change through exploring technology's role in empowering learning via organizational restructuring.

Practitioners could take the following steps:

1. Practitioners could convene a representative group of influential leaders from education, business, government, the media, and the community. The purpose would be to form a critical mass of resources to initiate large-scale innovation. The agenda would be to unite

— collective design principles for the restructuring of educational encounters throughout society for the purpose of learning through technology;

— shared long-range visions for educational practice based on those principles;

— detailed models of the first stage of education's evolution, to be implemented at a variety of demonstration sites; and

— a process for monitoring the evolution of these activities and pe-

20. John R. Frederickson and Allan Collins, "A Systems Approach to Educational Testing," *Educational Researcher*, 18(9):27-32 (1989).

21. Dede, "Imaging Technology's Role"; idem, "Emerging Technologies."

riodically reformulating design principles and long-range visions.

2. Practitioners could mount a coordinated campaign to inform all who have an interest in high-quality education both about why an immediate transformation of our current paradigm for teaching and learning is essential and about the evolutionary process that the coalition of influential leaders has initiated.

3. They could lobby all types of regulatory bodies that govern education for waivers from current regulations to allow experimentation with alternate paradigms for teaching and learning.

4. They could develop an overall research design for a set of high-risk, high-gain experiments with unusual institutional structures and innovative technologies. These studies would attack major problems that have been intractable in the current paradigm for education. For example, artificial realities created through information technology might undercut drug use by providing students with a different way of getting outside the stresses of their everyday environment. The restructuring coalition would distribute these projects among its participants to minimize costs and risks, but it would centrally coordinate research designs and information gathering to maximize the knowledge gained.

5. The practitioners could devise technology partnerships between business and education. For example, corporations could help to develop innovative approaches for front-end funding of capital-intensive technology investments. Also, industry experts

on implementing information technology in workplace settings could be valuable resources.

6. Less formal methods for credentialing educational achievement could be developed. For example, cognitive audit trails embedded in workplace tools could document learning-while-doing activities.

7. Instruction on the intersection of learning, technology, and restructuring could be included in preservice and in-service training of teachers. By analyzing the outcomes of alternative implementation strategies for educational technology, the importance of powerful hardware, long lead time, and a critical mass of resources could be demonstrated.

8. The practitioners could form buying collectives that develop a set of specifications for advanced applications, then contract to expend a substantial amount of money if vendors develop products that meet those requirements.

Policy initiatives include the following:

1. Policymakers could implement incentives to attract scarce human expertise into learning-related applications of artificial intelligence, computer science, cognitive science, and organizational design. At present, few expert practitioners in those fields choose to become involved with educational innovation.

2. Greater research funding could be provided for

— sophisticated conceptions of human intelligence;
— innovative technologies for evaluating aptitude and achievement;

— empirical studies of tutoring and individual learning;

— new approaches to instructional design—for human teaching, standard computer-assisted instruction, and intelligent tutoring systems;

— core human skills for cognitive partnership with intelligent tools; and

— psychological and social impacts of the intensive use of instructional technologies.

3. Better measures could be developed of the economic utility to our nation of investing in human resources. The American public has much more knowledge of how many resources educational endeavors consume than of the long-range costs of an ignorant society.

4. The facilitation of learning could be promoted by educational agents other than schools, such as families, communities, workplaces, and the media. For example, businesses could receive tax credits via technology partnerships with schools that go beyond the donation of obsolete equipment.

These lists are illustrative, but they indicate the types of actions central to an evolutionary process of restructuring education via technology.

CONCLUSION

In the 1990s, the United States has a rare window of opportunity to implement alternative paradigms for education. Reformers can bring to bear a lot of leverage: trends that undermine the traditional model, public dissatisfaction with fine-tuning existing approaches, and the growing power of the technology and restructuring movements. Nonetheless, a future of little or no change in American education is all too probable; similar past opportunities for innovation have always slipped away. Ultimately, a future discontinuous with the traditional paradigm of education is as much a matter of faith as of forecasting.

Aging America

By WALTER A. HAHN

ABSTRACT: Aging is among the more powerful and ubiquitous structural trends occurring in the United States. An increasingly large proportion of the population is middle-aged, young old, or old old. Dual views of aging from the inside and as generations moving through time are offered. The persistent and popular myth is that elders—persons 65-85 years old—are mostly old fogies, forgetful, sick or of limited ability, and generally out of it. While this indeed may describe some seniors, the reality is that almost the reverse is true for most. This article includes four sample "future history" scenarios from the viewpoint of elders for four time periods: Toward 1999, 2001+, 2020, and 2040. An example of a number of issues acting in concert is also presented. Last is a do-it-yourself futures exercise for the reader that may be both helpful and fun.

Walter Hahn has worked at the National Research Council, General Electric, the National Aeronautics and Space Administration, the White House National Goals Research Staff, as deputy assistant secretary of commerce for science and technology, and at the Congressional Research Service. His most recent position, prior to becoming a free-lance elder, was as futurist-in-residence at the George Washington University. Hahn is a senior fellow of the National Academy of Public Administration and serves on the board of the Congressional Institute for the Future.

AGING is among the more powerful and ubiquitous structural trends occurring in the United States. Present public policymakers and private institutional managers often behave as if they are unaware of the existence, size, or potential consequences of the aging trend. Most likely, they are postponing dealing with it, leaving it for their successors. The economic, social, political, and environmental impacts of this irreversible trend will continue to affect all of us well into the next century. What follows is a look at this trend from the viewpoint of a participant-observer futurist and elder—the term "senior citizen" can have negative connotations—who is both part of the problem and desires to be part of the solution.

This article opens with the parameters of the aging trend and rejection of the myth of the old fogy, passive, . . . senior. The impacts of the trend on the nation will be noted in five areas: society, technology, environment, the economy, and politics. Then the focus narrows to elders, with specific examples of their thinking which may in part shape their and younger persons' futures. To give policymakers a substantive view of the aging trend over the next several decades, next are examples of the use of one of the futurist's more powerful tools, scenarios. Four time periods are covered: Toward 1999, 2001+, 2020, and 2040. These dates coincide with the time when, starting with the present, each succeeding generation[1]

of elders is active on the national scene. Note that it will be the elders of the time stated who are speaking.

THE TREND(S)

Just what is this structural trend on aging in America that is receiving increased attention? First, the global context. There are almost 5.5 billion people on Earth today and another billion will be added by the year 2000. Of these, the U.S. population is about 250 million and will be about 299 million by the year 2010. By 2010, 1.4 billion Chinese and 4.4 billion other Third World people will share the globe with us. It is sobering to note that Third World birth rates exceed 2 percent while ours is 0.8 percent. What "Aging America" is specifically about is that increasingly large proportion of us in the U.S. who are middle-aged, young old, or old old. The median age of 33 in 1990 will advance to 36.5 in 2000.[2] Life expectancy is increasing, especially for women. Also, the aged are aging as we all live longer. In 1990, 12.4 percent of the population was over 65. By 2040 it will be over 20 percent. The number of those aged 85 to 94 will grow from 2.9 to 4 million between

1. William Strauss and Neil Howe, *Generations: The History of America's Future, 1584 to 2069* (New York: William Morrow, 1991). The writer of this article owes three debts to Strauss and Howe: stimulation to use the concept of generations, a plethora of facts and relationships too numerous for individual citations, and a great read. It is recommended as a refreshing and detailed view of American history from a novel standpoint.

2. *What Lies Ahead: Countdown to the 21st Century* (Alexandria, VA: United Way of America, 1989). A still up-to-date product of the United Way's Environmental Scan Committee, this document is a source of much of the information used in this article. It is an excellent example of the quality of the scanning that modern futurists can perform.

1990 and the year 2000. But it is not only those numbers, ratios, and rates that make the difference for the future. We need to be aware of the impacts these changes are having on us at present and may have in the future. We also need to know what choices we have for affecting changes: positively, negatively, and for avoidance.

The qualitative view of "Aging America" is as dramatic as the quantitative. Past policies and institutional arrangements now present us with some very difficult situations. Although made with the best of intentions, most past decisions were based on the pervasive youth model of our society and without clear views of their future consequences. Take Social Security. We now have a large cadre of aging seniors, increasing in size. Due to the way we chose to fund Social Security, this group must now, and in the future, be supported by a much smaller group of current wage earners. Increases in both benefits and eligibility have exacerbated this situation. We are in a similar bind with health care benefits. Increasing costs for longer living by less well persons, the skyrocketing costs of new technology defensively applied, and a crushing load of paperwork combine to overload both the public and private capacities to pay for it all.

In the marketplace we now see sophisticated hearing aids and telephones, turn-off irons, riser chairs and beds, large-print reading materials, and a plethora of health aids. Ethically and legally, we observe the clash of two strongly held and pervasive values: the aged want all the medical help available to live a "square wave" life, that is, functional living, terminated by a quick and painless death with dignity. The medical profession, in its own professional style and for legal protection, supports elders living well and longer but resists removing the tubes or aiding suicide. Legislation like the Older Americans Act of 1965, the Employee Retirement Income Security Act of 1974, and that which established individual retirement accounts—all amended from time to time—have helped the aging but may require rethinking in the face of the future challenges posed by the aging of America. Politically, Congress recently found out the strength and swiftness of elders as a coherent force when the legislature monkeyed with Medicare. Also as a group, more elders show up at the polls at election and referendum times. In late 1991, an assisted suicide proposition in the state of Washington was narrowly defeated.

Immersed in next-quarter profits and with youth-cult mind-sets, the private sector has been slow to realize the potential of growing senior markets. Marriott and other developers now offer a wide variety of retirement communities. But they seem to be unaware that as people age in these new Edens, problems of access, assisted living, medical services, and so forth will arise. Do they just want to sell the dwellings over and over as the aged are forced to move on? To where? Hyatt Corporation is offering top-of-the-line rental retirement and assisted-care housing. Manor Care and others keep expanding their profitable nursing home empire but can't keep up with demand. Travel agents now offer Granny Tours.

Elderhostel education for the sixties-plus is now a global not-for-profit enterprise. Lending institutions now offer government-backed reverse mortgages—loans against home equity—but what does this do to the inheritance of succeeding generations? Long-term-care policies are now marketed intensively, but costs are high, coverage spotty, and the stability of the insurers is in question. The American Association of Retired Persons, with over 33 million members, has become a marketing, service, information, and political force to be reckoned with nationwide. It seems that neither politicians nor entrepreneurs are yet fully aware of the nature and potential of aging America.

New and unfamiliar questions are arising. For many, retirement is an outmoded concept, yet it is enshrined in law, practice, and language as if it were immutable. We are at last becoming aware of the breakup of the traditional, single-locus, 2+2 (nuclear family with two children) family, as we see four-generation geographically distributed families becoming a reality. Can elders with dependent elders simultaneously deal with their boomerang kids' returning home to live? Will ethnic conflict enhance generational conflict and accelerate cocooning? Elders pay and have paid taxes, and consume and will consume revenues. But there is considerable argument about the net balance, especially since it is distributed over such a very long time. Elders have concern for preserving and enhancing natural environmental quality and especially that of indoor and in-transit spaces.

Many elders agree with Charles Krauthammer that "environmentalism . . . is not for nature's sake but for our own."[3] But generally, elders seem to accept the idea of environmental stewardship over dominion.

ELDERS

As conveyed in the introduction, this article includes a view of aging in the U.S. from the inside out in parallel with the more familiar outside-in perspective. Beyond their numbers, what is different about elders, seniors, the aging, or as the French call them, Third Agers? Who are they?

Here the term "elder" refers to persons 65 to 85 years of age. Those 85 or over are the old old. One octogenarian said that an elder is a person of any age who has become aware of his or her own mortality. But that is a bit too loose. It is well known that a majority of elders are female. In the over-75 group the ratio is 2:1.[4] Note that while chronological age is a useful label, it can also be very misleading as to individuals and groups. Physical appearance can be equally misleading.

The persistent and popular myth is that elders are mostly old fogies, forgetful, sick or of limited ability, and generally out of it as far as society is concerned. The reality is that, while this indeed may describe some seniors, almost the reverse is true for most of this 10 percent of the current

3. Charles Krauthammer, "Saving Nature, but Only for Man," *Time*, 17 June 1991, p. 82.

4. U.S., Congress, Office of Technology Assessment, *Technology and Aging in America*, OTA-BA-264 (Washington, DC: Office of Technology Assessment, 1985).

population. Today's elders espouse three core and overriding values that will continue to affect their and younger people's futures: functional independence, remaining in control of self, and avoiding/minimizing pain, loneliness, and meaninglessness. It is recognized that some elders are institutionalized, many are poor, and others are discriminated against for both ethnic or racial reasons, as well as for being old. But this article focuses on the well and functional aged, including the many who are affluent. It will also highlight the core experiences, heritage, and actions of the current elders and of the next three generations of elders succeeding them.

Elders are also a much-neglected resource. We've pushed many out of the work force, both against their will and where their experience and steady work habits are sorely needed. As a society, we fail to recognize and use the accumulated experience of elders in dealing with current, and particularly emerging, issues. They have a broad perspective—they have been at it for four generations! Elders usually have more time and often can take larger risks in actions and words. Some have strong motivation to give back to the society that has done so much for so many of them. Voluntary sector activities attract many elders. Most of all, elders have learned to cope, and many have accumulated that rare commodity, wisdom.

Is it the youth myth cited earlier that prevents utilizing these talents and seeing these elders as role models? Today's elders still believe in most of their institutions (albeit with increasing doubts); cooperative action; and contributing their time, energy, and some resources to the less well-off. They hold on to significant ties to family and religion. They also feel strongly that they have paid their dues, and thus the many entitlements available are theirs to enjoy. They would like to receive more respect.

An example:
Four wills

It may be instructive to look at one very limited subject as an example of how elder thinking differs from that of younger persons. Some modern alert elders, concerned about their own future and that of their significant others, arrange to have four wills. Of most personal and timely importance is a living will. Effective before death, this document is now legal and enforceable in all states. In the face of a terminally ill or damaged person, it hopefully prevents being hooked up to the tubes, or at least provides authority to remove them. A living will is the documented decision to die naturally with dignity and minimum pain.

The second will, effective exactly at the time of death, usually does not carry the label "will." It is the organ-donor document, which permits the transfer or storage of usable organs for others. Thus, some of the functions of the donor continue "living" into the future, albeit in another person.

The third will is the familiar legal last will and testament, which conveys financial wealth and property.

Although sometimes accompanied by memorabilia, photographic and art images, and written or taped documents, this will is really rather bland and all about tangibles. That leads to a fourth will with a focus on the future.

Except for Hebrew Ethical Wills, this fourth document has yet to have a common label. "Intellectual Heritage" is one that captures the modern content of this practice going back to the early Christians, Arabs, and Jews and popular in the twelfth century and through the Renaissance. The Intellectual Heritage is from and about the deceased, but it is for the living. It is designed to contribute to their future well-being. It conveys "the image one wishes to leave of himself [and says] 'This is what I want of you, this is what I stand for, this is the counsel I transfer to you.' "[5] Though historically turgid and flowery, these documents may now appear in modern form as audio- or videotapes. They are often delivered sealed, with instructions for opening at a time after the emotions of the death have passed. Hearing, seeing, or reading the lessons and meaning of a lifetime as a "voice from the grave" requires detachment and perspective.

The foregoing is not to advocate four wills for everyone. That some elders do this may indicate their continuing desire to leave their imprint not only on the past and present but also on the future. It also may reflect a judgment by some elders that decisions to be made by their inheritors must be constrained so that things are done right. And it may just be a way of elders' making one last try to communicate their values and what they have contributed, feeling that the younger generations still do not understand or appreciate them.

SELECTED SCENARIOS

Scenarios help us to explore alternative futures for the enlightenment of policymaking and other decision makers. Scenarios are internally consistent stories, creative verbal snapshots in future time. They are not predictions or forecasts, but they help us to deal with both complexity and uncertainty. They usually respond to the question "What if . . .?" and focus on a few consistent assumptions and variables of specific interest. Mostly, they are used in groups of three to seven and are from one to tens of pages long. The set of four to be presented here is typical in that one scenario is a view of more of the same, one is optimistic, another pessimistic, and one is a wild card. Often, all of the scenarios in one set are for the same time period, say, 15 years in the future.[6]

The sample "future history" scenarios to follow, however, are each for a different time period: Toward 1999, 2001+, 2020, and 2040. The constant and unique factor will be that each scenario is told from the viewpoint of the generation of elders in the time period selected. The "we" in the text refers to each elder generation speak-

5. Israel Abrahams, ed., *Hebrew Ethical Wills* (Philadelphia: Jewish Hebrew Society of America, 1976), p. 17.

6. *Scenarios: A Tool for Planning in Uncertain Times* (Alexandria, VA: United Way of America, 1984).

ing as Americans of their time. These very brief one-page scenarios only signal the story line and leave out much more than they include. *Omni* magazine would call them "thought bites."

Some assumptions pertain to all of the scenarios presented: no global wars or nuclear holocaust; no major natural or human-caused catastrophes; global interdependence (acknowledged or not); global population growth and environmental deterioration; surprises; and change, change, change.

TOWARD 1999

Born between 1901 and 1924, we depression kids are better known as the GI generation. After all, we've seen five big wars and more little ones than we wanted to, but it was Pearl Harbor that defined us. We've also been through depressions, recessions, and some of the best times our country has known. We both shaped and were shaped by the twentieth century, and neither process is yet over for us. We are still 30 million strong. Some of us have imprinted lasting impressions on subsequent generations: Bob Hope, Billy Graham, Joe DiMaggio, Walt Disney, Ann Landers, John Wayne, and Tip O'Neill. We have supplied the last seven presidents and many of us may witness the election of the first non-GI president in 34 (or 30) years. Business as usual, more of the same, muddling through, and continuing to exercise our traditional values characterize our mood. Our world technological, economic, and political leadership positions are weakening but remain strong enough to be envied by most of the world's citizens. We watched passively while Germany and the European Community got together and the Soviet Union and Yugoslavia disintegrated. We are simultaneously a manufacturing, service, and agricultural nation with these sectors, respectively, declining, expanding, and hovering in precarious balance. We are weakened by structural employment, a ghetto underclass, growing illiteracy, huge debt, and massive apathy. Enough of us are personally well enough off, unthreatened, and hopeful of a better future to postpone dramatic reform. We support research in the billions for a Supercollider and in the low millions for dealing with the common cold. All this as drugs and rampant crime threaten our way of life. We have difficulty learning to live with our cultural diversity and to tolerate a widening range of life-styles and values. We want improved environmental quality while continuing to make exceptions and grant postponements in meeting standards. We desire more energy self-sufficiency as we expand imports and ease but not abandon conservation practices. We view with alarm the crumbling of urban and connecting infrastructures as we postpone the inevitable to the next guy's watch, forgetting—ignoring?—that it's our children who have the next watch. We push harder for our rights than we do in meeting our responsibilities, and we have yet to exercise foresight effectively.

2001+: LAUNCHING A NEW CENTURY

Sandwiched between the GI and Boomer generations, we radio kids were born between 1925 and 1942. The 40 million of us are now known as the Silent generation, which is a misnomer when noting some of our members: Gore Vidal, Ted Koppel, Pat Schroeder, Jesse Jackson, and T. Boone Pickens. We have lost John and Robert Kennedy, Martin Luther King, Marilyn Monroe, and (we think) Elvis Presley. We have early memories of V-E and V-J days and the A-bomb detonations, and later ones of Watergate and the Carter "malaise." As elders, we get to help launch both a new century and a new millennium. But our predecessors have left us some mega-messes for our point of departure. Domestically, we continue to face crushing debts, ubiquitous crime and drug assaults, dependence on fossil fuels, growing tribalism and reemergent racism, decayed and obsolete infrastructures, consumption without saving, and more. We are still fighting learning to live with nature—a late-'90s northeaster this time wiped out ex-President Bush's retirement home in Kennebunkport. Our Congress and the other 80,000-plus units of government are obsolete, overstaffed, underfunded, and increasingly incapable of both governance and service. Compensating for this is the increase of the vigor of the voluntary third sector in providing a wide variety of services. The one-term presidency and 12-year limit on legislators is helping to restore ethics in government. We still struggle under the staggering costs of the savings and loan crimes, cleaning up decades of toxic wastes, and dealing with acquired immune deficiency syndrome (AIDS). We are beginning to see the awesome bill for long-term elder care. Means-tested Medicare and taxing high-income-earner Social Security benefits have given us a modest start in vitalizing and extending those support mechanisms, but much remains. Lengthening the school year and other small changes have helped to educate the populace and the emerging knowledge-worker work force, but in the meantime we must suffer the pangs and losses due to illiteracy and an apathetic underclass. The 1998-99 tax increases have yet to generate sufficient income for reform. Globally, we have not reversed the decline in our technological and marketing leadership positions, not joined with other nations in pollution control and global management of critical resources like water and farmland, and not dealt with AIDS; we do not even have any assurance that peaceful coexistence with others will continue. Some launching!

2020: BOOMERS AS ELDERS

We Boomers, born from 1943 to 1960,[1] have always been the pig in the demographic python and still number about 25 million. Though variously called TV Babies, Hippies, Yuppies, or New Agers, we differ even more than a sample of our members would suggest: Oliver North, Donald Trump, Janis Joplin, Oprah Winfrey, Dan Quayle, John McEnroe, Al Gore, and Steve Jobs. Phrases like "Brown v. Board of Ed," "Kent State," "Woodstock," "Apollo landing," "Cold War," "Nam," "Earth Day," and "Watergate" recall vivid memories. The new United Nations Peace Force helps stabilize the still-turbulent global scene. Domestically, the Social Security system is stressed to its limits and senior discounts have disappeared under the weight of numbers. The GI generation ran things so long that the Silents before us never learned how to do it. Their pitiful attempts to revitalize America at the turn of the century have only delayed reform. But at last things have gotten so bad that Americans of all stripes are being typically American and are acting together to "fix it." We banned guns in 2015 but it will take decades to get them off the streets. Elder Boomers lead in restructuring the education system and in repairing and modernizing our infrastructures. This is dramatically evidenced in our new integrated national compunications (computers plus communications) networks and in developing an effective multimode transportation system increasingly independent of fossil fuels. Ethical standards and efficiency are evidenced in the new streamlined participatory democracy forms of government at all levels. Privatization helps, while government sets the standards and rules. We all enjoy more leisure, much of which is spent in the now continuous learning we all pursue. Knowledge work dominates this "post-business" society, as Peter Drucker called it three decades ago. Quality and civility now dominate quantity and me-ism in economic and political affairs. Maybe some of this is due not only to the hands-on experience women have gained over the last thirty years as managers and leaders but also to the fact that they now significantly outnumber males at the polls and in the power centers. We seem to be beginning to realize that our mutual interest is also our self-interest. There is a sense of positiveness and movement toward a more vibrant America—just in time!

---

1. The U.S. Bureau of the Census, among others, classifies the boomers as having been born between 1946 and 1964.

2040: THE GOOD OLD DAYS ARE HERE AGAIN

In the nineties we computer, latchkey kids had no catchy name as a group. We were just labeled "13ers" as the thirteenth American generation. We who were born from 1961 to 1981 now think of ourselves as the "Survivors." Recognizable names (as of 1992) include Michael J. Fox, Mary Lou Retton, Tom Cruise, Brooke Shields, and Mike Tyson, but many new famous have evolved in the ensuing 48 years. Our early memories are of Roe v. Wade, the Challenger disaster, Desert Storm and Panama, A Nation At Risk, Iran hostages, and the collapse of the USSR and the Cold War. Not all of the mega-messes of the turn of the century have been cleaned up, but we have survived the doomsday predictions of generations preceding us. We have inherited the new dynamics and style set by our immediate predecessors, which we feel bound to continue and to expand upon in building a revitalized America. AIDS was licked in the twenties and advanced knowledge of the human genome helps prevent similar scourges. National health care is improving and is now extended to all citizens. We elders are economically less well off than those before us, but culturally we have turned America's ethnic diversity to advantage. "Mosaic America" is a positive label these days. The economy is sound if not robust. The Canadian-Quebec-Mexican-U.S. North American Economic Community is at last functioning well. Also, we now focus more on the Pacific Rim and see a united, quasi-democratic China as a huge market. We now recycle more and pollute less, but we have decades of toxic wastes to deal with. Education is now seen as both a personal and national resource and is pursued on a life-long in-and-out basis in the now integrated public-private National Learning System. Globally, peace—as the absence of war—obtains but the Middle East continues to fester. The larger nations of the world threaten to splinter and many of the smaller ones constantly explore various forms of federation. Another step toward world governance was taken with the formation of the United Nations Green Force to set and enforce standards for global pollution and its cleanup. In the United States, we try to exercise our dual roles as American and Global citizens. We now recognize as a functioning generation the centurians, those within ten years (either way) of their hundredth birthday. The majority are women, of course.

SO WHAT?

America *is* aging. No one needs a futurist to see the numbers, but futurists can enhance policymakers' ability to see the scope and range of the impacts of the trend. The present and future aged are already born and there are lots of them. Some of you are reading this article. The large numbers of active, thinking elders will have consequences throughout society, the economy, and politics. Serious problems of housing, health care and delivery (who pays?), generational equity, social harmony (who decides?), and political action head a long list of yet-to-be-squarely-faced issues—and opportunities? More serious than being unaware of some of the consequences of America's aging is that many of the known issues are being ignored or postponed for successors to deal with. Whether the cause is current political or economic survival, or deeper feelings of being overwhelmed in the face of the insoluble, is not clear. It is no comfort to note that the aging issue must be handled in parallel with the other issues noted in this volume of *The Annals*.

Up to now, only one or two examples of the consequences of a trend or event have been offered, almost as if both the trends and the consequences were independent of each other. But, of course, we all know that everything is related to everything else. What might be the impacts of a number of the issues mentioned earlier if they were acting in concert? For example, consider the breakup of families, immigration, population mobility, more self-selected TV than directed reading. Also look at the breakdown in education, with almost no geography, with little mathematics or civics, and with attractive electives outcompeting the hard stuff. All the generations born after the GIs and the boomers suffer from almost all of the foregoing divisive, rather than integrating, common knowledge and life-style experiences. Additionally, ethnic, racial, and religious rivalries have splintered our former common base of shared knowledge and customs. We have all but lost our historical melting-pot drives and our base of shared knowledge and experience. Therefore, we must now turn to a weakened and directionless education system to restore our ability to live together, function economically, and to govern ourselves.

In the future, it will be necessary to think of formal education and literacy beyond the three *R*s. The proposition is that for us in America to work, play, and live in peace in the twenty-first century, everyone needs to be literate in both the *same* three *R*s and the *same* three *C*s. The three *C*s are culture, civics, and 'cience. Culture includes awareness and understanding of our heritage and values and the exercise of our intellectual and social creativity. Civics deals with how our public sector democracy works—its strategy, structure, and style. Lastly, 'cience concerns how nature, our artifacts, and our bodies and minds function. Additionally, of overriding importance is for every citizen to learn how to continue to learn.

Maybe the current generation of elders can help in the transition from a society that mostly grew up and grew older together to the more mosaic, individualized one of the present and future.

Most futurists are not doomsayers in spite of the continuing market for dire predictions. Futurists cannot force their awareness and alternatives on decision makers or the public, but they do keep trying. They argue that the exercise of foresight at least expands our range of choices and offers more time to exercise them. Similarly, pre-assessment of consequences may help to prevent costly mistakes and policy traps. The reader should neither reject nor accept the four scenarios of the 16 possible in the matrix of four assumptions by four time periods presented earlier. Write your own stories and form your own images of likely and desired futures based on your assumptions and for time periods of your choice.

The foregoing material has attempted to outline the present and future of aging in America in its global and national contexts. It has focused on the aged as part of the solution along with the usual approach of seeing the elders as the problem. As with other subjects, one of our critical needs is to not view the current and future situation only through the images and assumptions of the past. To deal with current and future problems and opportunities will require rethinking the conventional wisdom that constrains us from constructive innovation, action, and change. It is hoped that these dual views of aging from the inside and as generations moving through time will assist.

The major points of this article are:

1. Look again *at* the aging trend in America to assess the impacts, options, and requirements.

2. Look *into* the aging trend—for example, observe and listen to the elders—for increased breadth, insights, and applicable values for use in #1.

3. Look *to* the viewpoints, substance, and techniques of the futurists as sources of additional help.

A READER
ACTION ASSIGNMENT

The paragraph that follows offers one last suggestion for the reader: a do-it-yourself futures exercise that may be both helpful and fun. Reading an article like this is a passive activity, but futurists often try to involve their clients in more active and experiential processes. It is recommended that readers try this one to experience some of the fun and learning of futures activity. In the 1960s, while exploring alternative futures of the 1990s and the magic year 2000, we occasionally held a Futures Brunch. This is typically a group of 5 to 10 friends, gathered in a very informal and comfortable setting for two, or at the most three, hours. A future time period is selected, say, 1995. An imaginary humanoid enters the room. How did he/she/it arrive? Where from? Clothing? Political party? Profession? Body and speech? Work? Play? . . . Whatever! Or pick a topic like aging. The questions are only to start the dialogue for the time frame chosen. Only three rules apply: nothing is silly or stupid, no hogging the floor (all should speak, often), and no put-downs or arguments (alternative views are OK). Try this at home with family and friends. Better yet, also try it at a special faculty meeting, a business strategy session, or a community or special-interest organization gathering. Try it anywhere where a small group wants to explore some *real* futures already stored in the minds of the people who may live them. A tape recorder (after agreeing on rules against misuse) can provide a treasure of insights. One may not believe what their stodgy neighbor really said! It is often even more revealing about one's own utterances. Try it; you'll like it!

ANNALS, *AAPSS*, **522**, July 1992

Health Care and AIDS

By JONATHAN PECK and CLEMENT BEZOLD

ABSTRACT: The acquired immune deficiency syndrome (AIDS) is a harbinger for change in health care. There are many powerful forces poised to transform the industrialized health care structure of the twentieth century, and AIDS may act as either a catalyst or an amplifier for these forces. AIDS could, for example, swamp local resources and thereby help trigger national reform in a health care system that has already lost public confidence. AIDS can also hasten the paradigm shift that is occurring throughout health care. Many of the choices society will confront when dealing with AIDS carry implications beyond health care. Information about who has the disease, for example, already pits traditional individual rights against group interests. Future information systems could make discrimination based upon medical records a nightmare for a growing number of individuals. Yet these systems also offer the hope of accelerated progress against not only AIDS but other major health threats as well. The policy choices that will define society's response to AIDS can best be made in the context of a clearly articulated vision of a society that reflects our deepest values.

Jonathan Peck is the managing director and Clement Bezold, Ph.D., is the executive director of the Institute for Alternative Futures, Alexandria, Virginia. They are co-authors of The Future of Work and Health, *named one of the ten best books of the year in 1986 by* American Health *magazine.*

P OWERFULLY entrenched forces in the American health care system resist fundamental reform, but the spread of the acquired immune deficiency syndrome (AIDS),[1] combined with other developments, creates new forces for change. Public policy clashes will pit established interests against these new forces. The outcome is unpredictable. Everything about AIDS—from mutations of the virus to society's response—is permeated with enormous uncertainty. Moreover, the politics of health care makes most predictions more an exercise in ideology than forecasting. Nevertheless, we can look at an array of developments that will be triggered or amplified by AIDS and begin to see the dim outlines of a very different health care system that is likely to emerge in the early twenty-first century.

HOW WE GOT WHERE WE ARE

Over the past century, important political victories helped transform a health care system fit for an agrarian world into one compatible with today's medical-industrial complex.[2] The most powerful players in health care all won significant political battles during this century to achieve their current positions. It is relevant to sketch some of the key state and federal policies that created the power structure undergirding our health care system today.

1. Throughout this article, we will use the term "AIDS" to encompass not only diagnosed disease but also infection with the human immunodeficiency virus and disease related to this virus.

2. Paul Starr, *The Social Transformation of American Medicine* (New York: Basic Books, 1982), pp. 60-449.

Physician licensure

In the nineteenth century, physicians had neither today's lofty status nor their high incomes. The rise of physicians to a position of power can be traced to the time when states began using licensure to regulate who could practice medicine. Following the Flexner report in 1910, the state-sanctioned monopoly to practice was effectively narrowed to physicians who were taught in university-based medical schools wedded to scientific research.[3] Now policymakers, consumers, and payers are asking whether doctors wield too much influence and earn too much money, making challenges to licensure more likely.[4]

Health insurance

Every time it became a national issue, compulsory health insurance was successfully opposed by insurers, doctors, pharmaceutical manufacturers, and employers. Unlike countries with compulsory insurance programs, which pool together those who are considered to have high risks for serious illness with those who have low risks, U.S. insurance companies are able to use experience rating. This method allows U.S. insurers to effectively avoid selling policies to people at greater risk for high medical costs. The resulting inequities in access to care, combined with the administrative complexity of U.S. insurance policies, have created a large

3. Ibid., pp. 116-21.

4. For a discussion of professional roles, see Jonathan C. Peck and Ken Rabin, *Regulating Change* (Washington, DC: Food and Drug Law Institute, 1989), pp. 72, 73.

reservoir of ill will toward the insurance industry.

Tax policy

Health benefits are subsidized through tax policy. As a result, employers have expanded benefits substantially since World War II. Unions accepted benefits in place of wage increases. The benefits have encouraged high utilization of health care services and an unquestioning attitude toward physician and hospital costs. Now, however, employers are enlisting labor support to challenge medical decisions, and many people are questioning the wisdom of our tax policy. The contrast between insurance haves and have-nots also raises questions about the fairness of the tax policy.

Hospital support

The industrial era that moved work into factories also moved health care into hospitals. Federal commitment to high-technology medicine in hospitals after World War II came with the Hill-Burton program, which encouraged construction of hospitals.[5] Efforts to constrain the resulting rise of inpatient costs have come more recently, most notably in 1983, when Medicare adopted diagnostic-related groups (DRGs) as the basis for capitated payments. Hospitals now feel the squeeze on inpatient care, and many are expected to fail in the coming years. Many will question whether the historical accidents and market forces that guided hospital

growth should also determine which hospitals fail in the years ahead. Uncompensated care for AIDS is likely to play a role in many hospital failures.

Federal research policy

The government made a major commitment to basic research starting in the 1950s through the National Institutes of Health (NIH). The NIH has favored the study of illness more than health, treatment more than prevention, and biomedical more than behavioral approaches. AIDS has affected research funding but has yet to affect the basic agenda of the NIH.

Health-services research that is designed to assess the value of medical treatments has been attacked by powerful interest groups. Until recently, the federal government had left this research underfunded as a result. The 1989 creation of the Agency for Health Care Policy and Research foreshadows a broader questioning about the value of high-technology medicine that could ultimately extend to national research policy.

Medicare and Medicaid

The government's major effort to give health care to the elderly and the poor dramatically has accelerated the growth of high-tech care. These programs have reinforced the emphasis on physician-oriented inpatient care and have failed to focus on health promotion. Medicare is the federally financed program primarily intended to supply the elderly with inpatient and outpatient treatment.

5. Starr, *Social Transformation of American Medicine*, p. 348.

Medicaid is the fragmented state and federal program that pays for services to a portion of the population in poverty, including the elderly in nursing homes. The uncoordinated patchwork nature of these programs creates a nonsystem that invites reformers to design alternatives.

THE CURRENT SYSTEM

The health care system that American public policy helped build provides the most costly health care on the planet. In 1991, the United States spent 12.2 percent of its gross national product on health care, while the average for developed countries was only 7.4 percent.[6] Despite this high amount of money spent on health care, there are still well over 30 million Americans who do not have health insurance and thus have limited access to health care. It is often pointed out that no other industrialized nation except South Africa does not have a national health insurance program. It is the uninsured population and Medicaid that will bear the brunt of AIDS infections in the early 1990s.

The international comparisons are made difficult by the fact that the major correlate of ill health, namely, poverty, is not dealt with as well in the United States as in other advanced nations. In effect, we give the poor less effective general assistance, allowing disease to become more prevalent and more intense. Then we often attack the acute stages of disease "with both guns blazing at the symptoms."[7] Thus comparisons of gross outcomes such as life expectancy and infant mortality, which clearly put the United States way behind other developed countries that spend far less of their gross national product for health care, are simplistic.[8] Nonetheless, it is true that, while the U.S. system is the best in the world, at the cutting edge of high technology, it does not serve the whole U.S. population effectively. Thus, while we may lead the world in finding new treatments for AIDS, we lag in public health measures to halt the epidemic.

Opinion polls show that Americans realize that they are ill served by their health care system. While consumers and payers alike express dissatisfaction with health care, there is some ambivalence over the potential for reform to improve that care.[9] The depth of the dissatisfaction is hard to fathom, particularly for politicians and their advisers who have the 1992 and 1996 presidential elections in mind. One plausible scenario is that a continuing recession makes domestic issues the battleground for the presidential elections, and health care reform becomes politically irresistible. In this scenario, AIDS could be a catalyst for public

6. George J. Schieber, Jean-Pierre Poullier, and Leslie M. Greenwald, "Health Care Systems in Twenty-Four Countries," Health Affairs, 10(3):24 (Fall 1991).

7. Jeffrey Goldsmith, Ph.D., coined this description of the approach of modern medicine to disease.

8. Schieber, Poullier, and Greenwald, "Health Care Systems," pp. 34-37.

9. Cindy Jajich-Toth and Burns W. Roper, "Americans' Views on Health Care: A Study in Contradictions," Health Affairs, 9(4):149-57 (Winter 1990). See also Joel C. Cantor et al., "Business Leaders' Views on American Health Care," Health Affairs, 10(1):98-105 (Spring 1991).

calls for reform, perhaps by causing a collapse in a major urban hospital system.

AIDS could be just one of many developments pushing the political system toward health care reform, or it could become the trigger for political action. To date, the polity has responded only marginally to AIDS, but we are still early in the epidemic. When AIDS first struck the gay community, we had a conservative Republican administration elected with the help of the "moral majority." It was expedient to pay little attention to the disease. President Reagan did not talk about AIDS to the American public until 31 May 1987, after 20,849 Americans had died from the disease. He never mentioned gays in the speech.[10] The anger of the gay minority in this country was expressed in 1987 by Randy Shilts in his book *And the Band Played On*:

The numbers of AIDS cases measured the shame of the nation. . . . The United States, the one nation with the knowledge, the resources, and the institutions to respond to the epidemic, had failed. And it had failed because of ignorance and fear, prejudice and rejection. The story of the AIDS epidemic . . . was a story of bigotry and what it could do to a nation.[11]

In the 1990s, the growth in the number of AIDS cases will overcome a new population of victims—poor, minority users of illicit drugs and the people closest to them. These groups may be as marginal politically in the second phase of the epidemic as gays were in the first. As one public health expert notes:

It has remained clear that the future course of the AIDS epidemic will be determined by the creation of a social and institutional milieu within which radical voluntary changes in behavior can occur and be sustained. Educational campaigns and counseling programs, most effectively undertaken by groups linked to the populations at risk, have remained the centerpiece of that preventive effort. . . . The most striking failure in the preventive realm, however, is rooted in the unwillingness to commit the resources necessary to treat drug abuse.[12]

While AIDS primarily hits politically marginal groups, most of the population, the media, and elected officials concentrate on other issues. It is easy to conclude, then, that AIDS will not trigger a movement for health care reform, at least until the epidemic threatens the general population in the political mainstream. This conclusion, however, ignores some of the challenges that AIDS will pose in a changing health care system.

NEW HEALTH CARE PARADIGM

AIDS will foment further change by exposing weaknesses in the most fundamental structure and practices of the health care system. The foundation of this system is a paradigm that was cracking even before the AIDS epidemic. Many of the twentieth century health care concepts tied to this paradigm, which place sick people in hospitals and have doctors making medical decisions, are under attack. AIDS becomes one more force applying pressure to shift from the old paradigm described in Table 1 to

10. Randy Shilts, *And the Band Played On* (New York: St. Martin's Press, 1987), p. 596.

11. Ibid., p. 601.

12. Ronald Bayer, "AIDS: The Politics of Prevention and Neglect," *Health Affairs*, 10(1):93 (Spring 1991).

TABLE 1

CHARACTERISTICS OF OLD AND NEW HEALTH CARE PARADIGMS

Old Paradigm	New Paradigm
Health is in the body	Health is spirit, mind, and body
Health equals absence of disease	Health equals maximum potentials and performance
Examines individuals	Examines society
Causal model	Multifactorial models
Pathogen focused	Systems view
Allopathic	Holistic
Physician dominated	Consumer oriented
Inpatient	Outpatient
Medical	Behavioral
Mass produced	Customized

a new paradigm. Unless the old paradigm creates a dramatic cure for AIDS or an effective vaccine in fairly short order, AIDS will likely be a strong force for a paradigm shift in health.

AIDS has unleashed a consumer movement that seeks the power, information, and choice that was assigned to higher authorities operating under the old paradigm. AIDS activists have created patient information networks, drug-purchasing groups, and a striking example of how motivated consumers can change health care. Regulatory authorities at the U.S. Food and Drug Administration were shocked by protesters who angrily rejected many fundamental rules of drug development. Physicians who treat AIDS and human immunodeficiency virus (HIV) infections have been surprised by patients who come to them knowing more about treatment options and experimental therapies than the doctors themselves. Pharmaceutical companies have been astounded that AIDS activists can gain access to corporate plans for developing drugs,

using an underground of informants. The growing power of AIDS groups has created more than just envy among other advocacy groups; it has created a model for activism.

If future AIDS activists from the inner cities take their cue from the current groups, then pressure will continue to push toward the new health care paradigm. In part, that shift is motivated by the desire to provide a more potent response to the rising epidemic. The new paradigm enlists all human resources in the struggle to thrive. The spirit and the mind are particularly important allies for HIV-infected individuals who may see victory not as eliminating the disease but as maintaining or recovering their self-esteem and their ability to function in spite of the disease. Some people with AIDS go so far as to place all their hope in faith healing or other approaches that are completely outside the traditional medical paradigm. Most people infected with HIV, however, do not ignore the offerings of the medical establishment; they just look for more than what medicine can offer.

BIOMEDICAL
ADVANCES AND AIDS

Fortunately, biomedical advances will offer better treatment for AIDS. Molecular biology promises to achieve more in the next decades than in any previous era of scientific history. New tools—the scanning-tunneling microscope that can manipulate single atoms, super-computers, monoclonal antibodies, and a raft of others—will help researchers create new knowledge and discover new therapeutics. Molecular biology will enable scientists to model organ systems. The scientists will be able to create simulations so real that their experiments can mimic disease processes and then reveal therapeutic approaches.[13] The understanding of disease processes will open up enormous potential for designing new interventions.

Already AIDS provides a dramatic view of the speed and direction of basic research. So much has been learned about HIV in such a short time that AIDS has itself become a force propelling research. Virologists can already describe the atomic structure of HIV, including the shape of the surface protein—gp 120—and the existence of two outer coats, called capsids. Their knowledge empowers other researchers to devise strategies to develop drugs that take advantage of the structure of HIV and, hopefully, to weaken or disarm it.[14] As more money pours into AIDS research, a scientific agenda that goes beyond AIDS comes into view. The frontiers of virology open not only to the study of retroviruses, but a host of other simple, relatively unknown life forms that will be implicated in a growing number of disease and life processes.

An even larger scientific agenda opens in immunology, where basic knowledge can be marshaled not just against AIDS but also against the larger, more established killers like cancers and heart disease. Immune-system research continues advances in the allopathic approach, or reductionist research, which has achieved such impressive results as the characterization of key constituents in the immune system such as T-4 cells, macrophages, interleukins, and other cytokines. Undoubtedly, the positivistic and reductionist approach of traditional medical research will continue to add knowledge to the medical arsenal needed to fight AIDS.

This allopathic approach has, however, split the body and mind and focused on empirical research. Health care is thus set up to ignore what we can do with our minds, how our emotions affect our health and illness, and how our personal and spiritual growth can also affect our health. Scientific studies that use empirical research to explore these issues emerged rapidly in the 1990s from the field of psychoneuroimmunology. This research will encourage the use of what we describe as soft technologies, such as visualization and meditation.[15]

13. Peck and Rabin, *Regulating Change*, p. 19.

14. See, for example, Ron Cowen, "The Shell Game: A Common Cold Virus Offers Clues to Sabotaging AIDS," *Science News*, 28 July 1990, pp. 56-57.

15. Clement Bezold, Rick J. Carlson, and Jonathan C. Peck, *The Future of Work and Health* (Dover, MA: Auburn House, 1986), pp. 125-31.

Many people with AIDS will use soft technologies along with the latest drugs to both strengthen their immune response and attack the invading virus. These people will encourage a synthesis of the reductionist and holistic practices that are often in opposition to each other in current medical practice.

AIDS will also affect other areas where scientific progress is accelerating. Pharmacology has entered a new era that will be dominated by rational research rather than random searches for pharmacologically active compounds. With rational research, scientists begin with a knowledge of the disease process, human organ systems, and cells, right down to the molecular shape of receptors at the cellular level. With such knowledge, pharmacologists can look for molecules with the right shape to bind with receptors. They can manipulate atoms to create the right shape, eventually even designing drugs atom by atom.

This new research approach is expensive, however, and the new drugs that result will be far more expensive than older drugs. The first drug approved for AIDS, azidothymidine (AZT), shocked payers and patients alike with a price tag that most individuals simply cannot afford. AIDS groups have pressured manufacturers, politicians, and third-party payers to help make expensive drugs available. The issue of how to pay for increasingly expensive drugs will be more visible as new treatments for many different diseases are developed. AIDS could well be the disease, however, where activist patients have the capacity to confront the public

with the need to change the financing system for drugs.

The new medicines developed later in this decade will be further enhanced by the understanding of genetics coming from the human genome project. The mapping of the human genome will affect every other type of biomedical research. Most powerfully, it will customize mass-produced knowledge about diseases to the biochemically unique characteristics of an individual person. Every drug on the market, whether for AIDS or any other condition, is developed for a statistical average patient. Doctors can adjust their prescribing to account for any individual variations that are known to affect how the drug works. To date, however, not much has been systematically learned about those individual variations. Some group factors such as race, age, and renal impairment are already known to affect drug response. Much more will be learned about group as well as individual differences when information from the genome project comes on line.[16]

The information systems that could take genetic knowledge into medical practice are revolutionary in themselves. AIDS can influence the course of the information revolution in health care because it raises crucial ethical and political issues. Even today's fragmented data bases, which are sure to look primitive in just a few years, frighten people with AIDS. The ownership of information about infected individuals is still open to question. Public health concerns

16. Peck and Rabin, *Regulating Change*, p. 25.

clash with individual rights when AIDS registries are kept or when contact tracing notifies sexual partners of infected individuals. Insurance companies that test for HIV infection own the results, leaving the individual vulnerable to discrimination, loss of confidentiality, and laboratory error.

Given these current realities, the AIDS community must look carefully at new information systems capable of changing the delivery and financing of health care. On the positive side, the speed at which medical knowledge accumulates and improves medical practice could increase dramatically with new information systems. The computer-based patient record, for example, is "an essential technology for health care" for which there are no technological developmental barriers.[17] Health outcome measures are also developing that could link health care inputs with multidimensional outcomes, including cost, health status, and quality-of-life dimensions. In addition, expert systems for diagnosis and treatment protocols show great promise for establishing standards of care.

Taken together, these technologies have the potential to empower patients. The complexity of medicine will no longer make the notion of the informed consumer of health care an unrealizable ideal. The coming generations of computers will cope with the complexity for people. Patients conceivably will be able to use computers instead of physicians as the

17. Institute of Medicine, *The Computer-Based Patient Record: An Essential Technology for Health Care* (Washington, DC: National Academy Press, 1991).

"learned intermediaries" who guide health decisions. There will still be important roles for physicians and other professionals as healers, health coaches, and perhaps guides for decision making, but the roles will change and so too will the rules of the system. If consumers use the emerging information systems to gain decision-making power, physicians will lose the monopoly that is granted them through licensure. Yet, doctors are also likely to lose their terrible liability burden as well. Patients will have to accept the risks and responsibilities that are unavoidably a part of the ongoing experiment we call medicine.

If medicine is an experiment, it has been limited by the fact that most results are not systematically collected to create new knowledge. The health care system of the twenty-first century will have a capacity to gather an enormous amount of data to answer questions we cannot even ask now. Twenty-four-hour monitoring; lifelong data bases on behavior, environment, genetics, and health care; and artificial-intelligence tools called knowbots and knowledge navigators that search all medical knowledge to answer an individual's question are some of the bright possibilities now seen by the visionaries in medicine.

There is, however, a darker side to the technological potential of information systems. The specter of information systems used against individuals rather than disease evokes images from Orwell and Kafka. Individuals with the AIDS virus could, conceivably, not know they are infected; they could suffer from discrimination based upon health records they never see. With advancing genetic information available through tests, this type of discrimination could broaden beyond AIDS to affect people having predispositions to any number of diseases. Even the threat of such abuses of medical confidentiality could be used by established interests to block their loss of power to the emerging information infrastructure.

These essentially political issues contribute to the great uncertainty facing our health care system as it responds to the AIDS epidemic. As futurists, our response to uncertainty is to explore the range of potential changes using alternative scenarios. These scenarios help point to the key choices facing our society, including those defining the delivery, financing, and use of technology.

The way that our society makes these choices by formulating policy is itself changing. Policy makes things happen. Tools are emerging that allow us to explore what might happen far more effectively. These include the type of futures research that the Institute for Alternative Futures and other health futurists provide.

But equally important, since we continually create the future by what we do and what we fail to do, is the emergence of processes for the development of our vision. Vision in this context is what we see with our eyes closed, that is, our preferred future, the future we want to create. Work on visions in a number of public and private sector organizations has shown that a great deal of personal power can be unleashed if people share a vision of the positive role their organization is playing and if attention is being given to using visioning techniques to enhance the conscious, inspiring, and compelling creation of a society that reflects our deepest values.

What should our vision be? This question becomes an invitation to design the best that can be. In health care, our vision is to move away from an expensive, often insensitive, narrowly focused health care system. We see the possibility of a system that is more caring and more focused on prevention; a system that helps each individual manage health, healing with the body and the mind; a system that measures what works in order to keep learning more about health; a system that recognizes the inevitability of death and helps us prepare for it. AIDS is one of the challenges that will help create such a health care system.

ANNALS, *AAPSS*, 522, July 1992

The Good-Books Imperative: Keeping up in Futures Studies

By MICHAEL MARIEN

ABSTRACT: Keeping up with the literature is imperative in any field. It is especially so in the loose, multifaceted realm of futures studies, where there is much to read, much of which becomes outdated in only a few years following publication. Newer is not necessarily better, but in futures thinking it often is. Books mentioned here have been selected from more than 11,000 abstracts and reviews published in *Future Survey* since 1979. They provide an introduction to much of the contemporary futures thinking in the United States, but they do not cover all sectors and all issues. The hundred-plus recommended book titles are a start in appreciating futures literature.

Michael Marien, a futures overviewer and critic, is founding editor of Future Survey. *His special interests are the quest for a sustainable society, information overload, and social and technological change.*

KEEPING up with the literature is imperative in any field. It is especially so in the loose, multifaceted realm of futures studies, where there is much to read, much of which becomes outdated in only a few years following publication. Newer is not necessarily better, but in futures thinking it often is.

The scope of futures-relevant books, reports, and articles is profoundly multidisciplinary, and the boundaries are fuzzy, greatly complicated by the fact that no credentials are needed to be a futurist. Futurists are people from a wide variety of backgrounds who say that they are futurists or who are seen as such. But many people who think intelligently about what is probable, possible, and/or preferable do not call themselves futurists. Rather, they are known as, and see themselves as, planners, policy analysts, consultants, environmentalists, social scientists, journalists, systems thinkers, political leaders, activists, technology assessors, and social thinkers. None of these serious futurists or cryptofuturists should be confused with the clairvoyants and astrologers of the supermarket tabloids, who unfortunately are much more visible to the general public, or with the well-defined field of science fiction, devoted to escaping the real world, rather than coping with it.

Ideally, the best futures thinkers specialize in big-picture overviews in time and space. They take a long view into the past and then forward into time, and a broad view across sectoral and disciplinary boundaries of society and often across national boundaries. They are specialists in generalities, integrators of knowledge, thinkers who emphasize breadth, and educators at large. They are at the leading edge of ideas that are shaping, will shape, or may shape society. To be at the leading edge, they frequently prod people to think about the unthinkable.

In practice, however, it is impossible to be on top of all trends and prospects in our turbulent era of multiple transformations, let alone appreciate the multiple perspectives on any problem area. Many futures thinkers are boxed into today's conventional wisdoms, which may or may not be warranted. And most futures thinkers necessarily specialize in the problems of several sectors, or only one sector, or even a subsector.

To think broadly, though, it is important to keep informed of the thinking in other sectors. And to think sharply, one must be exposed to multiple views. If one cannot read everything, one can at least read the good books of the moment—not necessarily the great books, but the best tools available to challenge thinking and expand horizons in time and space.

The books recommended here have been selected from more than 11,000 abstracts, many with critical comments, published in *Future Survey* since 1979. They provide an introduction to much of the contemporary futures thinking in the United States, but they do not cover all sectors and all issues.

ENVIRONMENTAL ISSUES
AND SUSTAINABILITY

The category of environmental affairs is placed first in this bibliographic review because it is a major and growing part of the futures literature, because it deals with basic long-term questions of human life that sooner or later must be addressed, and because it is still neglected or underappreciated by many people who should be giving it more attention—including many of the contributors to this issue of *The Annals*.

The most authoritative overview of world population, urbanization, food, resources, atmospheric warming, pollution, and policy responses is provided by *World Resources 1992-93*, a biennial report from the Washington-based World Resources Institute in collaboration with the U.N. Environment Programme and the U.N. Development Programme.[1] It provides more than suggested by the bland title, including many tables of valuable data. In contrast, the annual *State of the World* report from Lester Brown and his Worldwatch Institute colleagues provides less than the title suggests.[2] Still, *State of the World*, which now appears in 27 languages and claims to be the most widely distributed policy document in the world, offers leading-edge overviews of important selected issues. *The Global Ecology Handbook*, a tie-in with a Public Broadcasting Service television series, nicely covers these issues for college-level au-

diences.[3] For those who still have difficulty in grasping the message, *It's a Matter of Survival*, derived from a major radio series of the Canadian Broadcasting Corporation, describes global population, resource, and environment issues in even more basic language, with the added benefit of large type.[4]

Infoglut reigns in this area, with dozens of general save-the-planet books available. And there are hundreds of books that focus on specific problems, such as global warming,[5] population growth,[6] the threat to biodiversity,[7] the ineffectiveness of protecting endangered species to date,[8] soil conservation,[9] groundwater pol-

1. World Resources Institute, *World Resources 1992-93: A Guide to the Global Environment* (New York: Oxford University Press, Mar. 1992). This is the fifth edition of a biennial series.

2. Lester R. Brown et al., *State of the World 1992: A Worldwatch Institute Report on Progress toward a Sustainable Society* (New York: Norton, 1992). This is the ninth in an annual series.

3. Global Tomorrow Coalition, *The Global Ecology Handbook: What You Can Do about the Environmental Crisis* (Boston: Beacon Press, 1990).

4. Anita Gordon and David Suzuki, *It's a Matter of Survival* (Cambridge, MA: Harvard University Press, 1991).

5. Cheryl Simon Silver with Ruth S. De-Fries, *One Earth, One Future: Our Changing Global Environment* (Washington, DC: National Academy Press, 1990). See also Jeremy Leggett, ed., *Global Warming: The Greenpeace Report* (New York: Oxford University Press, 1990).

6. Paul R. Ehrlich and Anne H. Ehrlich, *The Population Explosion* (New York: Simon & Schuster, 1990). An excellent update of projections is provided by the annual *World Population Data Sheet* (Washington, DC: Population Reference Bureau).

7. E. O. Wilson, ed., *Biodiversity* (Washington, DC: National Academy Press, 1988). See also Boyce Thorne-Miller and John Catena, *The Living Ocean: Understanding and Protecting Marine Biodiversity* (Washington, DC: Island Press, 1991).

8. Richard Tobin, *The Expendable Future: U.S. Politics and the Protection of Biological Diversity* (Durham, NC: Duke University Press, 1990).

9. Frederick R. Steiner, *Soil Conservation in the United States: Policy and Planning* (Bal-

lution,[10] global threats to wetlands[11] and fisheries,[12] toxic waste,[13] and solid waste.[14] These books and many others all point to a vast cluster of intertwined problems created by industrial civilization and industrial-era thinking that ignored environmental matters. Sooner or later, our societies and our thinking must become oriented toward sustainability.

Thinking about sustainable development began as a trickle in the 1970s and picked up speed with publication of the World Commission on Environment and Development's report in 1987.[15] Since then, a special issue of *Scientific American* has been devoted to global sustainability,[16] as have books from the American Assembly[17] and the Trilateral Commis-

sion.[18] Transition to a sustainable society will involve much learning,[19] "making peace" between the ecosphere and technosphere,[20] and reformulating economics so that it relates to the real world.[21] The "environmental factor" pervades all aspects of business,[22] and transition to alternative or sustainable agriculture would appear to be inexorable.[23] There has been no recent counterargument of any note to this sustainable-society thinking; unlike the spirited debates on limits to growth in the 1970s, political conservatives and narrow-gauge social scientists have largely ignored the environmentalist thinking of recent years.

GLOBAL ISSUES

The second cluster of noteworthy titles involves other global issues in

timore, MD: Johns Hopkins University Press, 1990).

10. Sierra Club Legal Defense Fund, *The Poisoned Well: New Strategies for Groundwater Protection* (Washington, DC: Island Press, 1989).

11. Michael Williams, ed., *Wetlands: A Threatened Landscape* (Cambridge, MA: Basil Blackwell, 1990).

12. James R. McGoodwin, *Crisis in the World's Fisheries: People, Problems, and Policies* (Stanford, CA: Stanford University Press, 1990).

13. Lauren Kenworthy and Eric Schaeffer, *A Citizen's Guide to Toxic Waste Reduction* (New York: INFORM, 1990).

14. Richard A. Denison and John Ruston, eds., *Recycling and Incineration: Evaluating the Choices* (Washington, DC: Island Press, 1990). See also Louis Blumberg and Robert Gottlieb, *War on Waste* (Washington, DC: Island Press, 1989).

15. World Commission on Environment and Development, *Our Common Future* (New York: Oxford University Press, 1987).

16. *Managing Planet Earth*, special issue of *Scientific American*, 261(3):46-175 (Sept. 1989).

17. Jessica Tuchman Mathews, ed., *Preserving the Global Environment: The Chal-*

lenge of Shared Leadership (New York: Norton, American Assembly, 1990).

18. Jim MacNeill, Pieter Winsemius, and Taizo Yakushiji, *Beyond Interdependence: The Meshing of the World's Economy and the Earth's Ecology* (New York: Oxford University Press, Trilateral Commission, 1991). MacNeill was the main author of *Our Common Future*.

19. Lester W. Milbrath, *Envisioning a Sustainable Society: Learning Our Way Out* (Albany: State University of New York Press, 1989).

20. Barry Commoner, *Making Peace with the Planet* (New York: Pantheon Books, 1990).

21. James Robertson, *Future Wealth* (New York: Bootstrap Press, 1990). See also Herman E. Daly and John B. Cobb, Jr., *For the Common Good: Redirecting the Economy toward Community, the Environment, and a Sustainable Future* (Boston: Beacon Press, 1989).

22. Michael Silverstein, *The Environmental Factor: Its Impact on the Future of the World Economy and Your Investments* (Chicago: Longman Financial Services, 1990).

23. National Research Council, Board on Agriculture, *Alternative Agriculture* (Washington, DC: National Academy Press, 1989).

which the environment is only part of the analysis. Perhaps the best overview is *Global Outlook 2000*, a synthesis of trends prepared for the U.N. General Assembly.[24] Other useful overviews from the United Nations include the *Human Development Report*,[25] which introduces a broader and more realistic measure of development than mere gross national product, and the annual *State of the World's Children* from the United Nations Children's Fund.[26] The Club of Rome's leaders present a cogent overview of the global revolution, now just under way, that is forming a new type of world society.[27] Wagar provides broad integrations of the future of Earth, wealth and power, war and peace, and culture.[28] Kidder distills basic global goals: closing the North-South gap, halting environmental degradation, and finding ethical ways to balance rights and responsibilities.[29] Drucker offers a

thoughtful global tour of "new realities" such as privatization, the growth of the nonprofit sector and continuing education, and reality outgrowing economic theory.[30] In a tour of the emerging postmodern worldview, Anderson sums up what many have yet to accept: "reality isn't what it used to be."[31]

One of the major pivotal events of recent years, unanticipated by virtually all observers, was the sudden end of the Cold War and, seemingly, the threat of worldwide conflict. Large-scale conventional war may be at an end, but low-intensity conflict is rising,[32] fueled by hungry arms suppliers.[33] We are still stuck in Cold War thinking[34] and have yet to take a look at short- and long-term actions needed for survival.[35] Much of the suffering and expense of war could be avoided if we addressed our thinking to this end.[36]

24. United Nations, *Global Outlook 2000: An Economic, Social and Environmental Perspective* (New York: United Nations Publications, 1990).

25. United Nations Development Programme, *Human Development Report 1991* (New York: Oxford University Press, 1991).

26. James P. Grant, *The State of the World's Children 1991* (New York: Oxford University Press, 1991).

27. Alexander King and Bertrand Schneider, *The First Global Revolution: A Report by the Council of the Club of Rome* (New York: Pantheon Books, 1991).

28. W. Warren Wagar, *The Next Three Futures: Paradigms of Things to Come* (New York: Praeger, 1991). Many of these ideas are presented by Wagar in an extended scenario, *A Short History of the Future* (Chicago: University of Chicago Press, 1989).

29. Rushworth M. Kidder, *Reinventing the Future: Global Goals for the 21st Century* (Cambridge: MIT Press, 1989).

30. Peter F. Drucker, *The New Realities: In Government and Politics/in Economics and Business/in Society and World View* (New York: Harper & Row, 1989).

31. Walter Truett Anderson, *Reality Isn't What It Used to Be: Theatrical Politics, Ready-to-Wear Religion, Global Myths, Primitive Chic, and Other Wonders of the Postmodern World* (San Francisco: Harper & Row, 1990).

32. Martin van Crevald, *The Transformation of War* (New York: Free Press, 1991).

33. James Adams, *Engines of War: Merchants of Death and the New Arms Race* (New York: Atlantic Monthly Press, 1990).

34. Robert S. McNamara, *Out of the Cold: New Thinking for American Foreign and Defense Policy in the 21st Century* (New York: Simon & Schuster, 1989).

35. Frank Barnaby, ed., *The GAIA Peace Atlas: Survival into the Third Millennium* (New York: Doubleday, 1988).

36. Harry B. Hollins, Averill L. Powers, and Mark Sommer, *The Conquest of War: Alternative Strategies for Global Security* (Boulder, CO: Westview Press, 1989).

It is undeniable that we are in an emerging global economy[37] and that the influence of the superpowers has declined.[38] Development of a common market in Europe offers a challenge to the United States.[39] We will also be challenged to prepare our citizens for twenty-first-century global capitalism.[40] Urbanization into giant cities is an inexorable force.[41] With the advent of the global economy, nation building becomes more and more synonymous with city building, and cities become the nexus of global society.[42]

DOMESTIC ISSUES

The third cluster of good books concerns domestic issues. Perhaps the best recent overview of the emerging global economy and a broad range of U.S. issues is *2020 Visions*.[43]

A more optimistic view is presented in *American Renaissance*[44]; a much more gloomy view—still quite applicable—is offered in Richard Lamm's *Megatraumas*.[45] The well-known, happy-face best-sellers on the top ten "megatrends"[46] are interesting to read but intellectually inferior to the three preceding titles.

A broad and accessible overview on economic changes, perhaps a bit dated and overly sanguine in parts, is provided by *America's New Economy*.[47] More recent overviews include an optimistic view of economic renaissance in the 1990s by a former vice president of the Hudson Institute,[48] a generally gloomy view by a rising MIT economist,[49] and prescriptive views of how a more democratic and egalitarian economy could reduce waste[50] and how a new "social self-

37. William Brock and Robert D. Hormats, eds., *The Global Economy: America's Role in the Decade Ahead* (New York: Norton, American Assembly, 1990). For a more worried view, see Dennis C. Pirages and Christine Sylvester, eds., *Transformations in the Global Political Economy* (New York: St. Martin's Press, 1990).

38. James Laxer, *Decline of the Superpowers: Winners and Losers in Today's Global Economy* (New York: Paragon House, 1989).

39. Michael Calingaert, *The 1992 Challenge from Europe: Development of the European Community's Internal Market* (Washington, DC: National Planning Association, 1990).

40. Robert B. Reich, *The Work of Nations: Preparing Ourselves for 21st Century Capitalism* (New York: Knopf, 1991).

41. Mattei Dogan and John D. Kasarda, eds., *The Metropolis Era*, vol. 1, *A World of Giant Cities*; vol. 2, *Mega-Cities* (Newbury Park, CA: Sage, 1988).

42. Richard V. Knight and Gary Gappert, eds., *Cities in a Global Society* (Newbury Park, CA: Sage, 1989).

43. Richard Carlson and Bruce Goldman, *2020 Visions: Long View of a Changing World* (Stanford, CA: Stanford Alumni Association, Portable Stanford, 1990).

44. Marvin Cetron and Owen Davies, *American Renaissance: Our Life at the Turn of the 21st Century* (New York: St. Martin's Press, 1989).

45. Richard D. Lamm, *Megatraumas: America at the Year 2000* (Boston: Houghton Mifflin, 1985).

46. John Naisbitt, *Megatrends* (New York: Warner Books, 1982); John Naisbitt and Patricia Aburdene, *Megatrends 2000* (New York: William Morrow, 1990).

47. Robert Hamrin, *America's New Economy: The Basic Guide* (New York: Franklin Watts, 1988).

48. Irving Leveson, *American Challenges: Business and Government in the World of the 1990s* (New York: Praeger, 1991).

49. Paul Krugman, *The Age of Diminished Expectations: U.S. Economic Policy in the 1990s* (Cambridge: MIT Press, 1990).

50. Samuel Bowles, David M. Gordon, and Thomas E. Weisskopf, *After the Waste Land: A Democratic Economics for the Year 2000* (Armonk, NY: M. E. Sharpe, 1991).

governance" paradigm could make a difference in economic policy.[51]

Some important works on selected aspects of the economy include an overview of seven forces reshaping work that employs impeccable futures methodology,[52] a proposed "life-cycle approach" to work force improvement,[53] a broad overview of social welfare policy and the "mounting social deficit,"[54] a long-term warning about the rising cost of government entitlements,[55] and a proposal for widespread voluntary national service[56]—an old idea that could very well be taken seriously in the 1990s.

The spiraling cost of America's health care, now at 12 percent of the gross national product and notably higher than in any other country, will be a major issue in the next few years. In *Serious and Unstable Condition*, Aaron describes this problem as well as anyone.[57] Califano's broad and accessible overview of changes in health care is still useful,[58] and Callahan discusses the troubling paradoxes of medical progress.[59] *Healthy People 2000* suggests the health goals that we could pursue on various fronts in the 1990s.[60]

The concept of investing in "human capital" provides an excellent overview of education at all levels.[61] Zigler and Lang have written the best introduction to the child-care crisis at what is now called the preschool level.[62] School reform is a major concern, with scores of books on what should be done. *Educational Renaissance* offers a broad and upbeat overview,[63] and Roland Barth

51. Severyn T. Bruyn, *A Future for the American Economy: The Social Market* (Stanford, CA: Stanford University Press, 1991).

52. Joseph F. Coates, Jennifer Jarratt, and John B. Mahaffie, *Future Work: Seven Critical Forces Reshaping Work and the Work Force in North America* (San Francisco: Jossey-Bass, 1990).

53. R. Scott Fosler and Jack A. Meyer, *An America That Works: The Life-Cycle Approach to a Competitive Work Force* (New York: Committee for Economic Development, 1990).

54. Ford Foundation Project on Social Welfare and the American Future, *The Common Good* (New York: Ford Foundation, 1989).

55. Peter G. Peterson and Neil Howe, *On Borrowed Time: How the Growth in Entitlement Spending Threatens America's Future* (San Francisco: ICS Press, Institute for Contemporary Studies, 1988).

56. Charles C. Moskos, *A Call to Civic Service: National Service for Country and Community* (New York: Free Press, Twentieth Century Fund, 1988).

57. Henry J. Aaron, *Serious and Unstable Condition: Financing America's Health Care* (Washington, DC: Brookings Institution, 1991). See also Dean C. Coddington et al., *The Crisis in Health Care* (San Francisco: Jossey-Bass, 1990); Karen Davis et al., *Health Care Cost Containment* (Baltimore, MD: Johns Hopkins University Press, 1990).

58. Joseph A. Califano Jr., *America's Health Care Revolution* (New York: Random House, 1986).

59. Daniel Callahan, *What Kind of Life: The Limits of Medical Progress* (New York: Simon & Schuster, 1990).

60. Michael A. Stoto et al., eds., *Healthy People 2000: Citizens Chart the Course* (Washington, DC: National Academy Press, 1990). Stoto was study director of the Institute of Medicine Committee on Health Objectives for the Year 2000.

61. David W. Hornbeck and Lester M. Salamon, eds., *Human Capital and America's Future: An Economic Strategy for the Nineties* (Baltimore, MD: Johns Hopkins University Press, 1991).

62. Edward F. Zigler and Mary E. Lang, *Child Care Choices: Balancing the Needs of Children, Families, and Society* (New York: Free Press, 1991).

63. Marvin Cetron and Margaret Gayle, *Educational Renaissance: Our Schools at the*

provides an authoritative primer on characteristics of good schools.[64] In the realm of higher education, Harvard's Derek Bok rightly wonders why America's highly touted universities are not doing all they can and should to help America,[65] while Ernest Boyer points to what is needed, namely, more equal valuing of four types of scholarship: the scholarship of integration—illustrated in this review essay—the scholarship of application, and the scholarship of teaching, as well as the overvalued scholarship of discovery.[66] At the adult-education level, Chisman proposes an agenda to tackle the increasingly serious U.S. literacy problem.[67]

TECHNOLOGY

The fourth grouping of recommended books involves technology, often considered the only major driving force in human affairs. It is indeed one driving force, but ideas and events are equally important in shaping our destiny.

The extremes of optimism and pessimism are especially pronounced when considering what technology has done and might do. One of the most thoughtful overviews of technological impacts, and also one of the most pessimistic, comes from the French sociologist Jacques Ellul.[68] Less scathing and more balanced views, on the need to consider "technological risk"[69] and to make wise technological choices,[70] offer contrasts to Ellul in style and substance. The history of thinking about technology in America has generally been one of exuberant optimism,[71] and many technological forecasts are not realized because of this bias.[72] But like it or not, we will live in a technological world, and more technology is to be expected, both for better and for worse.

When we think of modern technology, we are prone to initially consider information technology (IT), which has reshaped our lives over the past few decades and is still developing new tools and techniques that promise profound impacts. *Technology 2001* is an authoritative but uncritical guide to emerging IT.[73] Equally

Turn of the Century (New York: St. Martin's Press, 1991).

64. Roland S. Barth, *Improving Schools from Within: Teachers, Parents and Principals Can Make the Difference* (San Francisco: Jossey-Bass, 1990).

65. Derek Bok, *Universities and the Future of America* (Durham, NC: Duke University Press, 1990).

66. Ernest L. Boyer, *Scholarship Reconsidered: Priorities of the Professoriate* (Princeton, NJ: Carnegie Foundation for the Advancement of Teaching, 1990).

67. Forrest P. Chisman, ed., *Leadership for Literacy: The Agenda for the 1990s* (San Francisco: Jossey-Bass, 1990).

68. Jacques Ellul, *The Technological Bluff* (Grand Rapids, MI: William B. Eerdmans, 1990). This updates and extends Ellul's best-known work, *The Technological Society* (New York: Knopf, 1964), first published in France in 1954.

69. H. W. Lewis, *Technological Risk* (New York: Norton, 1990).

70. Edward Wenk, Jr., *Tradeoffs: Imperatives of Choice in a High-Tech World* (Baltimore, MD: Johns Hopkins University Press, 1986).

71. Joseph J. Corn, ed., *Imagining Tomorrow: History, Technology, and the American Future* (Cambridge: MIT Press, 1986).

72. Stephen P. Schnaars, *Megamistakes: Forecasting and the Myth of Rapid Technological Change* (New York: Free Press, 1989).

73. Derek Leebaert, ed., *Technology 2001: The Future of Computing and Communications* (Cambridge: MIT Press, 1991).

uncritical is the idealized view of the global information society that will result.[74] Another upbeat forecast, of automatic-interpretation telephone systems by the year 2000, is far more plausible because it comes from the head of Japan's powerful NEC and is a major corporate goal.[75] Forester's anthology on computers provides an even-handed assessment of the pros and cons of this most powerful and celebrated of our new tools.[76] More specifically, the Massachusetts Institute of Technology's Management in the 1990s Research Program has found that IT enables fundamental changes in the way work is done, but only a few firms—so far—are demonstrably better off after deploying IT.[77]

Another major technology revolution, just under way, concerns biotechnology. One major subcategory involves creation, modification, or manipulation of plant and animal species. Goodman et al. provide a very broad and long-range view of the emerging factory farm and integrated biomass production systems,[78] while Busch et al. focus on social consequences.[79] Another major area of biotechnology involves applications to human beings, such as the various consequences likely to result from reliable genetic testing.[80] New technologies involving human reproduction are already creating a host of issues.[81] Future Man offers a very long-term and provocative view of where biotechnology may lead us in the centuries ahead.[82]

Because of environmental-protection imperatives, many changes in energy sources and usage are certain in the decades to come. A special issue of Scientific American spells out the problem and some of the prospects,[83] and a massive symposium at the Massachusetts Institute of Technology in 1990 resulted in over 1000 pages of views by more than 100 contributors.[84] More specifically, Daniel Sperling offers the best guide to al-

74. Yoniji Masuda, Managing in the Information Society (Cambridge, MA: Basil Blackwell, 1990). This is an augmented edition of The Information Society as Post-Industrial Society, first published in Japan in 1980.

75. Koji Kobayashi, Computers and Communications: A Vision of C&C (Cambridge: MIT Press, 1986). Kobayashi is chairman and chief executive officer of NEC Corporation, formerly Nippon Electric Company.

76. Tom Forester, ed., Computers in the Human Context: Information Technology, Productivity, and People (Cambridge: MIT Press, 1989). Forester also edited The Information Technology Revolution (Cambridge: MIT Press, 1985).

77. Michael S. Scott Morton, ed., The Corporation of the 1990s: Information Technology and Organizational Transformation (New York: Oxford University Press, 1991).

78. David Goodman, Bernardo Sorj, and John Wilkinson, From Farming to Biotechnology: A Theory of Agroindustrial Development (New York: Basil Blackwell, 1987).

79. Laurence Busch et al., Plants, Power, and Profit: Social, Economic, and Ethical Consequences of the New Biotechnologies (Cambridge, MA: Basil Blackwell, 1991).

80. Neil A. Holtzman, Proceed with Caution: Predicting Genetic Risks in the Recombinant DNA Era (Baltimore, MD: Johns Hopkins University Press, 1989).

81. Robert H. Blank, Regulating Reproduction (New York: Columbia University Press, 1990).

82. Brian Stableford, Future Man (New York: Crown, 1984).

83. Energy for Planet Earth, special issue of Scientific American, 263(3):54-163 (Sept. 1990).

84. Jefferson W. Testor, David O. Wood, and Nancy A. Ferrari, eds., Energy and the Environment in the 21st Century (Cambridge: MIT Press, 1991).

ternative transportation fuels,[85] and Deborah Gordon provides an excellent overview of the deteriorating U.S. transportation system and why we will have to choose new vehicles and fuels.[86] A case can still be made for reviving nuclear energy,[87] but it is important to understand previous flaws in the decision-making process and our passivity in the face of shaping technology, as splendidly presented by Morone and Woodhouse.[88]

Some other important frontiers of science and technology include the quiet and noncontroversial but highly beneficial materials revolution,[89] the far-off but exciting prospect of material abundance produced by molecular machines,[90] the old standbys of creating robots[91] and ex-

ploring outer space,[92] and the possibility of a successful search for extraterrestrial intelligence (SETI).[93]

METHODS TO
SHAPE THE FUTURE

The fifth and last cluster of good books involves methodology—not only forecasting what is probable and possible but actions to create preferable futures through planning, policymaking, and the skills of leadership. Makridakis provides perhaps the best recent overview in this area, albeit one addressed to business managers and weak on environmental aspects of the long-term future, a common failing of economists and business consultants.[94] In contrast, Schwartz's engaging introduction to scenario writing, also addressed to those in the business sector, focuses on the single method that informed observers now choose as most useful

85. Daniel Sperling, ed., *Alternative Transportation Fuels: An Environmental and Energy Solution* (Westport, CT: Greenwood Press, Quorum Books, 1989).

86. Deborah Gordon, *Steering a New Course: Transportation, Energy, and the Environment* (Washington, DC: Island Press, 1991).

87. Bernard L. Cohen, *The Nuclear Energy Option: An Alternative for the 90s* (New York: Plenum Press, 1990).

88. Joseph G. Morone and Edward J. Woodhouse, *The Demise of Nuclear Energy? Lessons for Democratic Control of Technology* (New Haven, CT: Yale University Press, 1989).

89. Tom Forester, ed., *The Materials Revolution: Superconductors, New Materials, and the Japanese Challenge* (Cambridge: MIT Press, 1988).

90. K. Eric Drexler and Chris Peterson, *Unbounding the Future: The Nanotechnology Revolution* (New York: William Morrow, 1991). This is an updated and popularized version of Drexler's *Engines of Creation: The Coming Era of Nanotechnology* (New York: Doubleday, Anchor Press, 1986).

91. Joseph Dekin, *Silico Sapiens: The Fundamentals and Future of Robots* (New York: Bantam New Age Books, 1986). See also Hans Moravec, *Mind Children: The Future of Robot*

and Human Intelligence (Cambridge, MA: Harvard University Press, 1988); Joseph F. Engelberger, *Robotics in Service* (Cambridge: MIT Press, 1989), which forecasts that service robotics will outstrip industrial robotics before 1995.

92. *Pioneering the Space Frontier: The Report of the National Commission on Space* (New York: Bantam Books, 1986). For a clear-headed view of costs, see also John S. Lewis and Ruth A. Lewis, *Space Resources: Breaking the Bonds of Earth* (New York: Columbia University Press, 1987); Thomas R. McDonough, *Space: The Next Twenty-Five Years* (New York: John Wiley, 1987).

93. Frank White, *The SETI Factor: How the Search for Extraterrestrial Intelligence Is Changing Our View of the Universe and Ourselves* (New York: Walker, 1990).

94. Spyros G. Makridakis, *Forecasting, Planning, and Strategy for the 21st Century* (New York: Free Press, 1990).

for futures thinking.[95] An anniversary issue of *Technological Forecasting and Social Change* provides a good critical overview of recent thinking on forecasting.[96]

Futures thinking should not, however, be confined merely to the necessary but hazardous task of trying to forecast what will happen. This can easily invoke passivity, at a time when there is much that can and should be attempted to create a better future. Several well-known futurists have published books in recent years on leadership and the importance of formulating and realizing some positive vision of the future.[97] Futures thinking is also intimately linked to planning,[98] issues management,[99] social marketing,[100] models

for national decision making,[101] and the growth of think tanks.[102]

The diversity of futures thinking is amply illustrated by the directory issued by the World Future Society.[103] The core of good futures thinking is suggested in *What Futurists Believe*,[104] with portraits and analyses of 17 leading futurists, albeit aging white male Americans, and in *What I Have Learned*,[105] providing 16 essays by leading thinkers on what has been learned over the past two turbulent decades. None of these thinkers, however, mentions the simple method of reading good books. Perhaps it is too obvious and inelegant to deserve mention, but the growing fragmentation of ever-narrow perspectives in an increasingly complex world suggests that the good-books imperative should be made explicit and ranked foremost in anyone's professional toolbox.

CONCLUSION

The hundred-plus book titles listed here are a start in appreciating

95. Peter Schwartz, *The Art of the Long View* (New York: Doubleday Currency, 1991).

96. Harold A. Linstone, ed., *Forecasting: A New Agenda*, special 20th anniversary issue of *Technological Forecasting and Social Change*, 36(1-2) (Aug. 1989).

97. John W. Gardner, *On Leadership* (New York: Free Press, 1990). See also Burt Nanus, *The Leader's Edge: The Seven Keys to Leadership in a Turbulent World* (Chicago: Contemporary Books, 1989); Warren Bennis, *On Becoming a Leader* (Reading, MA: Addison-Wesley, 1989); Harlan Cleveland, *The Knowledge Executive: Leadership in an Information Society* (New York: Truman Talley Books, E. P. Dutton, 1985).

98. Melville C. Branch, *Planning: Universal Process* (New York: Praeger, 1990). See also Guy Benveniste, *Mastering the Politics of Planning: Crafting Credible Plans and Policies That Make a Difference* (San Francisco: Jossey-Bass, 1989).

99. Joseph F. Coates et al., *Issues Management: How You Can Plan, Organize and Manage for the Future* (Mt. Airy, MD: Lomond, 1986).

100. Philip Kotler and Eduardo L. Roberto, *Social Marketing: Strategies for Changing Public Behavior* (New York: Free Press, 1989).

101. Gerald O. Barney, W. Brian Kreutzer, and Martha J. Garrett, *Managing a Nation: The Microcomputer Software Catalog*, 2d ed. (Boulder, CO: Westview Press, 1991). See also Lindsay Grant, *Foresight and National Decisions* (Lanham, MD: University Press of America, 1988).

102. James Allen Smith, *The Idea Brokers: Think Tanks and the Rise of the New Policy Elite* (New York: Free Press, 1991).

103. *The Futures Research Directory: Individuals 1991-92* (Bethesda, MD: World Future Society, 1991). A companion directory to organizations will be published in mid-1992.

104. Joseph F. Coates and Jennifer Jarratt, *What Futurists Believe* (Mt. Airy, MD: Lomond, 1989).

105. Michael Marien and Lane Jennings, eds., *What I Have Learned: Thinking about the Future Then and Now* (Westport, CT: Greenwood Press, 1987).

futures literature. Still, these titles do not fully cover the territory: major missing topics include various world regions and nations, the development fiasco (all of the recent literature is harshly critical of simplistic development thinking in the post-World War II period), crime and justice, the so-called war against drugs, the acquired immune deficiency syndrome (AIDS) pandemic, the disturbing plight of many American children and teenagers, race and gender issues, housing, problems and prospects at the state and local level, and government and politics. Several other topics have been touched on only lightly.

This introductory list is too brief for many people, yet it is already much too long for those considering futures literature for the first time. Such would-be students will rightly ask for a single book that magically sums everything up and towers above the others. No book comes close to this ideal; *Megatrends*, unfortunately, has provided an illusory solace for many. There are, however, entry points for plunging into this book pile—by picking one book in each of the five categories, preferably one of the overviews mentioned in the first paragraph in each section. Many of these books are available from the World Future Society Book Service, which publishes catalogues of offerings, updated every spring and fall.[106]

Beyond this initial introduction as of late 1991—much of it will be somewhat out-of-date in several years—would-be readers are urged to consult the monthly issues of *Future Survey* as well as the *Future Survey Annual* cumulations.[107] One can do so to help choose among the titles mentioned here or to dig still deeper and find leads to other important books and articles. There is much for all of us to learn, and our future depends on our doing so.

106. *The Futurist Bookstore: Books, Videos, and Other Products from the World Future Society* (Bethesda, MD: World Future Society, Spring 1992).

107. Michael Marien, ed., *Future Survey Annual: A Guide to the Recent Literature of Trends, Forecasts, and Policy Proposals*, vol. 12 (Bethesda, MD: World Future Society, 1992). A subscription to the monthly *Future Survey* includes a copy of this annual cumulation.

Book Department

INTERNATIONAL RELATIONS AND POLITICS

GLASER, CHARLES L. *Analyzing Strategic Nuclear Policy.* Pp. xii, 378. Princeton, NJ: Princeton University Press, 1991. $45.00. Paperbound, $16.95.

GERTSCHER, FRANK L. and WILLIAM J. WEIDA. *Beyond Deterrence: The Political Economy of Nuclear Weapons.* Pp. xlv, 362. Boulder, CO: Westview Press, 1990. $42.50.

Editor's Note: This review was written in the summer of 1991, before the dissolution of the USSR.

It is generally assumed that the Cold War belongs to the past and that the two major superpowers, the United States and the Soviet Union, no longer threaten each other and their respective allies with mutual assured destruction (MAD). At the moment, this assumption is probably correct. Whatever the reasons for the decisive changes of Soviet foreign policy, the disastrous state of the Soviet economy was certainly one of the most significant factors behind them. They allowed the East European countries to terminate their Communist political systems and to embark on the painful transition from their command economies to free-market systems.

Moscow's New Thinking in foreign affairs also made it possible to settle peacefully a number of serious regional conflicts and to conduct various arms-reduction negotiations. All these developments were symptomatic of the changed overall situation.

In spite of the dramatic events that improved American-Soviet relations, it appears that two major concerns continue to haunt U.S. security and nuclear weapons strategists. The first concern is caused by the uncertainty of the outcome of the internal changes in the Soviet Union. The government of President Gorbachev, attempting to implement *perestroika* and economic reforms, might be replaced by military hard-liners. Second, the Soviet Union still possesses a powerful military establishment, which has in its arsenals about 30,000 nuclear warheads and effective delivery systems.

The two books under review are therefore of utmost importance, as they provide for a better understanding of the major issues involved in developing an effective and viable security and nuclear weapons policy. The fact that the books do not include the most recent changes in American-Soviet relations does not diminish the value of these two thoroughly researched studies.

Charles Glaser's main objective is to find which nuclear strategy and forces can provide the greatest security for the United States. He proceeds on the widely held assumption that nuclear weapons play a central and controversial role in protecting U.S. interests and that their deterrent effect reduces the likelihood of a military confrontation of the two major superpowers.

It certainly is understandable that the current strategy of deterrence, based on MAD, encourages various analysts to search for an alternative nuclear world. The most frequently advanced alternatives are (1) a mutual perfect or near-perfect strategic defense, such as the Strategic Defense Initiative (SDI); (2) U.S. superiority; and (3) nuclear disarmament. The latter is based on the notion that living in a disarmed world would be safer than living with MAD.

Glaser examines four controversial policy issues inherent in the U.S. nuclear strategy and forces in MAD:

1. Should the United States deploy counterforce weapons designed to destroy Soviet nuclear forces?
2. Does the United States need land-based ballistic missiles, namely, intercontinental ballistic missiles?
3. Should the United States deploy a ballistic missile defense with limited missions but incapable of protecting U.S. cities?
4. What types of arms control agreements should the United States negotiate with the Soviet Union?

The answers to these questions are contained in the two broad conclusions that Glaser draws concerning U.S. nuclear strategy and force posture. First, the United States should explicitly reject efforts to escape from MAD because this strategy provides more security than the other three basic alternatives.

Second, after the United States has committed itself to MAD, it should reject a counterforce strategy. Glaser is convinced that a counterforce strategy adds little or nothing to deterring a Soviet attack against the United States and U.S. allies. The United States should maintain the ability to threaten attacks against Soviet society—countervalue—because this would offer essentially all required deterrent capability. A flexible assured destruction can support the current U.S. strategy of threatening strategic nuclear first use in order to extend deterrence to America's allies. It would also satisfy the strategic nuclear requirements of the North Atlantic Treaty Organization's (NATO's) doctrine of flexible response.

Glaser is convinced that a counterforce strategy is dangerous because preemption would never be the best U.S. option. In a severe crisis situation, however, U.S. decision makers may fail to fully realize this. Correctly understood, MAD makes both superpowers' first-strike incentive too small to risk the launching of a preemptive attack.

According to these views, the United States could reduce its counterforce systems, discontinue the development and production of new strategic bombers, and cease being concerned about the survivability of its intercontinental ballistic missiles. The question remains if the Soviet Union would do the same.

Glaser favors arms control efforts, but he believes that they should be directed primarily to limit counterforces. Arms control proposals attempting merely to reduce the arsenals of the superpowers fail to perceive the real dangers and misdirect our attention. The great economic advantages of a substantial reduction of strategic nuclear weapons, which is the objective of the current START negotiations, appears not to be a priority issue for Glaser. Some analysts may also take issue with the author's assertion that U.S. nuclear policy could significantly influence Soviet images of the United States. It can safely be assumed that most Soviet leaders' perception of U.S. foreign policy objectives were, and probably still are, primarily influenced by ideological considerations.

Beyond Deterrence by Frank L. Gertscher and William J. Weida uses a political economic approach and, in contrast to Glaser's analysis, provides a most welcome and detailed history of post-World War II international power relations, marked by the emergence of the military confrontation between the United States and the Soviet Union. The book analyzes the growing Soviet threat against the United States, and its allies, as perceived by military planners in the West and describes the emergence of NATO, the Western defense alliance. Gertscher and Weida explain that the development and production of modern nuclear weapons and ballistic defense systems were the results of decisions made by the governments of the United States, the Soviet Union, and the other nations of the nuclear club.

For over forty years, the United States defense strategy, designed to counter the perceived Soviet nuclear threat, has been based on deterrence and has remained essentially unchanged. The objectives of this strategy are to preserve the independence, institutions, territory, and worldwide interests of the United States and to influence an international order in which U.S. institutions and freedom can flourish. U.S. policymakers were faced with the challenge of developing specific strategies to implement these broad policy objectives. They basically had the choice of proposing a strong strategic retaliatory force that could deter a Soviet nuclear attack or they could introduce new ballistic missiles and air defenses to intercept incoming Soviet nuclear warheads or they could recommend a combination of both strategies. Economic and political considerations have influenced the decision to rely for the time being on the anticipated deterrent effect of punitive retaliation. President Reagan's speech on 23 March 1983, proposing to develop technologies for an effective ballistic defense system, presents a new approach for achieving American security. SDI is supposed to eliminate or substantially reduce the vulnerability of the United States to Soviet nuclear attacks. The authors prudently refrain from discussing the feasibility of SDI and concern themselves with the probable Soviet reaction to a unilateral U.S. development of this type of weapons systems. It certainly could destabilize the balance of power between the United States and the Soviet Union. President Gorbachev acknowledged in November of 1987 that the Soviet Union was also engaged in strategic defense research and probably had begun this activity before similar efforts were initiated by the U.S. government.

Up to the present time, U.S. offensive nuclear weapons, like their Soviet counterparts, remain the instruments for the United States to assure, in case of war, mutual assured destruction of the opposing civilian population. According to the authors, however, MAD never was the sole basis of U.S. operational strategy. The U.S. Strategic Integrated Operations Plan always contained some counterforce targets for at least two reasons. First, it is doubtful that a U.S. president would order the destruction of the Soviet civilian population in case of a deterrence failure. Second, the Soviet leadership places top priority on the survival of its military and civilian control functions rather than on the survival of its civilian population; therefore, these command and control centers became significant strategic targets.

Gertscher and Weida are aware of the possibility that terrorists may acquire nuclear weapons or commit sabotage of nuclear facilities. They believe, however, that the U.S.-Soviet nuclear confrontation and the problem of nuclear proliferation among nations overshadow by far the potential problem of nuclear terrorism. The acquisition of nuclear weapons by adversaries of an American regional ally could indeed create serious problems for U.S. policymakers and might even lead to direct involvement of U.S. military forces. For example, the acquisition of nuclear weapons by Iraq or Libya could threaten the national survival of Israel and possibly of Egypt. It should be noted that this concern was expressed by the authors long before the recent Persian Gulf crisis and the launching of Scud missiles against Israeli cities.

The United States, the Soviet Union, and the other nuclear powers must maintain enormous and costly infrastructures to support the operation and production of nuclear weapons. The United States employs between 115,000 and 120,000 persons for this purpose. The 1988 U.S. budget for its strategic nuclear operations and maintenance was about $45 billion. The economic cost to the Soviet Union is estimated to be considerably higher than that of the United States. About 420,000 persons are employed in Soviet nuclear weapons operations. On the other hand, nuclear weapons are a relatively inexpensive alternative to conventional forces providing equal military strength. Therefore, if the United States would have to rely on expensive conventional forces, required for its worldwide commitments, then the country's economic decline, caused by enormous defense spending, would greatly accelerate.

The authors found that Soviet military spending has impaired the civilian economy to the extent that the economy is often unable to support Moscow's military requirements. The Soviets are forced to acquire expensive technology from outside, frequently by stealing it. This practice might in the short run solve resource-allocation problems, but, in the long run, it is bound to create dependencies on Western technology.

Gertscher and Weida believe that, as the twenty-first century approaches, the United States will continue to upgrade its strategic forces. At the same time, the U.S. government will attempt to negotiate with the Soviet Union in order to reach cost-saving arms reduction agreements.

The U.S. defense budgets in the 1990s will be influenced by the difficulty, due to the vested interests in Congress and in the Bush administration, of stopping the momentum of the arms buildup started by the Reagan administration. On the other hand, the changed perception of the nature of the Soviet challenge and the erosion of public support for defense spending will also be reflected in the budget decision-making process.

In the conclusions to the two books, the authors recommend a reevaluation of the worldwide defense commitments of the United States. They also believe that increased assistance from the NATO allies should be obtained, realizing that U.S. allies have always differed from the U.S. views about the priority spending for defense at the expense of taking care of the social needs of the population. The readers of these two books will greatly benefit from the carefully selected bibliography and source references in the footnotes.

ERIC WALDMAN

University of Calgary
Alberta
Canada

HOWARD, MICHAEL. *The Lessons of History*. Pp. 217. New Haven, CT: Yale University Press, 1991. $27.50.

In this volume, Sir Michael Howard, Robert A. Lovett Professor of Military and Naval History at Yale University, has collected various essays that he published in the 1980s when he held the Regius Chair of Modern History at Oxford University. These 13 self-contained essays deal largely with nationalism and war in the late nineteenth and twentieth centuries. Professional historians, as well as the educated public, can profit by reading these elegantly crafted pieces.

Sir Michael's essay "Structure and Process in History" is his contribution to a debate that divides historians who choose to think about the meaning of their craft. He shuns the structuralist view of history epitomized by the French scholars of the *Annales* school. To Howard, history, especially twentieth-century history, is the story of events and decisions; to reject this as mere *histoire évènementielle* is to reject reality. He asserts that history contains "freely-willed human activities," for good or evil. It is the historian's duty to record those decisions that might have afforded the possibility of incremental progress. Inescapably, the historian becomes a moral judge. This places Sir Michael closer to Lord Acton, his nineteenth-century predecessor in the Oxford chair, than he is willing to admit.

His essay "Empire, Race and War in Pre-1914 Britain" is an incisive introduction to British imperialism. He suggests that the confidence to build and maintain an empire was sustained by a sense of cultural or racial superiority. This illusion ended in the chaos of World War I. The empire could not long be maintained, since, as Sir Michael put it, "the consciousness of being an 'Imperial Race' was not widespread among the British after 1918." True enough. But what of the energy and creativity of the indigenous peoples of the empire who strove to throw off the imperial yoke?

In "Churchill and National Unity," Sir Michael addresses the impact on Western societies of the third industrial revolution, that of computers and microtechnology. He emphasizes that communities whose livelihood depended on obsolescent processes face possible social extinction. Not only does this produce human tragedies, but it might incite a nationalistic backlash against the new economic internationalism. He argues that "National unity" requires a sense of compassion "from the top"; governments should act to ease the transition.

Sir Michael's essays are written from the viewpoint of a humane and enlightened conservatism. Popular protest is not always misguided and uninformed, however. There was a good case for the Campaign for Nuclear Disarmament of the 1980s, as there was for those who opposed the Edwardian naval arms buildup. Sir Michael would be the first to admit that these would not be the lessons he had drawn from history.

EDMUND S. WEHRLE

University of Connecticut
Storrs

AFRICA, ASIA, AND LATIN AMERICA

BATES, ROBERT H. *Beyond the Miracle of the Market: The Political Economy of Agrarian Development in Kenya*. Pp. xv, 203. New York: Cambridge University Press, 1989. No price.

LEONARD, DAVID K. *African Successes: Four Public Managers of Kenyan Rural Development*. Pp. xxxi, 375. Berkeley: University of California Press, 1991. $55.00. Paperbound, $18.95.

In *Beyond the Miracle of the Market* and *African Successes*, Robert Bates and

David Leonard examine the roots of Kenyan exceptionalism—why rural development has been relatively successful. Both assert the importance of institutions in shaping political and economic outcomes, but each uses a different methodological approach.

Bates, consistent with his earlier work in public choice, offers the proposition that public policies result "from a struggle among competing interests that takes place within a setting of political institutions, rather than markets." This argument is substantiated by case studies. For example, during the colonial era, Mau Mau pitted those who developed a stake in commercial agriculture against those who had been disinherited. This struggle laid the foundation for African politicians with ties through the political parties to administrative districts and specific tribes. These individuals with particular economic interests show preferences for certain organizational structures. Bates then offers his analysis of institutions designed to deal with problems with the deficiencies of markets.

Although Bates's argument is clearly and forcefully summarized, the book itself is disjointed, with three substantive appendices inserted in the text and several chapters standing almost independently. The theme, however, remains a critical one: institutions play a central role in the political economy of development.

Why some of Kenya's economic institutions have successfully played such a key role is, indeed, the subject of David Leonard's book. He explores questions of the dynamics of the policy process by tracing the lives of four top administrators: Charles Karanja of the Kenya Tea Development Authority; Harris Mule, Finance and Planning; Ishmael Muriithi, Veterinary Department; and Simeon Nyachae, Civil Service. By examining the public and private lives of these men and their different approaches to administration,

Leonard shows why these individuals were successful in their tasks. Their individual and collective successes provide the roots of Kenya's exceptionalism. Yet, although individual leaders—active and entrepreneurial—make a difference, other factors also explain the relative success: the existence of a rather strong state supported by matajiri class interests and strong professionalism in the civil service. Indeed, as Leonard concludes, "successful policy outcomes derive from the intersection of interests, institutions, and individuals."

Leonard's book is engrossing. The reader becomes caught up in the lives, the strengths and struggles of these men. Yet, happily, attention to individuals does not detract from the analysis of the broader issues of the role of institutions in shaping, both positively and negatively, the development process.

KAREN A. MINGST

University of Kentucky
Lexington

BURKI, SHAHID JAVED and CRAIG BAXTER, with contributions by ROBERT LaPORTE, Jr. and KAMAL AZFAR. *Pakistan under the Military: Eleven Years of Zia ul-Haq*. Pp. viii, 212. Boulder, CO: Westview Press, 1991. $29.50.

This volume is presented as a series of assessments of the 11-year rule of Mohammad Zia ul-Haq, Pakistan's most durable ruler, who died when an explosion destroyed the military aircraft that was returning him to Islamabad. The volume has two senior authors and two supporting contributors. The principals have each produced two chapters and the others one apiece. In the preface, the reader is informed that the "strength of the book is that it reflects differing views of the Zia period in Pakistan's history." Unfortunately, what the several authors identify as strengths are also weaknesses.

The decision to produce a volume in which the various chapters are individually framed and presented without consideration of the totality of the rendering diminishes the success of the effort. Moreover, the authors appear driven more by personal recollections of their meetings with President Zia than by the substantive character of the subject matter. As a consequence, they draw upon the highlights of the Zia years but seldom pause to take the measure of what they are describing. Indeed, there is too little analysis in this book. Not insignificantly, the title of the book is somewhat misleading. The principal theme is "Pakistan under the military," and yet the military is not examined, nor is there a chapter analyzing the military institution.

Zia ruled Pakistan longer than any of his predecessors. The institutional base that provided for his longevity still awaits examination. It can be hypothesized that Zia did not govern Pakistan alone. The authors are more inclined to compare Zia with Ayub Khan than they are to disclose the source of his authority. Although Zia was seldom given high marks as a politician, the reader can conclude from this volume only that he was as adroit a politician as the Muslim country has yet experienced.

This is a small book, with no more than 153 pages of narrative. The narrative is followed immediately by 27 pages of chronology described as containing the important events of the Zia years, 10 pages of biographical sketches, and 13 pages of bibliography. The brief, introductory chapters attempt to frame Zia's background and political experiments, another focuses on constitutional issues by returning to the first years after independence, while two others sketch economic and administrative developments before and during the Zia administration.

Although the book does not seriously tackle the role of the political opposition, the development of fundamentalist Islamic organizations, or even Zia's strenuous effort at transforming Pakistan into an Islamic state, there is a chapter devoted to Pakistan as an international actor. While acknowledging the importance of the externalities of the Zia program, this chapter simply is too thin to be useful to the serious student of the region.

The strength of this volume should be in its utility to the totally uninformed, beginning student in an undergraduate Asia-survey class. The several authors, all among the most notable scholars on Pakistani subjects, will no doubt release a more creative study for those readers who still await a probing and detailed investigation of the Zia years.

LAWRENCE ZIRING

Western Michigan University
Kalamazoo

COLLIER, RUTH BERINS and DAVID COLLIER. *Shaping the Political Arena: Critical Junctures, the Labor Movement, and Regime Dynamics in Latin America.* Pp. xii, 877. Princeton, NJ: Princeton University Press, 1991. $75.00. Paperbound, $19.95.

In *Shaping the Political Arena*, Collier and Collier's purpose is to provide an analytical framework for comparing the legacies of alternative strategies for harnessing labor unrest in Latin America. Based on an investigation of the dynamics of intra-elite politics and on the critical junctures and choices shaping the political arena, two broad types of control are distinguished: state incorporation of the labor movement by traditional and modern elites aimed at preserving the oligarchic state through depoliticizing labor demands and institutionalizing channels for the resolution of labor conflicts; and party incorporation by new middle-sector elites aimed at transforming the oligarchic state through mobilizing labor support behind a program of major social reforms.

The eight countries chosen for comparison represented in 1979-80 some 84 percent of the population of the 20 countries defined as Latin America and, excepting Cuba, 92 percent of the gross domestic product. These are classified into four pairs based on similar experiences and trajectories: (1) state incorporation (Chile, 1920-31; Brazil, 1930-45); (2) incorporation via electoral mobilization by a traditional party (Uruguay, 1903-16; Colombia, 1930-45); (3) incorporation by new populist parties with ties to urban labor organizations (Peru, 1939-48; Argentina, 1943-55); and (4) incorporation by new populist parties advocating agrarian as well as labor reform (Mexico, 1917-40; Venezuela, 1935-48).

Ironically, within the period studied, state incorporation created more opportunities for the later radicalization of the labor movement than did the more radical method of party incorporation. Although the aftermath of reaction to incorporation in Chile and Brazil was an aborted populism, the long-term outcome was a multiparty politics of polarization between Left and Right; in Uruguay and Colombia, a reinforcement of the traditional two-party system marked by social conflict; in Peru and Argentina, an electoral ban on the populist parties ending in political stalemate; and in Mexico and Venezuela, a weakening of the populist coalition through appeasement of the conservative opposition. Thus Chile and Brazil show a leftward shift by organized labor, whereas military coups and/or a conservative counterresponse elsewhere contributed to eroding the autonomy of organized labor.

Despite its scope, this study is confined to changes in state-labor relations initiated by nonlabor elites from above rather than by worker self-mobilization and protest from below. However, Collier and Collier find no clear pattern in these mobilizations or any systematic relationship between labor movement strength and type of incorporation period. Nor are they confident enough to forecast the trajectories of state-labor relations into the twenty-first century. At most, they anticipate a new cleavage and new critical juncture in response to the strong downward pressure on wages during the 1980s, the retreat from Keynesian policies of class compromise between labor and capital, the mushrooming of the debt crisis, declining growth rates, and the shift from inward-oriented growth to production for export and increased dependence on foreign markets. Thus the authors' analytical framework is useful for classifying and in part explaining the trajectories of state-labor relations since the turn of the century, but it has virtually no predictive power.

In a work of this magnitude, one might expect factual errors. In the case of Argentina, Collier and Collier claim that the Peronist Resistance to the electoral ban ended by 1960, but participants in the events cite the period from 1968 to 1973 as the crown of the Resistance that made possible Perón's third presidency. We are also told that it was the military government, which ousted the Peronists in March 1976, that launched the infamous "dirty war." In fact, the "dirty war" dates from February 1975, when the government of Isabel Perón gave a carte blanche to the armed forces to " 'carry out the military operations necessary to neutralize and/or annihilate subversive elements' " (Hodges, *Argentina's "Dirty War"* [Austin: University of Texas Press, 1991], p. 175). But these are minor faults in a work that is already a tour de force and promises to become a classic on Latin American politics.

DONALD C. HODGES

Florida State University
Tallahassee

HARDEN, BLAINE. *Africa: Dispatches from a Fragile Continent*. Pp. 333. New York: Norton, 1990. $22.50.

Blaine Harden, a veteran reporter for the *Washington Post*, spent four years trying to understand the causes of the problems that sub-Saharan Africa is facing. In this candidly and persuasively written book, Harden utilizes the skills of a seasoned journalist, rather than the insights of an experienced scholar, to portray a continent that not only is in political and socioeconomic disarray but that also is dying a slow and painful death.

Although Harden focuses on Liberia, Ghana, Nigeria, the Sudan, Kenya, and Zambia—and it is not hard to understand why he selected these countries—his characterization of these countries gives the reader a vivid portrait of a continent that is indeed fragile in many ways, both physically and in terms of the values of its institutions. For example, the rapidly increasing population has left the resources of the continent depleted. The Sahara Desert is steadily moving southward and the Kalahari Desert is steadily moving northward. Unless African nations do something soon to stop this perilous development, when the two deserts converge the entire continent will be reduced to nothingness. The life-giving and sacred Nile has been subjected to incredible abuse, the equatorial rain forest is diminishing at an alarming rate, the mineral wealth that nineteenth-century European entrepreneurs exploited with a brutal senselessness for their own profit has not been replaced by any viable alter-

natives to sustain a national character so essential to the survival of the continent.

With regard to the institutional values of Africa, Harden decries the decay, the steady decline in the basic system of values that sustained the structure of the African culture and society. First, the failure of the colonial governments to recognize the viability of African cultural traditions led to a psychological game-playing to make the Africans believe that they were inferior because their culture was inferior. Then, after the colonial systems had come to an end, the euphoria that characterized the enthusiasm of the new breed of national leaders such as Kwame Nkrumah, Jomo Kenyatta, Milton Margai, and William Tubman for creating a new climate of African greatness quickly gave way to a new political Machiavellian grandstanding that derailed the objectives and principles outlined at the inception of independence. Nkrumah himself, Milton Obote, Mobutu Sese Seko, Daniel arap Moi, Hastings Kamuzu Banda, and Kenneth Kaunda all became victims of the power they possessed and introduced a new order of things under dictatorial systems they put in place. One-party systems, presidencies for life, manipulation of elections, and corruption combined to betray the hopes and aspirations of the people.

The consequences of this political betrayal have been severe. As coups and countercoups have become the order of the day, political institutions have ceased to function. Corruption by government officials has robbed the people of their legitimate right to a decent life. Poverty, urban decay, crime, and dysfunctional operations have taken an incalculable toll. Social services, such as transport, medical care, housing, education, and communication have been transformed from the season of hope into an abyss of despair. The epidemic of acquired immune deficiency syndrome (AIDS) has been devastating in many ways. It has posed fundamental questions about cultural values and kinship structures. It has robbed the people of both their will to survive and the vital resources they need to lead a profitable life. It has placed enormous restraints on family relationships. The sad result of all this is that the African leaders still find it politically expedient to blame the colonial systems they replaced. They do not have the courage to face the reality that they themselves are part of the problem.

To read this book is to witness a call for action to save a continent from dying. Harden's account of the fragile continent, however, must not be regarded as an indictment of the old guard but as a challenge to the African nations to rise to the occasion and do something that only Africans can do before time runs out. The starting point of this challenge is for African leaders to take a hard look at themselves and their style of leadership and step aside to allow new leadership to emerge so that national resources are mobilized and the confidence of the people can be restored. Once this is done, the task of rebuilding the nations of Africa can begin in earnest.

This is a book that all African leaders and their people as well as those who are interested in the development of Africa must read with an intense interest.

DICKSON A. MUNGAZI

Northern Arizona University
Flagstaff

INDEN, RONALD. *Imagining India.* Pp. vii, 299. Cambridge, MA: Basil Blackwell, 1990. $39.45.

The book under review deals with a whole range of important topics in an original and often thought-provoking manner. Its main proposition is that, after the Enlightenment, the orientalist construction of knowledge about India deprived Indians and their institutions from being agents in the making of their history.

The best part of the book, in my view, is the first chapter, which discusses agency and essentialism. In general, Inden follows Collingwood's views on agency in the sense that he argues for (1) the complexity of agents and (2) the replacement of notions of "society" or "social system" with the notion of "polity." As far as the first argument is concerned, it seems clear that Inden himself is a complex agent in the field of South Asia studies. There is no reference here to earlier arguments he has made—with McKim Marriott as his coauthor—about the divisibility of the Indian person. Nevertheless, his present argument "that persons as agents are themselves composed of entities that overlap" seems remarkably similar to the earlier one. In fact, his entire argument in this book could be read as another, almost hidden, vindication of the Chicago-style ethnosociology of India with its emphasis on "native categories." Moreover, his second argument about "social system" and "polity" seems similar to the move from "ethnosociology" to "ethnohistory" and from "caste system" to the "state" that originates in B. S. Cohn's work and has been followed by Appadurai and recently Dirks and Raheja. Inden's refusal to place his current argument in the context of a particular development of historical and anthropological thinking on India often makes evaluation of it difficult. This difficulty is compounded by the fact that, despite the emphasis on the notion of "polity," there is, in a way, very little sense of a broader institutional history of colonialism and postcolonialism in Inden's reconstruction of orientalism's intellectual history.

The general theoretical introduction is followed by separate chapters on the most important essentialisms that have resulted in the image of an eternally un-changing India. These are "caste," "Hinduism," "village India," and "divine kingship." Inden has something interest-ing to say about all of them, and I cannot do justice to his discussion in this brief review. Instead, I want to offer a critique that pertains to the entire discussion. Although Inden wants to recover Indian agency through the deconstruction of ori-entalist essentialisms, he falls into the same trap as Edward Said in *Orientalism* by remaining confined to the Western history of ideas. Inden does not take into account the extent to which orientalist images of India have been produced in interaction with Indian discursive tradi-tions rather than only through a Western hegemonic discourse originating in the Enlightenment. I would suggest, for ex-ample, that the discussion of the meta-phor of Hindu India as feminine would have gained had it been related to Hindu discourses on femininity. This failure to see Indian agency also in the construction of orientalism is not redeemed by what Inden offers as an alternative to oriental-ist writings, namely, his reconstruction of the Rashtrakuta imperium in the second half of the first millennium A.D.

Despite the several reservations I have voiced, I would again want to em-phasize the significance of Inden's cri-tique of orientalist essentialism. I do think that his is a book that should be read by every student of India—whatever his or her specific field—and will, I hope, result in spirited discussions in many classrooms.

PETER VAN DER VEER

University of Pennsylvania
Philadelphia

POMFRET, RICHARD. *Investing in China: Ten Years of the Open Door Policy.* Pp. xiv, 152. Ames: Iowa State University Press, 1991. $22.95.

PEARSON, MARGARET M. *Joint Ventures in the People's Republic of China: The Control of Foreign Direct Invest-ment under Socialism.* Pp. xiv, 335. Princeton, NJ: Princeton University Press, 1991. $39.50.

Richard Pomfret, professor of interna-tional economics at the Johns Hopkins School of Advanced International Stud-ies, asserts that the most extensive expe-rience of investing in a Communist country comes from China, which opened its door to direct foreign investment (DFI) in June 1979. Hence a decade of interac-tion between Chinese policymakers and foreign companies can offer lessons to Eastern Europe.

Based on interviews and other re-search conducted mainly in China be-tween September 1988 and June 1989, this slim volume focuses on the role of DFI in China's economic development in the decade following 1978. Before that year, Chinese officials regarded exports as the means to obtain imports needed to fulfill the economic plan, and they re-jected out of hand foreign loans and in-vestments. But China abandoned this autarkic policy after 1978 when it liber-alized import controls and actively pro-moted exports. Moreover, it sought to attract DFI with its Law on Joint Ven-tures (1979). In 1980, China joined the World Bank and the International Mone-tary Fund. As the decade progressed, re-form in China led to shifts from plan to market mechanisms, from moral to ma-terial incentives, and from decision mak-ing centralized in Beijing to decision making decentralized in the provinces. By the end of 1984, over a thousand sep-arate entities conducted foreign trade.

Although attracted by the large size of China's domestic market, foreign firms encountered many problems in operating joint ventures, including poor infrastruc-ture, the lack of internal markets, over-valuation and inconvertibility of the yuan, and a poorly defined legal structure. But the most serious problem was the contradiction between China's desire to use DFI as a source of technology and exports and the desire of foreign investors to use DFI to exploit China's internal market. Chinese officials tried to limit access to that market and also required foreign firms to earn through exports the foreign exchange needed to pay for their imports and the repatriation of earnings. This contradiction was never finally resolved, but to obtain the investment it wanted, China was compelled to offer incentives to foreign investors in 1986-87 and to allow investors lacking foreign exchange to buy it with local currency from other investors.

In successive chapters, Pomfret details several aspects of the open-door policy and its consequences: the chronology, location, sectoral distribution, and size of joint ventures; the shift to a more positive attitude toward DFI; the characteristics of joint ventures; and the problems of manufacturing joint ventures. To Pomfret, the first 10 years of the open-door policy were a "resounding economic success." In sum, he has written a small book that packs a great deal of information but could be more analytical in examining the economic benefits and costs of DFI to China.

The origin of Margaret Pearson's book is her doctoral dissertation, written while at Yale's Department of Political Science. The book fully reflects its origin: an abundance of highly detailed footnotes, running from pages 237 to 299 in small type; a substantial bibliography, running from pages 301 to 320 in small type; and a careful, measured prose style. Pearson sets three goals for her work: (1) a thorough description of measures taken by the Chinese government to control equity joint ventures and how they changed over time, (2) an understanding of the various forces that shaped the open-door policy throughout the 1980s, and (3) an examination of the effectiveness of a socialist state in carrying out a dual policy of control and encouragement of DFI.

Pearson fulfills the first two goals in a comprehensive fashion. But the third goal requires an assessment of China as a test case of the ability of socialist states to manipulate their positions in the international economy. In my judgment, the author fails to demonstrate that a socialist state is any more able than a nonsocialist state to sustain a dual policy of control and absorption of foreign investment. Indeed, the lesson of both Pomfret's and Pearson's books to policymakers—socialist and nonsocialist—is a simple one: if a country wants to attract foreign investors, it must offer them an opportunity for profits in an economic and political environment that compares favorably with that of other countries.

FRANKLIN R. ROOT

University of Pennsylvania
Philadelphia

WALLER, DEREK. *The Pundits: British Exploration of Tibet and Central Asia.* Pp. viii, 327. Lexington: University Press of Kentucky, 1990. $30.00.

The latter half of the nineteenth century witnessed the seemingly inexorable advance of two imperial colossi, Great Britain, represented by the Indian Raj, and czarist Russia, into the politically fragmented and little-known expanses of inner Asia. The maneuverings for position and power that characterized this process were seen by informed Britons of that period as moves in what was then called the "Great Game." Among its significant players was a group of specially trained surveyors, recruited, with two notable exceptions, from the ethnic groups inhabiting the relevant portions of the then Indian frontier. Although these surveyors were dubbed "pundits," suggesting that they were drawn solely from

Hindu peoples, their ranks also included Muslims and Buddhists. Identified by code names, they traveled in disguise over vast stretches of what are now Afghanistan, Soviet and Chinese Turkestan, Tibet, and Myanmar. Their task was twofold: to extend the geographic knowledge gathered by the Great Trigonometric survey of India—later merged with the Survey of India—as far as possible and simultaneously to gather as much information as they could about the political and economic conditions of the countries they traversed. As Waller's engagingly written and meticulously documented history makes clear, their forays into the unknown, along with those of a number of British military personnel, were attended by unremitting drama, considerable intrigue, prodigious feats of daring and endurance, and, with rare exceptions, uncanny devotion to duty.

Several pundits, such as Nain Singh, Kishen Singh, and the learned Bengali Sarat Chandra Das, were abundantly honored for their achievements by the Royal Geographical Society and by the authorities in India—sometimes only after secrecy in regard to their missions was no longer essential, the need for secrecy being a much-debated issue. Others, however, languished in obscurity. Perhaps none was less well served than Kintup, officially known as KP. A precis of his story will convey some sense of Waller's narrative. A highly intelligent but illiterate tailor from Darjeeling, KP was, strictly speaking, not himself a surveyor but rather an aide to the only ethnic Chinese pundit. The two were assigned to trace the Tsangpo, the great river of Tibet, downstream to whatever south-flowing stream it may have joined. Faced with having his mission and disguise as a lama discovered, the nameless Chinese sold KP into slavery and absconded with all their surveying instruments and supplies. It was more than four years before KP made his way back to Darjeeling. During that period, 1880-84, he effectively completed the mission to which his superior had been assigned, exploring the Tsangpo deep into the great gorge through the Himalayas, an area ruled by the wild Abor tribe, and came to within 25 miles of the farthest point on the Brahmaputra reached by military expeditions proceeding north from Assam. Endowed with a superb memory, KP related, with astonishing detail and accuracy, the nature of the country through which he had passed, but, because of his inability to provide a written record, his account was accorded little credence. Not until a military expedition of 1913 were KP's observations fully verified. The following year the long-forgotten and impecunious tailor received a modest cash award. A few months later he expired.

Waller, whose overriding concern is with exploration, has no political ax to grind. Nevertheless, his account provides a litany of evidence of British high-handedness in their dealings with Asians during the heyday of imperialism. Small wonder that the Chinese in particular should now view as invalid in principle every international boundary that was negotiated in the aftermath of the many unauthorized European incursions into what China regarded as its territory. The validity of China's own territorial claims in places such as Tibet, however, is an issue that Waller has chosen not to examine. Nor does he discuss, despite the benefit of hindsight, whether there was any legitimate basis for the pervasive British perception that a Russian military advance on India was a genuine threat. My own assessment is that officials who should have known otherwise purposely perpetuated that erroneous notion as a means of justifying their own expansionist agenda.

An important feature of *The Pundits* is its abundant cartographic documentation. An attractive shaded relief representation of the entire area that Waller considers occupies the front and rear inside covers of the book, and nine slightly enlarged excerpts from that map form the background against which the routes of some 25 expeditions are plotted. Waller's intent is certainly laudatory and goes well beyond what many other historians would have offered. Still, I remain less than satisfied. The maps are insufficiently detailed to enable the narrative to be closely followed. Far too few rivers, which so often formed the course of the routes followed, are shown, much less named, and scores of places alluded to in the text find no place on any map. The solution to the problem of crowding place names on a map would have been to identify those places on the map seriatim by key numbers and to append a key to each map so constructed. Sometimes the routes portrayed simply are not credible; an example is the near beeline on map 5 on Kishen Singh's route across four mountain ranges from Batang to Rima in eastern Tibet. Elsewhere there are major editorial blunders. The most serious was to misidentify, on map 6, Kishen Singh's explorations in the Takla Makan and Ladakh as the totally different route of M. S. (Muktar Shah) and to completely omit the actual route of the latter. Elsewhere, on map 2, the plotting of the route of the Afghan mission of "the Mirza" differs markedly from the description in the text. Careless textual errors are also not infrequent. In particular, Waller is prone to reverse east and west; for example, Aligarh lies southeast of Delhi, not, as stated on page 240, southwest.

Whatever its editorial shortcomings, *The Pundits* is a most enjoyable and, on balance, a very scholarly work. It effectively synthesizes and critically discusses a vast array of material from numerous archives in England and India. Moreover, it may be read with profit not only for its historical content but also for the sense of high adventure that it conveys. Finally, it is a worthy tribute to the spirit of a remarkable group of men.

JOSEPH E. SCHWARTZBERG

University of Minnesota
Minneapolis

WURFEL, DAVID. *Filipino Politics, Development and Decay*. Pp. xiv, 361. Ithaca, NY: Cornell University Press, 1991. Paperbound, $12.95.

This is the single best study of contemporary Philippine politics in print today. David Wurfel has long written skillfully and with insight about the Philippines, particularly its tortured and flawed agrarian policies. In this book, however, his task is much more daunting: to provide a historical, cultural, and political framework with which to understand the last two decades of Philippine politics.

The book is sufficiently chronological in format and careful in its explanations so that nonspecialists can appreciate it fully. There are no real surprises or even provocative interpretations of events, but the scholarship is exhaustive, the documentation meticulous, and his personal sources so well connected that scholars in Philippine and comparative politics will find this volume a valuable reference.

The book is well organized and quite balanced in its treatment of the full spectrum of interests on the Philippine scene. It is particularly successful in chronicling the stages of martial law. The missed opportunities for reform and development in agrarian reform and bureaucratic reorganization, the avarice of the new elite, and the growing impoverishment of the population unfold in grim detail.

Wurfel's analysis is actually rather conventional, drawing as it does on terminology derivative of Samuel Huntington's classic, *Political Order in Changing*

Societies. Unlike Huntington, however, Wurfel is less sanguine about trade-offs between authoritarian rule and development. With the benefit of hindsight, Wurfel clearly demonstrates the limits of martial law and authoritarian leadership. In the Philippines, martial law did not bring order, institutional stability, or development. It brought modernization through crippling debt and dependency, fantastic wealth for a few at the expense of reform.

The chapters on the Aquino government will be the most interesting for political scientists because they illustrate so well both what is new and what is different about Philippine politics today. Unfortunately, the continuities and the differences are both disturbing. The old elite is once again entrenched in government, particularly the Senate, and as such remains an obstacle to agrarian reform and other social-justice issues. The military and the Catholic Church are more politicized than ever, with the former a threat to human rights and democratic government and the latter unwilling to permit the kind of population policies that will allow for any advances in quality of life. Corruption, nepotism, personality-based party alliances, and patronage politics are alive and well.

While the reader will finish *Filipino Politics* with none of the upbeat rhetoric of people power so common in 1986, they will have a far less transitory understanding of the dynamics of the Philippine political system.

LINDA K. RICHTER

Kansas State University
Manhattan

EUROPE

ADAS, MICHAEL. *Machines as the Measure of Men: Science, Technology, and Ideologies of Western Dominance.* Pp. xii, 430. Ithaca, NY: Cornell University Press, 1989. $29.95.

This excellent, well-titled, and well-subtitled book explores European rationales for the rise of the West to world hegemony from the 1500s through the Great War of 1914-18. It outlines the shift in European attitudes, chiefly French and British, toward Third Worlders, mainly Africans and Asians, over four centuries of cultural contact and increasingly heavy-handed exploration and exploitation. It demonstrates neatly the shift from religious and racial notions of the Western superiority complex to secular and quasi-scientific arguments for Europe's domination of the globe. Adas concentrates his attention on "The Age of Industrialization" to show how imperialist ideologies became based in the nineteenth century on the power of machinery and the authority of science-based technologies.

Adas's work grew out of Philip Curtin's Comparative Tropical History Program and is a part of George Fredrickson and Theda Skocpol's Cornell Studies in Comparative History. As such, it is well informed with regard to political and social scientific studies of modernization theory, but it definitely must be classified as sociocultural, and even intellectual, history rather than as a work in socioeconomic or synchronic political science or the history of technology. Indeed, its focus on the negative aspects of cultural imperialism is so forceful that readers may forget the positive aspects of the secularization process and of the globalization of science and technology.

Adas divides this study into three parts and only six chapters. So apt are the six chapter titles that they may serve as a summary; from first to sixth, they are "First Encounters: Impressions of Material Culture in an Age of Exploration"; "The Ascendancy of Science: Shifting

Views of Non-Western Peoples in the Era of the Enlightenment"; "Global Hegemony and the Rise of Technology as the Main Measure of Human Achievement"; "Attributes of the Dominant: Scientific and Technological Foundations of the Civilizing Mission"; "The Limits of Diffusion: Science and Technology in the Debate over the African and Asian Capacity for Acculturation"; and "The Great War and the Assault on Scientific and Technological Measures of Human Worth."

Expert in comparative social histories of Southeast Asia—witness his books The Burma Delta (1974) and Prophets of Rebellion (1979, 1987)—Adas writes well and is most persuasive in his treatments of European attitudes toward India and China. Having probed the travel literature in depth, he also examines the attitudes of armchair travelers around London and Paris. Voltaire, David Hume, and James and John Stuart Mill, for instance, receive more attention than do Matteo Ricci, Pierre Sonnerot, Mungo Park, or Captain James Cook. Yet Darwin and Wallace, Marx and Engels, Pierre Mille and Gustave Le Bon, for instance, represent symbolic stances of ethnocentrism more than enduring influences on racism.

The anthropological, missionary, and engineering literatures from far-flung fields abroad are not explored in this book to any remarkable extent. Nor are the problems of the design versus the mastery of machines and the inspiration of instruments for measurements in both the natural and human worlds adequately treated. But as an introduction to European ideologies in the last two centuries of industrial imperialism, this is a very good book. Its perspectives, although partial, are trustworthy, and its production, aside from a few typos, is handsome.

LOYD S. SWENSON, Jr.

University of Houston
Texas

MÜHLBERGER, DETLEF. Hitler's Followers: Studies in the Sociology of the Nazi Movement. Pp. xii, 276. New York: Routledge, 1991. No price.

Detlef Mühlberger has provided a thought-provoking analysis of his research dealing with the social makeup of the Nazi Party prior to the Nazi seizure of power in 1933. He disputes the generic approach of classifying membership that has dominated the historian's thinking for the past 45 years. The traditional thesis was that the German middle class dominated the ranks of the prewar NSDAP. Mühlberger argues that historians have not refined the classes of the German population; such an analysis would more clearly distinguish class membership. He suggests that those who were recruited often claimed their occupation in general terms, thereby skewing the results of later researchers.

Mühlberger uses numerous examples obtained from regional records in Gau Württemberg, Gau Hesse-Nassau-South, and Gau South-Hanover to support his thesis. Through the use of statistical tables that utilize percentages to indicate numbers of different German work groups, Mühlberger focuses on the more specific occupations and delineates between the types of workers within those occupations. For example, he suggests that often the responses made by young men about work were too generic to truly identify class. This is supported by the examples of respondents saying they were farmers, craftsmen, or small businessmen, when in fact they were more probably laborers, apprentices, or clerks. This conclusion is predicated on the ages of the respondents, many of whom were under thirty years. This, Mühlberger argues, would indicate a lower to middle middle-class societal position rather than pure middle to upper class.

To many readers, these subtle changes to the generally accepted thesis are more finite than necessary. This, however, does not discount the need to more closely differentiate the German society that was the foundation of the Nazi Party of the late 1930s and 1940s. Mühlberger has done a credible job of focusing on the lower to middle middle-class through his extensive research and has provided important insight into the types of people who were the basic Nazi Party organizers and workers of the late 1920s and early 1930s. This book is an excellent source for specialists in modern Germany history and for those who are peripherally interested in the social relationships that led to such an important movement in the twentieth century.

RAND C. LEWIS

Duquesne University
Pittsburgh
Pennsylvania

SMITH, GEOFFREY. *Reagan and Thatcher: The Inside Story of the Friendship and Political Partnership That Changed World Events from the Falklands War to Perestroika.* Pp. viii, 285. New York: Norton, 1991. $22.95.

BARNEKOV, TIMOTHY, ROBIN BOYLE, and DANIEL RICH. *Privatism and Urban Policy in Britain and the United States.* Pp. xiv, 267. New York: Oxford University Press, 1989. $59.00. Paperbound, $16.95.

With the sounds of the Persian Gulf war, which featured British-American cooperation, and the crumbling of the urban infrastructure in both countries reverberating in our ears, it seems a welcome time to reexamine the very "special relationship" that developed between President Reagan and Prime Minister Thatcher during the 1980s. The works considered here take contrasting approaches: one provides a journalistic description of the relationship between the two leaders; the second offers a detailed comparative analysis of the impact of privatization, or privatism, on the metropolitan areas in the respective countries.

Geoffrey Smith, a political correspondent for the *Times* in London, presents a straightforward, essentially chronological narrative that lacks footnotes and has little supporting apparatus. Using interviews, he traces the origins of the affinity between Reagan and Thatcher to a meeting in April 1975. The warm relationship started almost immediately for, as Michael Deaver noted, the future president always had "a very soft spot for a lady." For her part, Thatcher found Reagan's beliefs about government, specifically domestic policy, compatible with her own. He also validated Britain's importance through the clear evidence of their partnership. As Smith notes, both were, at the time of the meeting, "out in the cold," and the experience of coming to power together "was critical to everything that came later." Though they did not share a belief in the importance of a work ethic and disagreed on more topics than is commonly realized, their basic compatibility made it possible for them to survive many subsequent crises.

They shared domestic ideas of encouraging the private sector through deregulation, in the American case, and sale of state enterprises, in the British. Yet Smith's analysis of the impact of these programs is not presented in the depth needed to understand their long-term implications. In addition, attributing the success of their ideologies to vague ideas whose time had come, as Smith does at one point, avoids basic issues and analysis. He is better on foreign affairs, but even in this area, despite such provocative chapter titles as "Irangate: What Thatcher Knew," more analysis would have been useful. Although the text is clear and the chronology useful as a handbook, there are few revelations.

On balance, Smith finds that the leaders of Britain and the United States gained different advantages from their friendship, but the results were generally favorable for both countries. Still, in concluding that England would be an ideal friend in the evolving Europe of 1992, the author lapses from being a reporter and becomes an advocate.

In assessing the Reagan-Thatcher era, the analysis by Barnekov, Boyle, and Rich of the public policy implications of privatizing urban services is likely to be more enduring. Written by a British-American team, it is solidly based on statistical and other sources and soundly analyzes the intermingling of ideas of privatism between the two countries during the period. It is an outstanding book on urban policy that is critical, at times highly so, of the policies in both countries.

Barnekov and his coauthors believe that a prominent characteristic of British policy during the period "was an attempt to replicate US urban redevelopment programs." Although they admire some aspects of the ensuing programs, they also note that Britain's historical context was significantly different from American experiences and that British planners did not have a clear understanding of what the impact of those policies had been in America. Therefore, inappropriate programs may have been devised and applied. For example, American local governments began competing with one another for locating job-producing factories or firms in their areas and frequently provided incentives or surrendered tax revenues. Privatization led to similar urban policies in England. Local government authorities, because of unrelenting economic pressures, increasingly competed with one another in a process that the authors refer to negatively as "marketing the city."

America's "new privatism" left cities more dependent on state government, and on federally mandated but underfunded programs, and an overall cutback in funding for domestic responsibilities resulted in a type of social Darwinism among cities. Privatism for privatism's sake did not enhance the life of urban dwellers but left many poorer if not bankrupt.

Even though occasionally dense and loaded with tables and data, this is a challenging work that should engender debate about national priorities and is essential for understanding urban policy development during the period. It would be useful to have additional studies comparing Liverpool or New York with, for example, the success of Paris during the period. Perhaps the decision by the French central government to pump in funds for cultural activities equal to the expenditures of the American government was a factor in that success.

ERWIN K. WELSCH

University of Wisconsin
Madison

WATKINS, SUSAN COTTS. *From Provinces into Nations: Demographic Integration in Western Europe, 1870-1960.* Pp. xvii, 235. Princeton, NJ: Princeton University Press, 1991. No price.

Writing a book in which people have been replaced by numbers can be an exercise fraught with peril. Susan Cotts Watkins has avoided the perils admirably in *From Provinces into Nations: Demographic Integration in Western Europe, 1870-1960.* She explains all statistical tests clearly and enumerates her findings without using jargon. The stories of individuals and groups enrich the analysis now and then. In addition, Watkins has inserted herself pervasively and gracefully into her text, allowing her lively historical imagination to bring her findings to life.

Watkins demonstrates that between 1870 and 1960, demographic diversity in levels of marriage, illegitimacy, and marital fertility between the provinces in western European nations was transformed into demographic nationalism. Where linguistic differences, local gossip networks, and isolation once created dissimilar geographic patterns of duration of breast-feeding, age at marriage, or acceptability of children born out of wedlock, by 1960 similar patterns of behavior existed throughout a nation. The differences between provinces within a country lessen, she argues, impelled by national market integration, nation building, and state expansion. As networks expand, owing to nationally prescribed education and increased communication and travel, localized patterns begin to disappear. The usual framework in which demographers work, Watkins asserts, is one in which the individual calculates "the costs and benefits of another child, or the costs and benefits of marrying earlier, later, or not at all." Her findings indicate that these decisions have been influenced more by the behavior of the group—before 1870, in the village or the province; by 1960, in the nation.

Comparisons with Eugen Weber's *Peasants into Frenchmen* are inevitable, acknowledged by Watkins in both her title and a chapter heading. *Provinces into Nations* is not the compelling literary and historical masterpiece that Weber produced, though it is a most useful analysis of the demographic changes that have occurred in Europe since 1870. Teachers will find it a helpful source of information, but it is not a book for the general reader.

The only disappointment in the book is the presentation of the tables. Though there are some good graphs and maps, most of the quantitative information in the text is laid out in lists of statistical test results, the meaning of which the nonexpert reader must search for in the text. Those tables should have appeared in the appendix, which contains many similar lists of use to the expert.

MARY BETH EMMERICHS

University of Wisconsin
Milwaukee

UNITED STATES

ALTSCHULER, BRUCE E. *LBJ and the Polls.* Pp. xvii, 137. Gainesville: University of Florida Press, 1991. $19.95.

SMOLLER, FREDERIC T. *The Six O'Clock Presidency: A Theory of Presidential Relations in the Age of Television.* Pp. xii, 158. New York: Praeger, 1990. $39.95.

LBJ and the Polls and *The Six O'Clock Presidency* are brief volumes that carve out rather thin slices of recent political history. Despite being slim, they help round out our understanding of some undercovered facets of the Johnson and Reagan presidencies.

The more useful of the two may be Bruce Altschuler's study of the use—or nonuse—made by President Johnson of a constant flow of statistical data delivered to him by his pollsters. Practitioners looking for hints that will help in advising presidents may not find much of use since the president disregarded most of the data delivered to him. Historians, however, will discover a fund of detail regarding another facet of the Johnson career. His strong will apparently overrode the recommendations concerning policy that he could have found in Oliver Quayle's extensive research efforts.

If there is a lesson to be learned, it is probably that when a political leader formulates policy, he would be better advised to rely on his own judgment and that of his principal advisers than on the whims of public opinion. There is, however, a caveat. A president cannot afford to be so bullheaded that he refuses to modify policies that the polls clearly show are not working. Polls are useful, according to Altschuler, to judge reaction to programs in being but not to formulate policy in unfamiliar areas.

The Six O'Clock Presidency deals with an entirely different facet of the presidency, its relationship to television news. Frederic Smoller has checked exhaustively into television's White House coverage patterns from 1982 to 1986. His account of the working routines of the White House correspondents, their relationships to assignment desks in New York, the types of subject matter that interest them, and the constraints they have to live with makes for interesting reading. The descriptions of the White House press room and the daily routines of the White House correspondent corps are equally informative.

Unfortunately, the patterns that prevailed in the period studied were ephemeral. Since those years, television news ratings have been declining steadily, news executives have been changing formats, and, perhaps most important, President Reagan is no longer in the White House. The White House press corps adapts its methodology to the style of the president it is covering. President Reagan permitted media contacts only in tightly controlled situations. President Bush has been much more open. He frequently comes to the press room to conduct informal press conferences. It is no longer necessary for Sam Donaldson to shout questions at the president over the noise of whirling helicopter propeller blades. This change in the accessibility of the president modifies not only correspondent attitudes but coverage methods as well.

As to the relative volume of coverage from the White House, it also is variable, depending in part on the president and his style, in part on the journalistic philosophies of the news executives in New York, and, most of all, on the flow of news, which is constantly changing.

Television news is a critical factor in the president's efforts to govern. It is worth studying for that reason, but one must remember that the news flow is uneven. The White House may be dominant today and secondary tomorrow. Putting the microscope on the years from 1982 to 1986 is a significant contribution to understanding one of the key processes of governing in the age of television, but it is a mistake to generalize from so short a span of history.

And could someone not have come up with a title a little less redolent of corn and more descriptive of the contents?

SIG MICKELSON

Louisiana State University
Baton Rouge

BAKKEN, GORDON MORRIS. *Practicing Law in Frontier California*. Pp. xvii, 192. Lincoln: University of Nebraska Press, 1991. No price.

KYNELL, K. S. *A Different Frontier: Alaska Criminal Justice, 1935-1965*. Pp. xiv, 369. Lanham, MD: University Press of America, 1991. $38.50.

As the academic literature on law and society has continued to grow, historians have drawn from analytical concepts in contemporary research to examine the development of judicial institutions and legal phenomena. Gordon Morris Bakken's *Practicing Law in Frontier California* examines the legal profession in California from 1850 to 1900. Although the study emphasizes the details of lawyers' activities in addressing the kinds of disputes—namely, debt collection, real estate, torts, and criminal justice—that inevitably occur on a developing frontier, Bakken also links his analysis to broader debates about the role of law in American society. Because of his reliance upon and liberal quotations from the letters of early California lawyers, he effectively conveys the perspectives of attorneys who shaped the development of law during that era. The book's primary flaw is its brief conclusion. Bakken could have synthesized the study's evidence more thoroughly in order to analyze the broad issues raised elsewhere in the book concerning lawyers' roles and social acceptance of legal norms. Despite this weakness, readers interested in the development of the legal profession will value the detailed accounts of early lawyers' working lives.

The study of early California lawyers overlaps with K. S. Kynell's Alaskan study only in its discussions about the treatment of criminals in miners' camps. Although Alaskan "miners' law" practices paralleled those in frontier California and elsewhere, A Different Frontier: Alaska Criminal Justice, 1935-1965 discusses how other legal developments in Alaska, specifically in the criminal justice system, generally differed from those described in studies of frontier justice in the American West. Geographic circumstances, federal government influences, and other factors led Alaska to develop as a unique frontier.

For the reader from outside Alaska, the book effectively describes the historical and environmental factors that shaped the state's social development. One suspects that Kynell's previous personal experiences as an Alaskan homesteader enhance his ability to illuminate the underlying texture of Alaska's twentieth-century frontier society. The analysis of crime and criminal justice institutions is well grounded in academic literature. The examination of crime patterns in Alaska adds to important scholarly discussions about the effects of such influences as urbanization and alcohol. In its weaker moments, the book slips into a mere cataloguing of important criminal justice personalities in Alaskan

history. Generally, however, the study makes a valuable contribution by applying analytical criminal justice concepts to an important but frequently unnoticed portion of the United States.

CHRISTOPHER E. SMITH

University of Akron
Ohio

LINK, ARTHUR S. et al., eds. The Papers of Woodrow Wilson. Vol. 63. Pp. xxii, 668. Princeton, NJ: Princeton University Press, 1990. $57.50.

LINK, ARTHUR S. et al., eds. The Papers of Woodrow Wilson. Vol. 64. Pp. xxii, 553. Princeton, NJ: Princeton University Press, 1991. $57.50.

These volumes are critical, as further volumes are likely to be, in developing a view of Wilson's public career as were the volumes that accompanied the assassinations of Garfield and McKinley. They help us observe another stage of the presidency in crisis. There is new evidence in an appendix to volume 64, from released papers of the family of Dr. Grayson, not only that Wilson was stricken by paralysis during his countrywide tour in behalf of League of Nations proposals but also that he had suffered carotid artery disease and "malignant hypertension" long before. The striking fact is that these physical troubles may have earlier contributed to his strong prose and public posture, before the breakdown that put his presidency at risk.

The editors find diminished power in the speeches that Wilson gave on his western tour. Certainly, they were received with enthusiasm. Almost any passage from them exemplifies his varied deliveries, to people on the street who were fearful of being dragged into new wars and to more sophisticated auditors who responded to his closer analyses. The League of Nations, he thought too sanguinely, would work in favor of what he and his coleaders in Paris drew up to ensure that their peace would be permanent.

Once he had broken down, and his special train brought him back to Washington and the White House, constitutional questions arose and would haunt the remainder of his term in office. Would he be able to carry out his executive duties? It is clear from the evidence that he was not, but two factors ruled against his office being turned over to the vice president, Thomas R. Marshall, a former Indiana governor and moderate reformer. One was the high regard and affection that Wilson's wife and such coadjutors as Joseph P. Tumulty had for him, leading to their reluctance to relinquish his power to any successor. The editors are emphatic in judging that Mrs. Wilson was far from running the White House, as legend has it. On the one hand, she would not let politicians, labor leaders, and others readily into her husband's presence to excite and possibly kill him with urgent messages. But she needed such associates as Tumulty, Secretary of the Interior Franklin K. Lane, and even Robert Lansing to handle matters with which he could not cope. Tumulty wrote Wilson's veto of the Volstead Act, which David F. Houston, then secretary of agriculture, went over for legal details. Wilson probably did not see the veto, a footnote reminds us, as was the case with many actions to which his name was added.

Tumulty, again, wrote his lengthy State of the Union message to Congress, snipping passages from Wilson's earlier writings for tone and opinion; sophisticated politicians went over it to distinguish his prose from Tumulty's own. Lane prepared important papers relating to strikes, public relations, and congressional associations.

To an extent, Dr. Grayson and other physicians suppressed information and so deceived the country. This course led the nation to expect that Wilson might be in charge of his office at almost any time. There is little doubt that, had crises materialized, there would have been demands for facts that could have forced Wilson's retirement.

Wilson's increased irascibility and suspicions did no good to his connections vital to public issues. A Foreign Relations Committee hearing with William C. Bullitt revealed that Robert Lansing had disagreed with Wilson's program in Paris, and it marked Lansing for dismissal, Wilson bitterly adding up all he had done for Lansing. Yet Lansing held on to handle awkward and dangerous European issues before quitting his office at the Department of State. On the League of Nations, Wilson's adamant all-or-nothing program kept his more flexible associates on a leash.

It can be concluded that the public behind congressional and other public actions was not so much kept in the dark as they were uncertain about what ought to be national policy. Colonel House, now banned from the White House, thought that Vice President Marshall should have been made acting president. In those last months before the 1920 Democratic Convention—not yet reached in these volumes—the government was in the hands of Wilson's cabinet and entourage. They made no decisions critical to America's role at home or abroad. Regarding the League of Nations, hindsight suggests that it may have been just as well that the government did not commit itself to full support of its leaders and their politics.

LOUIS FILLER

The Belfry
Ovid
Michigan

NEDELSKY, JENNIFER. *Private Property and the Limits of American Constitutionalism: The Madisonian Framework and Its Legacy.* Pp. xiii, 343. Chicago: University of Chicago Press, 1990. $29.95.

Many scholarly works on the intent and legacy of the United States Constitution have appeared at the time of the Constitution's bicentennial. One of the best studies is Jennifer Nedelsky's well-written *Private Property and the Limits of American Constitutionalism*. Drawing heavily upon a large number of published primary materials, Nedelsky demonstrates convincingly that a preoccupation with property rights has greatly shaped national political institutions and the extent of governmental power.

Such influence started largely with James Madison. Madison felt that the major responsibility for him and other delegates at the Constitutional Convention in 1787 was to ensure that republican government would not be a threat to property rights and cause a lot of instability and disorder. He strongly advocated certain checks on representative democracy to remove governmental activity as much as possible from the excesses of the propertyless majority. James Wilson had far different concerns. Nedelsky relates that Wilson did not worry about majority threats to property and saw the protection of the political rights of the people as the main object of government. He proposed an egalitarian structure consisting of internal controls that would prevent public officials from misusing power and would allow the majority wide participation in governmental affairs.

Little of Wilson's admirable model prevailed at the convention, however. Most of the delegates shared Madison's distrust of majority rule and accepted in the new constitution his constraints upon the operations of republican government. The development of Madisonian federalism discouraged any real effort to increase the political competence of ordinary citizens and readily delegated matters of economic importance to unaccountable members of the elite. Nedelsky eloquently describes the consequences: "Our tradition gives us a powerful set of concepts for understanding majority tyranny. It provides nothing comparable on the ways in which economic power may also threaten rights, the public interest, and the basic principles of republican government." The weight of property in many decisions of the Supreme Court in the nineteenth and twentieth centuries is impressive evidence of these conditions. Nedelsky shows that the Court has often ruled in favor of propertied classes at the expense of egalitarian values. The alternative to this disturbing predicament lies in a new model of constitutionalism in which individual rights and democratic principles could be mutually promoted and protected.

Nedelsky's incisive, thoughtful study should be the starting point for any serious debate on the difficulties and future of American federalism.

MARTIN J. SCHIESL

California State University
Los Angeles

RITCHIE, DONALD A. *Press Gallery: Congress and the Washington Correspondents*. Pp. xiv, 293. Cambridge, MA: Harvard University Press, 1991. $29.95.

LANOUE, DAVID J. and PETER R. SCHROTT. *The Joint Press Conference: The History, Impact, and Prospects of American Presidential Debates*. Pp. 173. Westport, CT: Greenwood Press, 1991. $39.95.

Few subjects generate more controversy based on less information than the issue of the mass media in American politics. Both of the books reviewed here attempt to add to the existing information on the dynamics of the media and seek to deepen the quality of debate rather than merely fuel the controversy.

Ritchie's book is both well written and well researched. He presents an engrossing account of the people in the media and Congress and their personal and professional relationships. Ritchie, like many scholars of the media, finds that despite an abundance of mutual suspicion and adversarial rhetoric, the relationships between members of Congress and members of the press during the nineteenth and early twentieth centuries were both close and mutually beneficial.

His study provides a wealth of information and insightful analysis concerning the politics of the mass media. His style is lucid and clear. Ritchie enlivens the topic with a variety of anecdotes and stories that instruct as well as entertain. The book adds a great deal of historical insight into the task of researching media relations with the Congress.

The Lanoue and Schrott book provides a very different treatment of the media and politics. Their focus is on presidential debates, and they usefully synthesize much of the social science literature concerning debates and their utility in informing and influencing votes and voters. Lanoue and Schrott provide historical context as well as contemporary examples in presenting their analysis.

For media scholars, the real interest of this book lies in the model of debate effects presented in chapter 5. Both direct effects—which Lanoue and Schrott consider more important for those with little information and fewer biases—and indirect effects—such as the mediated nature of debates—are taken into account. The authors recognize the importance of perceptual filters such as party identification, candidate preference, and issue positions, and they attempt to account for these filters in their model.

They conclude with a discussion of debates and the vote choice, possible changes in the format of debates, and the overall future of debates. Throughout the book, the authors' analysis is well grounded in social science literature but is nevertheless readable and accessible.

Both of these books have much to offer general readers as well as scholars on the topic of the role, functions, and relationships of the mass media in American politics.

MARY E. STUCKEY

University of Mississippi
University

ROSENTHAL, JOEL H. *Righteous Realists: Political Realism, Responsible Power, and American Culture in the Nuclear Age.* Pp. xxii, 191. Baton Rouge: Louisiana State University Press, 1991. $24.95.

Political realism has dominated American foreign policy in the second half of the twentieth century. For just as long, critics of political realism have attacked it as an amoral, if not immoral, political philosophy that runs counter to American values. *Righteous Realists* provides a much needed corrective to this misreading of realist political thought.

In an extensive review of the work of five major realist thinkers—Hans Morgenthau, George Kennan, Reinhold Niebuhr, Walter Lippmann, and Dean Acheson—Rosenthal argues that moral concerns were central to all five men. Although each rejected the crusading moralism so natural to many Americans, believing it would doom American foreign policy to failure, their vision of power politics proceeded from a moral foundation. Their works represent an attempt to marry moral concerns to traditional political realism—"to turn power politics into *responsible* power politics."

Rosenthal sets his task as "a description of how the realists went about integrating their moral concerns into their practical political judgments, rather than an evaluation of the realists as pure prescriptive theorists." He portrays realists as thinkers sensitive to the prospect that political action might have evil consequences and well aware that many countries play by rules alien to most Americans. Indeed, realists fervently criticized crusading moralism—on both the left and the right—precisely because it recognized neither the limits of good intentions nor the ill will of other countries. For many realists, then, the guide to moral action lay not in best intentions but in choosing the lesser of two evils (p. 32).

Righteous Realists is less convincing in its attempt "to present realism as a coherent whole." The effort to find common themes in realist thought is laudable, especially since so much of what is written on political realism takes on the much easier task of finding inconsistencies within and among realist writings. But, as Rosenthal himself amply documents, realists frequently found themselves on opposite sides of the pressing issues of the day, as Acheson and Kennan did on the decision to build the hydrogen bomb. Some readers may find disagreements of this sort to be differences in kind and not of degree. Even with this caveat, though, *Righteous Realists* stands as a valuable contribution to the literature on realist political thought.

JAMES M. LINDSAY

University of Iowa
Iowa City

SOCIOLOGY

BROOKS, ROY L. *Rethinking the American Race Problem*. Pp. xiv, 256. Berkeley: University of California Press, 1990. $24.95.

NIEMAN, DONALD G. *Promises to Keep: African Americans and the Constitutional Order, 1776 to the Present*. Pp. xviii, 275. New York: Oxford University Press, 1991. $29.95. Paperbound, $9.95.

These books provide unusual insights into the connections between race, class, law, and public policy in American society. Focusing on African Americans and the legal system from the beginning of the new nation to recent times, historian Donald Nieman emphasizes how law, society, and politics have interacted in shaping the black experience. He not only shows how the Constitution has been a malleable instrument, permitting a variety of groups—including African Americans—to use it to further their own interests, but also how legal principles and institutions played an equally powerful role in shaping the nation's social relations and politics.

For his part, law professor Roy Brooks addresses a straightforward question: how can African Americans be accorded genuine equal opportunity in American society? Using Gunnar Myrdal's classic study, *An American Dilemma: The Negro Problem and Modern Democracy* (1944), as a historical backdrop, Brooks argues that whereas political inequality constituted the pivot of racial issues in the past, socioeconomic or class inequality is the most salient feature of the racial question today. Thus, in his view, the status of African Americans "can no longer be defined solely in racial terms. Consideration of race and class now criss-cross into an often puzzling portrait."

In his excellent historical analysis, Nieman shows how race shaped the American constitutional order over a long period of time. The debate over slavery influenced the Constitutional Convention of 1787; shaped the development of constitutional doctrine through the midnineteenth century; and played a role in disrupting the constitutional order, which culminated in the Civil War. While the destruction of slavery ushered in fundamental changes in the legal status of African Americans, Nieman demonstrates that it did not end the pivotal and enduring role of race in the American legal system.

African Americans were not merely subjects of debates on law and race among whites; they were important "agents of change." From the outset of the new nation to recent times, Nieman illustrates how African Americans "embraced principles of equality and constitutional rights," employed them to assault the system of racial subordination, and helped to reshape the Constitution and American society. African Americans and their white allies not only established the legal foundations for full black citizenship rights but empowered the federal government "to protect the fundamental rights of citizens." In the wake of new racial restrictions and the rise of Jim Crow during the late nineteenth and early twentieth centuries, for example, African Americans soon challenged the repressive southern criminal justice system. They pressed the U.S. Supreme Court "to take a broader view of the Fourteenth Amendment's due process clause and the Bill of Rights," as indicated by antipeonage decisions in cases like *Bailey* v. *Alabama* and *United States* v. *Reynolds* (1914). The legal assault on inequality—which culminated in landmark court decisions and new civil rights laws in the 1950s and 1960s—was not the achievement of black elites and their white allies alone, Nieman argues; it also involved the masses of black working people. Although the U.S. Supreme Court rolled back increasing efforts to address racial inequality through the law during the 1970s and 1980s, Nieman predicts that race and blacks will continue to shape American constitutionalism during the twenty-first century.

In his careful *Rethinking the American Race Problem*, Roy Brooks analyzes the contemporary race question from the vantage point of the changing configuration of social classes within black America. He shows how a black middle class, a black working class, and what he calls a poverty-stricken class—with manifestations of an "underclass subculture"— "emerged with greater clarity and force" during the 1970s and 1980s. Using the notion of "subordination," Brooks systematically analyzes the social status of each class, showing how racial discrimination constituted a special problem for African Americans at each level of the social structure. While black poor and working people suffered greater socioeconomic and political disadvantages—in jobs, housing, education, and access to channels of influence—the black middle class also faced racial constraints on their ability to maintain and improve their position in the social structure. Unlike Nieman, however, Brooks is far less confident that blacks will be able to gain substantial assistance from the government. Thus he concludes with a call for a new era of African American "self-help," which he outlines in substantial detail.

These studies are not fully satisfactory. Nieman argues, for example, that the black working class helped to shape American law and practice, but the voices of black workers are barely audible in much of his account. On the other hand, while Brooks affirms the need for an ongoing campaign to secure government assistance, his emphasis on self-help tends to minimize the very important role that government must play. Moreover, his program of self-help is dependent on the black middle class, with little attention to the ways that the black poor can help themselves independent of middle-class guidance.

Nonetheless, taken together, these books advance our understanding of the complicated interplay of race, class, and public policy in American society. Nieman provides a rich and illustrative history of blacks and the legal system, while Brooks offers a vivid portrait of life in contemporary black America. Students of African American and American legal, public policy, and social welfare history should welcome these books.

JOE W. TROTTER

Carnegie Mellon University
Pittsburgh
Pennsylvania

HOLLINGSWORTH, J. RODGERS, JERALD HAGE, and ROBERT A. HANNEMAN. *State Intervention in Medical Care: Consequences for Britain, France, Sweden, and the United States, 1890-1970*. Pp. x., 266. Ithaca, NY: Cornell University Press, 1990. $46.50.

Health care reform is on virtually everyone's short list for the most important domestic issue of the decade. The American health care system is in a state of crisis: an estimated 32-35 million Americans have no health insurance, there are disparities in the quality and accessibility of care, and health costs are out of control. These problems have bedeviled policymakers for years. Hence the appearance of *State Intervention in Medical Care: Consequences for Britain, France, Sweden, and the United States, 1890-1970* by J. Rodgers Hollingsworth, Jerald Hage, and Robert A. Hanneman is timely and welcome. Although not everyone will agree with the authors' conclusions or policy prescriptions, no one interested in health policy can ignore them.

Simply stated, the authors have asked the right question: What mix of state and private sector health care involvement is most likely to maximize desirable outcomes, including controlling costs, im-

proving health, equalizing access, and facilitating medical innovations? The authors offer a provocative response: Active and substantial state intervention in funding, resource allocation, and delivery of health care, not privatization, best accomplishes these goals. They make their case in a sophisticated analysis of four systems, which range from highly interventionist, as in Britain, to highly privatized, as in the United States.

In addition to their main thesis, the authors question several widely accepted assumptions about health policy. For example, they challenge the notion that medical advances played only a minor role in reducing morbidity and mortality in the nineteenth century, and they present convincing evidence that increased medical specialization improves the health of a population rather than putting it at risk through unnecessary and often dangerous procedures.

It should be noted that there are some minor irritants in the book. First, contrary to its title, there is little here about the Swedish and French health systems; this is essentially a book about Britain and the United States. Second, I question the desirability of ending the analysis at 1970—a restriction the authors often ignore. Indeed, I would argue that health cost inflation really becomes a serious problem only after 1970. Most important, the analysis rarely looks at the impact of political factors on health policy. Thus, in discussing the diffusion of smallpox vaccination in the United States, the authors ignore the role of federalism, religious fundamentalism, and anti-vaccination interest groups. The authors' desire to find the answer to health policy differences in terms of market- versus state-oriented systems results in a neglect of cultural and political factors.

Despite these criticisms, *State Intervention in Medical Care* is one of the most imaginative and important contributions to the national, and international, dialogue on the future direction of health care in a long time.

HOWARD M. LEICHTER

Linfield College
McMinnville
Oregon

JOHNSTON, WILLIAM M. *Celebrations: The Cult of Anniversaries in Europe and the United States Today.* Pp. xii, 187. New Brunswick, NJ: Transaction, 1991. $29.95.

This book is a study of American and European cultural anniversary celebrations that were staged during the 1980s. Postulating that "we commemorate what we no longer wish to emulate," Johnston insists that celebrations thrived because they were characteristic of a postmodern Western perspective. Indeed, celebrations mimicked every style from every period of the past as a reflection of contemporary aimlessness, a waning faith in the future, and the absence of a cultural avant-guarde to forge the sorts of commemorations that would better serve our current needs. They have tended to be ephemeral, specialized, and arbitrary, substituting parts of a past personage or event for the whole, drama for accuracy, vividness for definitiveness, and accessibility for weightiness. With the abandonment of religious calendars, moreover, celebrations of the 1980s satisfied cravings for comparable if secular rhythms—assurance that the practices of nations and regions flowed in time and with some semblance of order.

Noting these general forces contributing to recent celebrations, Johnston stresses how varied they have been. In Europe, the government culture ministries that funded the arts used celebrations to establish national consensus by commemorating luminaries like Bach and Marivaux. But in the United States,

where private foundations have provided the preponderance of the funding and where the values of the marketplace and traditions of separation of church and state have been ascendant, luminaries have been ignored and, instead, events have been commemorated. In 1988, for example, eight states celebrated the ratification of the federal Constitution, but the births and deaths of cultural luminaries like Henry Adams and Bronson Alcott were ignored. A second interesting variation Johnston discusses concerns a comparison of celebrations in European countries. Anniversaries have flourished in Germany, France, and Austria, where national identity has rested on a recently forged civil religion. In contrast, Italy's Catholicism and municipal loyalties have run so deep that a developed cult of anniversaries has not been required.

Johnston also emphasizes the coming bimillennium. People are coming to feel increasing awe, he contends, as the year 2000 approaches. More and more, he insists, the Holocaust and Stalinism are being put behind us as the events of a prior century. As the 1990s progress, the floodgates of commemorative consciousness will open because the bimillennium stands to encompass every anniversary. Johnston hopes that organizers of commemorations in this decade will take advantage of this and take into account more than commercial expediency. He wants them to celebrate aspects of the past in ways that prompt consideration of the issues of survival and renewal in the twenty-first century.

Johnston is probably right in describing his book as the first "to interpret cultural anniversaries as characteristic of our time." But it is an inauspicious beginning. Themes are formulated vaguely and demonstrated by simple assertion more than through reasoned use of evidence. What data Johnston advances seem more directly compatible with the possibility that celebrations accommodate our simultaneous desires for stability and mobility than with illustrating a vaguely defined postmodernism. The research is skimpy by any standards, and secondary sources crowd out the primary ones. Although Johnston is a historian, he makes little of celebrations before the 1980s. Rather, he insists on the unparalleled intensity of late-twentieth-century celebrations and requires that they be differentiated from, say, American commemorations of the Fourth of July or of George Washington's birthday during the 1820s. Allowing his postmodernist perspective on our times to explain all, Johnston dismisses predecessors of celebrations in the 1980s as extraneous. Given all of this book's problems, it may be charitable to describe it as a polemical if interesting cultural commentary and not a work of scholarship.

LAWRENCE J. FRIEDMAN

Bowling Green State University
Ohio

JONSEN, ARTHUR. *The New Medicine and the Old Ethics*. Pp. xi, 171. Cambridge, MA: Harvard University Press, 1990. $18.95.

Arthur Jonsen is eminently qualified to address the topic of his book. Having a background in philosophy and religious history, he has immersed himself in medical education, the history of medicine, and medical ethics. Admittedly an avid "doctor watcher," he has integrated "historical approaches" to observe physicians with, in his words, a "bigger telescope." This approach has enabled him to reflect upon current ethical problems as new formulations of old problems. Thus the book focuses upon how the medical technologies work within an ancient ethical framework. His speculation that his work is a secular *aggadah*—a magical rabbinic mode of thought in which myth, theology,

poetry, and superstition robustly mingle —sets it apart from other works in the field and, at the same time, enables the reader to comprehend the issue raised.

In medicine's moral history, there is a central axis that forms at the point where altruism and self-interest meet. The moral archaeology of medicine exposes two traditions, one coming from ancient Greek medicine, the other from medieval Christian medicine. Hippocratic medicine was deemed a skill, its practitioners were craftsmen, and their objective was a good living. It was not until the second century A.D. that Christian ideals, such as that espoused in Jesus' parable of the Good Samaritan, fostered the spirit of altruism. As medical practice became dominated by the Judeo-Christian ethic, altruism and medical care became bound in a moral covenant.

Today these two traditions are blended. Modern society permits doctors to learn and use their skills in order to earn a living and simultaneously insists that these skills be used for the benefit of the entire society. In order to safeguard this dual goal, Western society has invented the medical license, which in a most peculiar way often reinforces the moral paradox of self-interest and altruism. This becomes more apparent when the organized—licensed—medical profession fears that its concerns are threatened and reacts by instituting policies that reflect its self-interest. According to Jonsen, a better sense of awareness may enable practicing doctors to better understand the nature of this paradox and live with it, enable medical education to better prepare medical students to deal with it, and permit patient-doctor relationships to be more honest.

As a result of the successful dialysis technique developed by Dr. Belding Scribner earlier in the century, public attention focused on the problems of "allocation of scarce medical resources," and the field of bioethics was born. In essence due to the new technologies, medicine faced an issue that the traditional ethics of medicine had not previously dealt with and for which it had no immediate remedy.

Jonsen's view is that the task of bio-ethics is to preserve the wisdom of the old ethics, in the hope of formulating a new ethic to deal with new medicine. Consequently, he launches on a journey of the mystical origins of the medical profession, from the myths of the Greeks to Roderigo a Castro's influential Medicus Politicus (1614) to the writings of Dr. Richard Cabot (1868-1939). From these origins the problem currently posed is whether there is an intrinsic limit to medical competence. Today, the moral crisis of medicine concerns the limits imposed on competence, which is driven not only by masters of science but also by an appreciation of the personal and social needs of the patient.

The Samaritan principle deserves to stand beside the Hippocratic principle of competence in its importance for medicine. In this way two ethical traditions flow through Western medicine: competence and compassion. The good Samaritan represents the good physician of today. As the modern physician espouses both the Hippocratic-Cabotian ethics, which prohibit exploitation of patients and demand competence, and the Samaritan ethics, which include compassion and nondiscriminatory service to those in need, the quandary of the modern physician is how to distribute the available resources of time, energy, and money among all who can benefit from his or her attention.

In recent years, the word "gatekeeper" has returned to designate the role of primary-care physicians as they direct patients through the medical care system in the most cost-efficient manner. The role of the good Samaritan as gatekeeper must be to make sure that the gate is never permanently locked, that all have reasonable access to medical care, and that the gate is opened and closed to admit all the needy in a timely and orderly fashion.

The essential moral problem of gatekeeping, however, concerns the degree of certainty required to judge a procedure as necessary and efficacious. According to Jonsen, the three sets of principles that have made up the ethics of medicine—Hippocratic, Samaritan, and Cabotian—converge toward the ethics of justice. If a physician has many virtues but lacks justice, his other virtues, or part of them, will fail him, for justice is the sum and source of all virtues.

Modern medicine is currently confronted by a massive army of persons unable to afford medical care as well as external institutions that regulate its activities. In the past, the ethos of the noble physician dictated its own conditions for service, choosing the ethos of noblesse oblige. Today, many of these terms are set by external institutions. For example, treatment must be given in hospitals, drugs must be bought at pharmacies, diagnostic equipment must be paid for, and so forth. According to Jonsen, if the institution of medicine is to survive, it must choose its ethos and remain faithful to it. The ethos of noblesse oblige, by itself, may not be strong enough to meet the challenge.

In a free society, medical care is neither a right nor a privilege but a service provided by doctors and others to people who wish to purchase it. This argument, stressing the economic rights of physicians, can be extended also to the rights of physicians to use their skills in accordance with their own best judgment of the patient's best interests. In recent years, challenges to this benevolent authority have increased due to the changing technological and scientific capacities of medicine. For example, resuscitative techniques can revive severely traumatized patients who formerly would have died but who now may continue to survive in a damaged state. These technological advances have aroused public concern about the appropriateness of leaving to the physician the crucial choices inherent in their use. As a result, it is felt that even the best-intentioned and most selfless physicians are not in a position to perceive or control the best interests of others.

Jeremy Bentham, the father of utilitarianism, promoted the idea that social reform in law, suffrage, criminal justice, education, medicine, and many other areas of life should promote the "greater good," which consists of maximizing pleasure over pain. According to Jonsen, the new medicine hears Bentham's ghostly voice urging all physicians to convert to utilitarianism at a time when allocation of scarce health care resources is a pressing problem. Conversion to this doctrine is not easy for doctors. Even though they may be deeply committed to the general welfare, they have been inculcated in the old ethics, which tell them their primary duty must be to their patients. Euthanasia, for example, for the sake of others not yet existing seems incredible—yet the philosopher will retort that, although incredible, it seems rational.

Physicians are heirs to an ethic that requires dedication to individual patients. Yet, in the new medicine, physicians think through diagnoses and devise therapy in a technological, statistical fashion. Thus, according to Jonsen, there are at least four problems at the interface between technology and medicine: the disparity between statistical thinking and personal dedication, the temptation to take precipitous action, the confusion between results and benefits, and the potential for conflict in organizations. To deal with this interface, we must first admit that in modern medical education there is very little teaching about technology, that is, about its importance for

human life and institutions and about its overt and covert effects on many practices. Technology and ethics are strangers to each other, yet they are neighbors in the world of human accomplishment. They face each other but do not interact. The personal face of ethics looks at the impersonal face of technology in order to comprehend technology's potential and its limits; the face of technology looks to ethics in order to be directed to human purpose and benefit.

It may be concluded that contemporary bioethicists do not need to create new ethics for medicine. They are bringing the old ethics into a new era and using them to address questions about problems they could not have imagined in detail but did anticipate in outline. With this in mind, Jonsen reviews the evolution of the old ethics from the origins of contemporary times, proposing that their earliest phase envisioned the nobility of service and that the final phase initiated a kind of democracy of medicine improving both physician and patient rights. The novel problems of genetics, transplantation, neuroscience, provision of services, and so forth are new in their technical, social, and economic detail. They are old in the ethical outlines of the mantra "beneficence, nonmaleficence, autonomy, and justice."

JOSEPH D. BRONZINO

Trinity College
Hartford
Connecticut

OSTERUD, NANCY GREY. *Bonds of Community: The Lives of Farm Women in Nineteenth-Century New York*. Pp. ix, 303. Ithaca, NY: Cornell University Press, 1991. $42.50. Paperbound, $14.95.

GABIN, NANCY F. *Feminism in the Labor Movement: Women and the United Auto Workers, 1935-1975*. Pp. xi, 257.

Ithaca, NY: Cornell University Press, 1990. $31.95. Paperbound, $12.95.

Osterud's *Bonds of Community* and Gabin's *Feminism in the Labor Movement* are among the growing number of volumes dealing with women workers in a manner sensitive to a feminist point of view.

Using local records and other historical data, including firsthand interviews with present-day descendants of the people of the Nanticoke Valley area of New York State, which is located near Binghamton, Nancy Grey Osterud adds vivid sections of nineteenth-century diaries and letters to provide a portrait of the life of women in the small New York towns of Maine and Nanticoke from the mid-nineteenth to the beginning of the twentieth century. The accompanying photographs of the plain, hard-working inhabitants of the area offer revealing reinforcements of Osterud's conclusions about the closeness of family life, the importance of gender relationships, the isolation of rural life, and the rural emphasis on cooperation. How women lived in rural America during this period—how they grew up, married, viewed family relationships and responsibilities; how gender operated within their culture—is the focus of this book.

Osterud takes as her base the concept that "gender is socially constructed and culturally constructed, not natural and universal." Conformity was mandatory, but within the pattern individuals and new conditions gradually acted to modify the norm. From 1880 on, as some left the valley, those families remaining became increasingly agricultural and the economy centered on gender-related activities. Land continued to be passed to and to be controlled by men; women attained status through organization, cooperation with kin in closely interrelated family groups, and sometimes through the cooperation of husbands and fathers.

In her conclusion to this perceptive study, Osterud notes the logical development of the growing independence of women in the suffragette movement, as expressed in the Convention of 1848 at Seneca Falls.

Nancy F. Gabin, in *Feminism in the Labor Movement*, considers the urban working woman in a much later period and in a setting markedly different from that on which Osterud bases her study. The theme of the pressure of the social order to establish and to maintain a gender-related structure is common to both volumes, however. Also, both authors are contributing views on women workers from areas not, perhaps, as carefully covered previously, with Osterud covering rural farm women and Gabin, women auto workers.

Gabin traces the development of women's activism in the United Auto Workers (UAW) from 1935 to 1975. She discusses the formation of the Women's Department of the UAW in 1944 and the constant struggle of women workers for recognition. Quoting the slogan of the Coalition of Labor Union Women in 1974, "A Woman's Place is in Her Union," Gabin points out that the union had at last reached a culminating point, recognized as such by the workers of both sexes. The author notes that in 1910 women auto workers numbered 1000; men, 42,000; and that by 1930, less than 3 percent of these wage-earning women were union members, though they composed 25 percent of the labor force, mostly in low-skill, poorly paying categories. By contrast, 300,000, or 21 percent of the total UAW membership, was composed of women by the 1970s. The union was now working on securing gains for women on such issues as sexual harassment; however, the union and management often united to establish wage differentials based on nonobjective standards of evaluation. For instance, job descriptions would be formulated to classify a woman in a lower-paying bracket than that of a man doing the same work. Women, especially Afro-Americans, were customarily denied seniority in favor of male workers, even those men with less training and skill. Eventually, and with the support of the union, these conditions were improved. In a careful, well-documented study, Gabin portrays the increasingly important role of women in industry, with attention to the opposition they faced from male workers, the effect of World War II, and the interaction between feminism and the UAW.

Students of labor relations, social historians, and those interested in feminist history will find the frank treatment given by Gabin and by Osterud valuable.

DOROTHY RUDY

Caldwell College
New Jersey

STANBACK, THOMAS M., Jr. *The New Suburbanization: Challenge to the Central City.* Pp. xv, 126. Boulder, CO: Westview Press, 1991. $34.50.

With a rich array of data, Thomas Stanback examines the changing nature of American metropolitan areas. Better said, he explores the challenge to the central city thrown down by suburban change.

The dynamics of challenge and change are by now familiar, and they organize Stanback's research:

1. Central cities and their suburbs are locked into a system of competitive economies. Market strategies drive these economies, no strategy being more important than the business firm's search for comparative advantage.

2. Contributing to challenge and change is a fundamental economic transformation from manufactures to services, especially intermediate services: transport,

communication, finance, consulting, advertising. Thus, Stanback points out, "the share of gross national product originating from these intermediate services has risen from 29 percent in 1947 to over 40 percent today."

3. Again, as both consequence and component of the foregoing, there is an expanding series of changes that affect suburbs, central cities, and, most important, their reciprocal relationships.

Among Stanback's most significant findings are that, first, over and above population growth, many suburbs now display the attributes and benefits of agglomeration—the clustering of similar economic enterprises—formerly the exclusive province of central cities. Second, and as a consequence of agglomeration, many suburbs now offer a wide range of service industries—hotels, theaters, conference centers—that rival, and thus displace, those of the central city's central business district.

Third are the labor market consequences of suburban agglomeration and the growth of service industries in both suburbs and central cities. These consequences include the loss of job opportunities for the illiterate and the unskilled. These were central-city job opportunities formerly provided by manufacturing. Their loss has the heaviest impact on the inner-city young. Another consequence is the growth of low-paying back-office jobs in the suburbs. Finally, there is a significant mismatch between job location and job seekers, a mismatch exacerbated by suburban housing costs and the lack of inter-urban transportation.

Among the several strengths of Stanback's research is his examination of the location quotient, or the share of employment in a given industry in specific urban areas. In the 14 central cities under study, three industrial groups are overrepresented when compared to the entire U.S. economy: (1) wholesaling; (2) finance, insurance, and real estate; and (3) other services. Equally important are data indicating that suburbs have become net exporters of services to the central city. This change is a reversal of traditional patterns and is of considerable significance for central-city employment opportunities.

Stanback's study expands our understanding of changes in suburbia, and it heightens civic anxieties over the future of the suburbs: poorly paid back-office workers, lack of affordable housing for those workers, commuters' gridlock, and endless sprawl. No less important, Stanback increases our appreciation of central-city problems: the paucity of employment opportunities for the unskilled; the difficulties faced by central-city workers in securing access to suburban jobs; the relatively low wages offered by the available service jobs. However much a deepened understanding may be the beginning of wisdom, we are, as Stanback clearly indicates, a long way from solving the problems of the new suburbanization.

LAWRENCE J. R. HERSON

Ohio State University
Columbus

ECONOMICS

DIETRICH, WILLIAM S. *In the Shadow of the Rising Sun: The Political Roots of American Economic Decline*. Pp. xvi, 343. University Park: Pennsylvania State University Press, 1991. $24.50.

George Bush, take note: instead of a "new world order," the United States confronts a "new economic order," in which Japanese banks and high-tech industries will dominate the global economy and threaten America's political independence. William Dietrich, a steel company executive who holds a Ph.D. in political science, forecasts a dark future, unless the federal government undergoes funda-

mental restructuring and adopts a Japanese-style industrial policy.

Pointing to the loss of U.S. leadership in steel, automobiles, and consumer electronics, Dietrich asserts that the dissimilarities between American and Japanese business and governmental policies fostered Japan's industrial superiority. He applauds Japan's tax and banking policies that promote selected manufacturers, and he admires the Japanese educational system, managerial philosophy, and professional bureaucracy. Japan's industrial policy, he writes, is "a strategic plan that affects every facet of the nation's economic system."

By contrast, an antistatist ideology in the United States has nurtured a diffuse economic and political system unable to compete effectively with the rising industrial nations of Asia. Drawing heavily from the writings of Louis Hartz and Richard Hofstadter, Dietrich identifies persistent sentiments against a strong central government as the legacy of Thomas Jefferson. He finds modern manifestations of that legacy in both the Republican right's free-market, free-trade illusions, and the Democratic left's attempts to insert a social-justice agenda into industrial policy.

Painstakingly clear, thoughtful, and convincing in his analysis of the Japanese and American political and economic systems—especially of the need for more active and positive government leadership in setting industrial policy—Dietrich is less persuasive when offering prescriptions for reform. After analyzing the deep roots and long evolution of American attitudes and institutions, he proposes scrapping them for a Japanese model. Convinced that only a strong central government can reverse America's economic decline, he would replace political appointees in executive agencies with a permanent, professional bureaucracy, reduce the power and staff of "a swollen and omnivorous Congress," and revise the

Constitution to free the economy from "the straitjacket of eighteenth-century political institutions." But his vision of grafting Japanese theories onto the American system seems likely to meet the same fate as American attempts to restructure Japan after World War II. Over time, and without bothering to amend the American-imposed constitution, Japanese society simply reverted to traditional patterns of behavior.

DONALD A. RITCHIE

U.S. Senate Historical Office
Washington, D.C.

GRAF, WILLIAM L. *Wilderness Preservation and the Sagebrush Revolution.* Pp. xviii, 329. Lanham, MD: Rowman & Littlefield, 1990. $38.50.

Approximately two-thirds of the land area of the United States is owned by the federal government. Just why this is so in a country that ostensibly relies upon private property for most resources and has a celebrated history of homestead settlement remains a fundamental question for research. Unfortunately, much of the literature on the federal lands is too normative to be of much help in addressing this question.

The issues are of more than historical interest. As chronicled by William Graf in *Wilderness Preservation and the Sagebrush Revolution,* federal lands have remained embroiled in controversy for over 100 years. Even so, we have surprisingly little information on the condition of these lands or of the net social value of alternative uses. Currently, it appears that management of federal lands by the Forest Service, the Bureau of Land Management, and the Park Service is molded by bureaucratic objectives and the shifting patterns of interest group politics, where the competing interests include conservation groups, timber and mining

companies, ranchers, and utilities. The public interest, however defined, seems to be little served by this institutional arrangement. William Graf's book provides a rich historical discussion of the political struggle over western lands and provides insights into the process by which current federal land policy has emerged.

The book is divided into four parts, each chronicling a "sagebrush rebellion." The first outlines conflict in the late nineteenth century over arid lands that did not blend well with the land policies devised earlier for small farms in the eastern United States. The land was better suited for ranching than for farming, and much larger plots were necessary for viable ranches than the 160 acres allowed by most land laws. For reasons that are still not clear, a political consensus for the liberalization of the land laws could not be mustered. Part of the political resolution of the problem was to finance irrigation projects that subsidized continued homestead settlement. The second rebellion involved competition for forest lands that could not be claimed within the agricultural focus of the land laws. Ultimately, the National Forests emerged, and Graf describes some of the personalities involved in the debate, including Bernhard Fernow, Gifford Pinchot, and Theodore Roosevelt. He also describes the slippery political maneuvering behind the General Revision Act and section 24, which created the forest reserves. Because this provision authorized federal retention of land, it represented a fundamental change from the past, and, accordingly, much more needs to be known about this action. The third rebellion involved access to and use of grazing lands from the 1920s through the passing of the Taylor Grazing Act in 1934, and the fourth was over wilderness lands, beginning with the Wilderness Act of 1964.

The contribution of this book lies in the placing of the political conflict over western lands into historical context. Its weakness lies in the absence of a theoretical framework for evaluating the claims of the competing parties and for assessing the social returns and costs involved. Essentially, federal lands remain common property, where property rights are unclear and uncertain. It is an indictment of this commons arrangement that conflict over access and use remains unresolved after 100 years. As a wealthy country, we are able to tolerate the resulting aggregate costs. By highlighting federal-land issues, William Graf's book usefully contributes to discussion of this chronic debate.

GARY D. LIBECAP

University of Arizona
Tucson

LINDBECK, ASSAR and DENNIS J. SNOWER. *The Insider-Outsider Theory of Employment and Unemployment.* Pp. xii, 285. Cambridge: MIT Press, 1988. $27.50.

Assar Lindbeck and Dennis J. Snower have nicely integrated a number of articles into a concise illumination of the theories of involuntary unemployment. The book is designed to be used in macroeconomic theory or labor economics classes; however, it is so well done that a noneconomist would greatly benefit from its insights. Although the nontechnical reader may need to pass lightly over several technical parts, the central themes of the book are so well established and explained that this is a most valuable source for anyone who wants a readable summary of basic macroeconomic research on the issue of employment and unemployment. The book will quickly become part of the required reading list for macro theory and labor economics classes.

The theory introduced in this work is that insiders who are experienced incumbent employees, protected by various job-preserving measures, have clout in the labor market, while outsiders, either unemployed or employed in the informal sector, have little wage or job security. Insiders participate in wage negotiations via unions or individually and influence production, profit, morale, turnover, strikes, and absenteeism in such a way as to determine market power not held by outsiders. The outsiders influence the employment and unemployment of the insiders only within the parameters that are determined to a large degree by the insiders, who can protect themselves from the underbidding of the outsiders by influencing labor-turnover costs.

The exercise of insider market power creates involuntary unemployment by raising the wage above the outsider wage without being in competition with outsiders due to the significantly higher turnover costs for the insider positions. This explains why outsiders are unable to replace insiders by underbidding and why wages remain above the market-clearing levels.

The various market-clearing versus non-market-clearing theories explaining unemployment are presented, critiqued, and compared to the insider-outsider theory. The micro foundations and the behavioral fit for the wage, job-security, work-rule, and employment decisions of the individual, the union, and the firm make the rent-seeking behavior in this theory and the efficiency-wage theory a persuasive explanation for involuntary unemployment. The chapter comparing and contrasting the efficiency-wage theory with the insider-outsider theory is particularly valuable. The chapter on harassment, cooperation, and involuntary unemployment tests numerous positions and can be useful without technical understanding.

The chapters on union behavior are both innovative and supportive of the main thesis that insiders have market power and are not wage takers. Union activity and power just enhance the effect on turnover costs by the insiders due to the strike threat and bargaining power. The policy implication of the theory is that demand management must be augmented by structural policies and some wage control. There is a glaring neglect of citation of the Piore-Doeringer work of two decades ago to the basic premises underlining this theory. Nonetheless, the book is a valuable contribution to the literature and will be a popular reader for aspiring economists.

W. E. SPELLMAN

Coe College
Cedar Rapids
Iowa

MASHAU, JERRY L. and DAVID HARFST. *The Struggle for Auto Safety.* Pp. xi, 285. Cambridge, MA: Harvard University Press, 1990. $29.95.

The Struggle for Auto Safety is a well-written and carefully documented historical account of the difficulties encountered by the National Highway Traffic Safety Administration (NHTSA) in its efforts to improve automobile safety. Two important themes run through the book that help explain these problems especially well. The first is that the agency's primary mission of improving on highway casualties was probably doomed from the start, given the fact that only a very small percentage of automobile accidents are due to mechanical defects in the vehicles. Yet, the mechanical focus tended to drive agency policy through much of its existence. The second significant theme is the difficulty of enacting regulatory policy in the all-pervasive political environment. The shifts in administrations and political winds often made both engineering and economic approaches to regulation unsellable to larger and more complex constituencies, whether they were industry related or pro-safety.

The book is especially useful to the student of public administration or the applied economist who must conduct cost-benefit analysis in a political environment. Chapter 9 is interesting in this regard in that it deals with bureaucratic-political struggles within the NHTSA and the varied perceptions of administrators toward cost-benefit and other analytical techniques. *The Struggle for Auto Safety* is important because it details how the courts, economists, engineers, and traditionally trained administrators view the complexities and approaches to regulation.

The account of the politics behind the decision to have the states implement mandatory seat belt laws is well written and informed. The authors agree, however, with an NHTSA study that suggests that mandatory seat-belt laws may be ineffective in reducing highway fatalities "unless usage approaches 100 percent." In many states where weak laws have been passed, this may well be the case, but the book does not take account of or document studies in states such as Michigan and New York, which have indicated reductions in both fatalities and injuries. While compliance was raised in these states, it was not anywhere near universal when the laws were passed.

This reservation aside, I recommend the book strongly to those interested in regulatory policy, automobile safety, public policy, and applied economics. It should be read by both practitioner and academic audiences.

JEROME S. LEGGE, Jr.

University of Georgia
Athens

MUCCIARONI, GARY. *The Political Failure of Employment Policy, 1945-1982.* Pp. xi, 317. Pittsburgh, PA: University of Pittsburgh Press, 1990. $34.95.

In 1945 a bill was set before Congress, entitled the Full Employment Act, which aimed to prevent the return of pre-World War II stagnation and mass unemployment through public investment financed by budget deficits. A coalition of Republicans and Southern Democrats defeated the bill, and this policy has never had a serious place on the national agenda since. Instead, a course was set that dealt with stagnation and unemployment as mere phases of a business cycle. Unemployment was defined as a "manpower problem" to be treated by programs targeted at special areas or at ethnic and racial minorities. These programs offered vocational training, retraining, counseling, and, to a very limited extent, the funding of new jobs. But even these programs finally fell victim to the growing power of conservatism. The culminating act, the Comprehensive Employment and Training Act (CETA), was terminated by the Reagan administration in 1982.

Gary Mucciaroni covers this period exhaustively in *The Political Failure of Employment Policy, 1945-1982*, and for the specialist the book is, undoubtedly, valuable. But the book is also relevant to our present political situation. Large-scale employment programs have been one of the mainstays of liberalism, and their defeat can be seen as both cause and effect of the decline of liberalism. To be sure, manpower programs reflect deeply held values regarding democracy and equality. But there is another value system, centering around capitalism and individualism, that is perhaps stronger at this time. The former dictates obligations to ensure equality of opportunity for weak and disadvantaged groups, but the latter confines manpower programs within the framework of market relationships.

Another factor leading to the failure of liberal manpower programs is the existing balance of class interests. The 1945 act had been strongly opposed by the business class, which saw it as a threat to its power to control investment decisions. The limited policies that were adopted, on the other hand, held little threat or even interest for the business class. Organized labor offered little support for these manpower programs. In some cases, these programs were considered a threat to organized labor; retrained workers might become members of a rival union, or, perhaps even more threatening to sections of the working class, trained minority workers might become threats to "white" jobs.

Finally, manpower programs ran afoul of the nature of our governmental institutions. Fragmented government levels, the federal system, and checks and balances all virtually guaranteed that, at most, underfunded, unenthusiastically supported programs would be unevenly and unjustly applied, inefficiently managed, and highly vulnerable to corruption. Thus this book can be recommended as a case study in the difficulties of bringing liberal reforms, let alone more fundamental changes, to this society.

EUGENE V. SCHNEIDER

Bryn Mawr College
Pennsylvania

MURPHY, MARJORIE. *Blackboard Unions: The AFT and the NEA, 1900-1980.* Pp. xiii, 284. Ithaca, NY: Cornell University Press, 1990. $28.95.

Marjorie Murphy argues that her book, *Blackboard Unions*, is a "standard account of unionization" but that what makes it "unusual" is that the "workers are teachers and the industry is education." This history of the American Federation of Teachers (AFT) and the

National Education Association (NEA) covers tremendous territory, weaving an intricate tale that examines teachers' attempts to empower themselves within a highly politicized industry. Expected to be professional as well as standard-bearers of the values that define the nation, this group of workers, suggests Murphy, has instead been divided by competing ideas of public service. Should they maintain a professional demeanor and stand apart from the communities to which they are assigned, or should they respond to the particular demands and needs of their local constituency?

Organized by teachers who opposed efforts to centralize school administration and policy, the AFT promoted a system of education that allied teachers' interests with those of the communities in which they worked. In contrast, the NEA began as a professional association composed of people drawn from all ranks of education. While the AFT pitted teachers against administrators, the NEA sought an alliance with the educational hierarchy, embracing professionalization and advocating a larger federal role in education.

The more expansive vision of the AFT was gradually eroded as the organization was weakened by sexism that privileged men over women for leadership positions and by "recurrent seasons of red baiting." As it eliminated its more radical members and strengthened its ties to the American Federation of Labor, the AFT focused more narrowly on issues of collective bargaining. Murphy finds that the AFT and the NEA, so different at the outset, have converged in recent years, emerging as public service unions and, as such, "narrow economic organizations." Ironically, it is the NEA, the more conservative of the two originally, which has proven more responsive to the most recent social challenges presented by the civil rights and feminist movements, accommodating the voices of minorities and women.

While her focus is on education, Murphy's analysis has larger implications for the study of public service employees generally. We expect our public servants to be highly trained professionals, but we allow them little autonomy and ask them to make do with shrinking resources. Murphy suggests that if teachers appear self-interested, it is largely the result of this society's expectations of them and our unwillingness to provide adequate financial support for the services they perform.

SUSAN M. YOHN

Hofstra University
Hempstead
New York

SERINGHAUS, F. H. ROLF and PHILIP J. ROSSON. *Government Export Promotion: A Global Perspective*. Pp. xx, 295. New York: Routledge, 1990. $49.95.

Export-promotion activities by government present a classic example of the difficulties of addressing firm-level problems with a national strategy. This book is a good introduction to the wide range of strategies of and problems in assessing the effectiveness of export-promotion activities. Written by two Canadian professors of marketing, the book offers a thorough, straightforward assessment of the practice of export promotion and its inherent difficulties. Given the importance of differentiated goods in international trade and the seemingly endless desire of governments to promote exports, the focus of the book is valuable and should be read by those concerned with its practical implications, by those many international economists who neglect the importance of marketing and distribution activities in determining the pattern of international trade, and by people concerned with commercial policy and trade negotiations.

The book is essentially divided into two parts. The first part describes the range of activities that make up export promotion and bears witness to the fact that export promotion is, in spirit and inevitably in part, against the principles of completely decentralized and unimpeded international trade. But there is always the moral problem of what one country should do when other governments indulge in these practices. The answer is to be more efficient, and the second part of the book addresses the fact that it is very difficult for government to hurdle the gap between a national government program and the customer who is an individual business. Probably, too, the customer is a small business with a niche market, since a great deal of international trade is conducted by multinational corporations. The first part is concerned with a consideration of the different kinds of promotional efforts and their compatibility with international trading agreements; the second part is more hands-on, provides a schema for increasing the effectiveness of promotional operations by a classification of export status, and includes a case study as well as a chapter on "measuring the impact."

Export promotion is a nontariff-barrier activity of relatively little importance, and the firm-government dichotomy may explain why this is so. Seringhaus and Rosson define export promotion very broadly and include such activities as information generation and the overcoming of a lack of motivation to test foreign markets on the part of corporate executives. The basic distinction is drawn between institutional support—not in contravention of the General Agreement on Tariffs and Trade—and financial support, which comes as tax remissions as well as direct contributions (subsidies). Failure to consider explicitly such organizations as the U.S. Export-Import Bank and its European and Japanese equivalents is surprising, but the reader could refer to Rita M. Rodriguez's very interesting book on this topic (*The Export-Import Bank at Fifty* [Lexington, MA: Lexington Books, 1987]). The range of ways by which a governmental agency can convey direct contributions is breathtaking.

In the end, it all comes back to trying, almost impossibly, to distinguish in principle between measures that make a competitive firm realize and exploit its bona fide competitiveness and those that run a substantial risk of being trade distorting by reducing the costs of exports. Probably, most government programs of export promotion are designed to achieve the first goal, but such programs will inevitably be perceived as effecting an increase in export promotion by virtue of subsidizing exports. It is a hard world for people engaged in this endeavor if only because they are set an inherently difficult task in bridging the gap between government and small business. This book makes one more aware of the difficulties that these people face.

H. PETER GRAY

Rensselaer Polytechnic Institute
Troy
New York

Rutgers University
New Brunswick
New Jersey

OTHER BOOKS

ALLEN, DOUGLAS and NGO VINH LONG, eds. *Coming to Terms: Indochina, the United States, and the War.* Pp. x, 350. Boulder, CO: Westview Press, 1991. $46.95. Paperbound, $16.95.

BAKER, LIVA. *The Justice from Beacon Hill: The Life and Times of Oliver Wendell Holmes.* Pp. xiv, 783. New York: Harper Collins, 1991. $29.95.

BALDWIN, PETER. *The Politics of Social Solidarity: Class Bases of the European Welfare State 1875-1975.* Pp. xiii, 353. New York: Cambridge University Press, 1990. $44.50.

BANFIELD, EDWARD C. *Here the People Rule.* 2d ed. Pp. xx, 405. Lanham, MD: American Enterprise Institute, 1991. $24.95.

BECNEL, THOMAS A. *The Barrow Family and the Barataria and Lafourche Canal: The Transportation Revolution in Louisiana, 1829-1925.* Pp. xii, 202. Baton Rouge: Louisiana State University Press, 1989. $27.50.

BENNETT, EDWARD M. *Franklin D. Roosevelt and the Search for Victory: American-Soviet Relations 1939-1945.* Pp. 243. Wilmington, DE: Scholarly Resources, 1990. $40.00. Paperbound, $13.95.

BERGERSON, PETER J. *Teaching Public Policy: Theory, Research, and Practice.* Pp. xiv, 225. Westport, CT: Greenwood Press, 1991. $42.95.

BIRNBAUM-MORE, PHILLIP H. et al., eds. *International Research Management.* Pp. x, 221. New York: Oxford University Press, 1990. $45.00.

BLAIS, ANDRE and STEPHANE DION, eds. *The Budget-Maximizing Bureaucrat: Appraisals and Evidence.* Pp. vii, 366. Pittsburgh, PA: University of Pittsburgh Press, 1991. $39.95.

BLECHMAN, BARRY M. *The Politics of National Security: Congress and U.S. Defense Policy.* Pp. xiii, 249. New York: Oxford University Press, 1990. $24.95.

BOSE, SUGATA, ed. *South Asia and World Capitalism.* Pp. xii, 405. New York: Oxford University Press, 1991. $36.00.

BRINKERHOFF, DAVID B. and LYNN K. WHITE. *Sociology.* 3d ed. Pp. xxix, 681. St. Paul, MN: West, 1991. No price.

BRINT, MICHAEL. *A Genealogy of Political Culture.* Pp. x, 147. Boulder, CO: Westview Press, 1991. $31.95.

BROOK, STEPHEN. *Winner Takes All: A Season in Israel.* Pp. xi, 363. New York: Viking, 1991. $22.95.

BROWN, LESTER R. et al. *Saving the Planet: How to Shape an Environmentally Sustainable Global Economy.* Pp. 224. New York: Norton, 1991. Paperbound, $8.95.

BRUN, ELLEN and JACQUES HERSH. *Soviet-Third World Relations in a Capitalist World.* Pp. x, 335. New York: St. Martin's Press, 1990. $55.00.

BURKE, PETER. *The French Historical Revolution: The Annales School 1929-89.* Pp. vi, 152. Stanford, CA: Stanford University Press, 1991. $27.50. Paperbound, $9.95.

COUGHLIN, RICHARD M., ed. *Morality, Rationality, and Efficiency: New Perspectives on Socio-Economics.* Pp. xii, 411. Armonk, NY: M. E. Sharpe, 1991. $45.00. Paperbound, $17.95.

COX, GARY W. and SAMUEL KERNELL, eds. *The Politics of Divided Government.* Pp. xvi, 270. Boulder, CO: Westview Press, 1991. $55.00. Paperbound, $15.95.

CROTTY, WILLIAM, ed. *Political Participation and American Democracy.* Pp. x, 233. Westport, CT: Greenwood Press, 1991. $47.50.

DANIELS, ROBERT V. *Trotsky, Stalin and Socialism.* Pp. xi, 208. Boulder, CO: Westview Press, 1991. $39.95.

DAVIDSON, CARL. *Recent Developments in the Theory of Involuntary Un-*

employment. Pp. vi, 171. Kalamazoo, MI: W. E. Upjohn Institute, 1990. $22.95. Paperbound, $13.95.

DE HAAN, H. H. *Alternatives in Industrial Development: Sugarcane Processing in India.* Pp. 178. Newbury Park, CA: Sage, 1988. $26.00.

DENTON, ROBERT E., Jr. and GARY C. WOODWARD. *Political Communication in America.* 2d ed. Pp. xix, 363. New York: Praeger, 1990. $49.95. Paperbound, $18.95.

EILBERG-SCHWARTZ, HOWARD. *The Savage in Judaism: An Anthropology of Israelite Religion and Ancient Judaism.* Pp. 304. Bloomington: Indiana University Press, 1990. $35.00. Paperbound, $17.95.

EWIN, R. E. *Virtues and Rights: The Moral Philosophy of Thomas Hobbes.* Pp. ix, 212. Boulder, CO: Westview Press, 1991. $39.50. Paperbound, $14.95.

FARHI, FARIDEH. *States and Urban-Based Revolutions: Iran and Nicaragua.* Pp. x, 147. Champaign: University of Illinois Press, 1990. $29.95.

FAURE, CHRISTINE. *Democracy without Women: Feminism and the Rise of Liberal Individualism in France.* Pp. viii, 196. Bloomington: Indiana University Press, 1991. $29.95.

FEENBERG, ANDREW. *Critical Theory of Technology.* Pp. xi, 235. New York: Oxford University Press, 1991. $35.00. Paperbound, $14.95.

FEHÉR, FERENC, ed. *The French Revolution and the Birth of Modernity.* Pp. 297. Berkeley: University of California Press, 1990. $39.95. Paperbound, $12.95.

FEHÉR, FERENC and ANDREW ARATO, eds. *Crisis and Reform in Eastern Europe.* Pp. ix, 531. New Brunswick, NJ: Transaction, 1991. No price.

FRIEDMAN, LAWRENCE J. *Menninger: The Family and the Clinic.* Pp. xix, 472. New York: Knopf, 1990. $29.95.

GAMBINO, RICHARD. *Racing with Catastrophe: Rescuing Higher Education in America.* Pp. 132. Lanham, MD: Freedom House, 1990. $39.75. Paperbound, $17.50.

GENOVESE, MICHAEL A. *The Nixon Presidency: Power and Politics in Turbulent Times.* Pp. xiii, 265. Westport, CT: Greenwood Press, 1990. $42.95.

GOLDMAN, RALPH M. *The National Party Chairmen and Committees: Factionalism at the Top.* Pp. xxii, 649. Armonk, NY: M. E. Sharpe, 1990. $49.95.

GOOD, KENNETH. *Into the Heart: One Man's Pursuit of Love and Knowledge among the Yanomama.* Pp. 349. New York: Simon & Schuster, 1992. Paperbound, $12.00.

GORMLY, JAMES L. *From Potsdam to the Cold War: Big Three Diplomacy 1945-1947.* Pp. 242. Wilmington, DE: Scholarly Resources, 1990. $40.00. Paperbound, $13.95.

HAMMER, DARRELL P. *The USSR: The Politics of Oligarchy.* 3d ed. Pp. xvi, 320. Boulder, CO: Westview Press, 1990. $46.50. Paperbound, $16.95.

HOFFMAN, PAUL E. *A New Andalucia and a Way to the Orient: The American Southeast during the Sixteenth Century.* Pp. xiii, 353. Baton Rouge: Louisiana State University Press, 1990. $42.50.

HUNLEY, J. D. *The Life and Thought of Friedrich Engels.* Pp. xiii, 184. New Haven, CT: Yale University Press, 1991. $22.50.

ITO, TAKATOSHI. *The Japanese Economy.* Pp. xvi, 455. Cambridge: MIT Press, 1992. $39.95.

JOHNSON, ANN BRADEN. *Out of Bedlam: The Truth about Deinstitutionalization.* Pp. xxvi, 306. New York: Basic Books, 1990. $22.95.

KANG, T. W. *Gaishi: The Foreign Company in Japan.* Pp. xxiv, 279. New York: Basic Books, 1990. $19.95.

KING, DESMOND S. and JON PIERRE, eds. *Challenges to Local Government.* Pp. vi, 298. Newbury Park, CA: Sage, 1990. $55.00.

KINGSOLVER, BARBARA. *Holding the Line: Women in the Great Arizona Mine Strike of 1983.* Pp. 230. Ithaca, NY: ILR Press, 1989. $26.00. Paperbound, $10.95.

KLAITS, JOSEPH and MICHAEL H. HALTZEL, eds. *Liberty / Liberte: The French and American Experiences.* Pp. ix, 218. Baltimore, MD: Johns Hopkins University Press, 1991. $35.00.

KOMIYA, RYUTARO. *The Japanese Economy: Trade, Industry, and Government.* Pp. xiii, 396. New York: Columbia University Press, 1991. $54.50.

KREML, WILLIAM P. *Psychology, Relativism and Politics.* Pp. xi, 274. New York: New York University Press, 1991. Distributed by Columbia University Press, New York. $40.00.

LEDERHENDLER, ELI. *The Road to Modern Jewish Politics: Political Tradition and Political Reconstruction in the Jewish Community of Tsarist Russia.* Pp. ix, 240. New York: Oxford University Press, 1989. $34.50.

LEFEBVRE, JEFFREY A. *Arms for the Horn: U.S. Security Policy in Ethiopia and Somalia 1953-1991.* Pp. xvi, 351. Pittsburgh, PA: University of Pittsburgh Press, 1991. $49.95.

LI, HE. *Sino-Latin American Economic Relations.* Pp. xii, 179. New York: Praeger, 1991. $45.00.

LIBBY, RONALD T. *Hawke's Law: The Politics of Mining and Aboriginal Land Rights in Australia.* Pp. xxvii, 175. Nedlands: University of Western Australian Press, 1989. Paperbound, $25.00.

LICHT, ROBERT A., ed. *The Framers and Fundamental Rights.* Pp. viii, 194. Lanham, MD: American Enterprise Institute, 1991. $19.95.

MACESICH, GEORGE. *Reform and Market Democracy.* Pp. xi, 145. New York: Praeger, 1991. $39.95.

MARTINELLI, ALBERTO and NEIL J. SMELSER, eds. *Economy and Society.* Pp. viii, 328. Newbury Park, CA: Sage, 1990. $60.00. Paperbound, $24.00.

MARZ, EDUARD. *Joseph Schumpeter: Scholar, Teacher and Politician.* Pp. xx, 204. New Haven, CT: Yale University Press, 1992. $30.00.

MATTHEWS, MERVYN. *Patterns of Deprivation in the Soviet Union under Brezhnev and Gorbachev.* Pp. xvi, 158. Stanford, CA: Hoover Institution Press, 1989. $26.95. Paperbound, $18.95.

McEACHERN, DOUGLAS. *The Expanding State: Class and Economy since 1945.* Pp. ix, 231. New York: St. Martin's Press, 1990. $39.95.

MESA-LAGO, CARMELO. *Ascent to Bankruptcy: Financing Social Security in Latin America.* Pp. xviii, 290. Pittsburgh, PA: University of Pittsburgh Press, 1990. $49.95.

MICHELMANN, HANS J. and PANAYOTIS SOLDATOS. *Federalism and International Relations: The Role of Subnational Units.* Pp. xii, 322. New York: Oxford University Press, 1991. No price.

MINOW, MARTHA. *Making All the Difference: Inclusion, Exclusion, and American Law.* Pp. xii, 403. Ithaca, NY: Cornell University Press, 1990. $29.95.

NARDINELLI, CLARK. *Child Labor and the Industrial Revolution.* Pp. x, 194. Bloomington: Indiana University Press, 1990. $25.00.

NATHAN, ANDREW J. *China's Crisis.* Pp. x, 242. New York: Columbia University Press, 1991. $12.95.

NEVITTE, NEIL and ROGER GIBBINS. *New Elites in Old States: Ideologies in the Anglo-American Democracies.* Pp. xi, 209. New York: Oxford University Press, 1991. $27.50.

OLSON, WILLIAM C. and A.J.R. GROOM. *International Relations Then and Now: Origins and Trends in Interpretation.* Pp. xvi, 358. New York: Routledge, Chapman & Hall, 1991. Paperbound, $18.95.

O'NEILL, WILLIAM L. *The Last Romantic: A Life of Max Eastman.* Pp. xix, 339. New Brunswick, NJ: Transaction, 1991. Paperbound, no price.

RAZ, JOSEPH, ed. *Authority*. Pp. 330. New York: New York University Press, 1990. Paperbound, no price.

RIVERA, MARIO ANTONIO. *Decision and Structure: U.S. Refugee Policy in the Mariel Crisis*. Pp. 263. Lanham, MD: American Enterprise Institute, 1991. $38.50.

ROGERS, DAVID E. and ELI GINZBERG, eds. *Improving the Life Chances of Children at Risk*. Pp. viii, 184. Boulder, CO: Westview Press, 1990. $34.95. Paperbound, $10.00.

SANTAYANA, GEORGE. *Character and Opinion in the United States*. Pp. xliv, 233. New Brunswick, NJ: Transaction, 1991. Paperbound, $19.95.

SAPIR, JACQUES. *The Soviet Military System*. Pp. 362. Cambridge, MA: Basil Blackwell, 1991. $49.95.

SCHELLENBERG, JAMES A. *Primitive Games*. Pp. xiii, 263. Boulder, CO: Westview Press, 1990. Paperbound, $24.95.

SCHWARTZ, WILLIAM A. et al. *The Nuclear Seduction: Why the Arms Race Doesn't Matter—and What Does*. Pp. xii, 294. Berkeley: University of California Press, 1990. $25.00.

SHANLEY, MARY LYNDON and CAROLE PATEMAN, eds. *Feminist Interpretations and Political Theory*. Pp. x, 288. University Park: Pennsylvania State Press, 1991. $35.00. Paperbound, $12.95.

SHARP, GENE. *Civilian-Based Defense: A Post-Military Weapons System*. Pp. viii, 165. Princeton, NJ: Princeton University Press, 1990. $19.95.

SHOEMAKER, CHRISTOPHER C. *The NSC Staff: Counseling the Council*. Pp. viii, 152. Boulder, CO: Westview Press, 1991. $29.95.

SHOEMAKER, DONALD J. *Theories of Delinquency: An Examination of Explanations of Delinquent Behavior*. 2d ed. Pp. xxvi, 329. New York: Oxford University Press, 1990. Paperbound, $14.95.

SIMONS, THOMAS W., Jr. *The End of the Cold War?* Pp. 210. New York: St. Martin's Press, 1990. $16.95.

SMITH, CHRISTOPHER J. *China: People and Places in the Land of One Billion*. Pp. xix, 355. Boulder, CO: Westview Press, 1991. $56.00. Paperbound, $24.95.

SORENSEN, GEORG. *Democracy, Dictatorship and Development*. Pp. xii, 214. New York: St. Martin's Press, 1991. $45.00.

STOKES, GALE. *Politics as Development: The Emergence of Political Parties in Nineteenth-Century Serbia*. Pp. xiv, 400. Durham, NC: Duke University Press, 1990. $49.50.

SULERI, SARA. *The Rhetoric of English India*. Pp. 230. Chicago: University of Chicago Press, 1992. $24.95.

TETLOCK, PHILIP E. et al., eds. *Behavior, Society, and Nuclear War*. Vol. 2. Pp. x, 367. New York: Oxford University Press, 1990. $49.95. Paperbound, $19.95.

THEOBALD, RONIN. *Corruption, Development and Underdevelopment*. Pp. xi, 191. Durham, NC: Duke University Press, 1990. $40.00. Paperbound, $15.95.

TOCH, HANS and KENNETH ADAMS. *The Disturbed Violent Offender*. Pp. xx, 183. New Haven, CT: Yale University Press, 1989. $22.50.

TOMA, PETER A. and ROBERT F. GORMAN. *International Relations: Understanding Global Issues*. Pp. xx, 485. Pacific Grove, CA: Brooks/Cole, 1991. Paperbound, $29.75.

TONNESSON, STEIN. *The Vietnamese Revolution of 1945: Roosevelt, Ho Chi Minh and de Gaulle in a World at War*. Pp. xiv, 458. Newbury Park, CA: Sage, 1991. $60.00.

VAN DYKE, CARL. *Russian Imperial Military Doctrine and Education, 1832-1914*. Pp. 216. Westport, CT: Greenwood Press, 1990. $55.00.

VILLARREAL, ROBERTO E. and NORMA G. HERNANDEZ, eds. *Latinos and Political Coalitions: Political Empowerment for the 1990s*. Pp. xxvi,

221. Westport, CT: Greenwood Press, 1991. $49.95. Paperbound, $17.95.

WARE, ALAN and ROBERT E. GOODIN, eds. *Needs and Welfare*. Pp. 218. Newbury Park, CA: Sage, 1990. $47.50. Paperbound, $19.95.

WASBY, STEPHEN L., ed. *"He Shall Not Pass This Way Again": The Legacy of Justice William O. Douglas*. Pp. xvii, 338. Pittsburgh, PA: University of Pittsburgh Press, 1990. $39.95. Paperbound, $19.95.

WEISS, CAROL H., ed. *Organizations for Policy Analysis: Helping Government Think*. Pp. xvi, 289. Newbury Park, CA: Sage, 1991. $30.00. Paperbound, $18.95.

WEITZER, RONALD. *Transforming Settler States: Communal Conflict and Internal Security in Northern Ireland and Zimbabwe*. Pp. xiv, 278. Berkeley: University of California Press, 1990. $29.95.

WHITE, STEPHEN, ALEX PRAVDA, and ZVI GITELMAN, eds. *Developments in Soviet Politics*. Pp. xvi, 310. Durham, NC: Duke University Press, 1990. $52.50. Paperbound, $19.95.

WHITNAH, DONALD R. and FLORENTINE E. WHITNAH. *Salzburg under Siege: U.S. Occupation, 1945-1955*. Pp. xiv, 163. Westport, CT: Greenwood Press, 1991. $45.00.

WILLIAMS, RORY. *A Protestant Legacy: Attitudes to Death and Illness among Older Aberdonians*. Pp. x, 371. New York: Oxford University Press, 1990. $72.00.

WILLIS, PAUL. *Common Culture: Symbolic Work at Play in the Everyday Cultures of the Young*. Pp. viii, 165. Boulder, CO: Westview Press, 1990. $48.50. Paperbound, $17.95.

WILSON, JAMES Q. *On Character*. Pp. ix, 211. Lanham, MD: American Enterprise Institute, 1991. $24.95.

WOLF, SUSAN. *Freedom within Reason*. Pp. xii, 162. New York: Oxford University Press, 1990. $24.95.

ZEMTSOV, ILYA. *Encyclopedia of Soviet Life*. Pp. ix, 376. New Brunswick, NJ: Transaction, 1991. $59.95. Paperbound, $44.95.

ZIMBALIST, ANDREW and JOHN WEEKS. *Panama at the Crossroads: Economic Development and Political Change in the Twentieth Century*. Pp. xi, 219. Berkeley: University of California Press, 1991. $40.00. Paperbound, $13.95.

INDEX

SOCIAL JUSTICE
World Order, Power & Politics in the 1990s

Vol. 19, No. 1

These essays pose questions essential for coming to terms with the post-Cold War and Gulf War era. What will be the new face of U.S. power— politically, economically, and militarily? What will be the ideological underpinnings of the reconstituted power arrangements? Does the "New World Order" mask a shift from East-West rivalry to intensified North-South conflict? How should the programs of the social movements address these new realities?

Social Justice
P.O. Box 40601
San Francisco, CA 94140

Individual Copies: $12
1-year subscription: $30 (4 issues)
Institutions: $68 per year
Add $4.00 for mailing outside the U.S.